"I began to wander at an earl, ...ge... my first getaway on my own took place in the summer of 1941 when I was less than four years old and living in the state's oldest inland city of Camden, where five of my first cousins also lived—three of them older and two younger with two more in the offing. . ."

"To the best of my knowledge, I've only saved one other person's life and, ironically enough in view of having been drowned myself not long before the event, I did it underwater. That may have been even more commendable because, as destiny or my gene pool would have it, I'm one of those people who, owing to body density or something of the sort, won't under any conditions bob back up like a cork. . ."

"Jim [Dickey], who knew no Russian, hadn't let that hinder his 'translations' of Yevtushenko's poems, and, on the occasion of the Russian poet's visit, things were at such a fever pitch that, before the evening was over, Yevtushenko had taken to drinking from my wife's shoe while crooning '*malen'kaya mama*' into her ear, literally 'little mother,' and comparing her to Natasha at the end of *War and Peace*."

"'What?'" I said with exclamation points. I was forty years old, I objected, reminding myself of the fact that, though I'd taken up distance running and sporadically practiced yoga over the years, I was lamentably middle-aged and couldn't imagine getting into splits. 'I'd look ridiculous,' I added, 'strutting about in tights.'"

"'Listen,' the mogul said, brushing a speck of dust from my state-owned cream-colored trousers, 'how'd you like to have lunch with François Truffaut?'. . . I managed to gasp I'd like that fine, and, only a few minutes later, we strolled along Fifth Avenue together, past the spot where horse-drawn carriages picked up tourists and would-be lovers for movie-like rides in the park, the place where I'd always felt on the edge of somebody else's dream. . ."

Revelations to ensue. . .

THE GLINT IN A FOX'S EYE

&

Other Revelations

a memoir by

Ben Dunlap

ISBN: 978-1-7374947-3-7

Grateful acknowledgement is made to RiskPress Foundation for making The Divers Collection possible.

Cover art by Laura Spong
All rights reserved by Personal Reflections, LLC

Author photo by Alchetron

Lines quoted in the dedication are from Stanley Lombardo's translation of Homer's *Odyssey*.

San Francisco, California

For Anne

For nothing is greater or finer than this,
When a man and woman live together
With one heart and one mind. . .

CONTENTS

Be like the fox
who makes more tracks than necessary,
some in the wrong direction.

—Wendell Berry

FOREWORD

A Pilgrim's Lack of Progress

I've never felt very comfortable about assuming dominion over every living thing, preferring that other tradition that defines us somewhat less presumptuously as "rational animals capable of laughter"—each word of which is fraught with chastening implications, especially the hedging implied by tossing in merely "capable." So, thanks to some ancient Greeks, I was more or less prepared when, during a break in one of my Aspen seminars, a clever and very successful young woman asked me in a playful semi-facetious way what animal I'd most want to be if I wasn't the one I was.

I honestly told her, "An elephant." It's the animal that I've always most admired—so much so that I'd once written the libretto for a comic oratorio to be entitled "On the Sixth Day," my theological premise being that, on the next to last day of the very first week, God's plan for the elephants (tenors and trumpets, of course) to serve as lords of creation had been thwarted by a dissonant chorus of fast-evolving apes usurping that role for themselves, thereby prompting divine misgivings about freedom of the will that have haunted us ever since. Needless to say, the composer, an adherent of the alternative version in Genesis, had never composed a note.

I reported that additional scrap of personal history to the relentlessly clever young woman, who then nodded and asked what I'd choose to be if I couldn't be an elephant. I said in that case I'd want to be a dolphin—no doubt a less than original choice since everyone likes dolphins. "And if you couldn't be a dolphin?" she asked. "An otter," I replied, a bit to my own surprise. . . whereupon she explained that my first answer was how I'd like to be perceived, the second was how I think I'm generally regarded, and the third was what, in my innermost self, I really believe I am.

I pondered that analysis for a moment, but, on the whole, I was okay with that. I'm otter-like in lots of ways. I'm monogamous and convivial and, despite this being an autobiography of sorts, I intend for what follows in these episodes to be far less about my own paltry accomplishments than about the resilient, creative, often unheralded outcasts and renegades whom I've encountered along the way, frequently in predicaments that were—in retrospect, at least—both hilarious and absurd. Come to think of it, otters are also frolicsome creatures that seem to have a sense of fun, so maybe there was some validity in my questioner's whimsical game. My life has not only included a great deal of fun but lots of people who were funny.

I should add that, aside from her light-hearted predilection for pop psychology, I knew she'd be stopping well short of any merely trendy cultural appropriation. But if she'd continued by posing questions about my spirit animal or whatever totemic guide had led me through life on my sometimes preposterous odyssey, I'd have told her it was none of the above while confessing pedantically that I'd only presume to call it an odyssey because my heart never fails to leap up at the opening lines of Homer's great epic (one of the works we'd been talking about that day) and especially at his use of πολύτροπον for his hero—a man "of twists and turns" in Robert Fagles' nimble translation or "wandering" and "versatile" according to others— and because, in a way more risible than heroic, I think the term suits me as well.

Not so coincidentally, perhaps, that word *polutropon* might also apply to otters, especially with regard to twisting and turning, though I should also note that the nomenclature on my birth certificate is not in the least otter-like because I was named for my father, whose middle name of Bernard had led to his nickname Bernie and inevitably to my being called "Little Bernie" which, even at a time when few felt qualms about using demeaning caricatures, struck me as far too similar to the dim-witted Little Beaver in the *Red Ryder* comic strip that had made its first appearance within a few months of my own.

Anyhow, as far as spirit animals go, I'd have had little interest in identifying with a beaver for the simple reason that, despite its seemingly higgledy-piggledy construction work, so straightforwardly purposeful a creature would never resort to such a convoluted jumble of words as my previous couple of paragraphs—which is pretty much how my brain has been functioning from birth or, at least, since I could talk. Nor was I attracted by the prospect of being a bear which, of course, was implicit in calling me Bernard.

That was something I learned in Rock Hill, South Carolina, from my father's sternly Victorian mother who informed me when I was five or six that, according to its Germanic or maybe Old Frisian roots, the name meant "bold as a bear," which had suited my father splendidly, she said, as it would in turn suit me. . . though I already had my doubts.

Not that I meant to disparage my unhappily profligate father whom I greatly admired and who'd been highly favored by the gods not only in intellect but in every collegiate sport from football, baseball, and boxing to basketball, tennis, and back—and, generally speaking, I have nothing but respect for ursine behavior of any sort, having myself at times been bold to the point of recklessness in clawing my way towards honey. But there's almost nothing about me that's lumbering or bear-like. Agility and speed have always been my forte from harum-scarum stunts as a kid to dashing about as a scatback in pads and on through leaping and spinning in tights. So despite a lifelong conviction that I'm a natural-born leftie, I decided I'd rather be called a "son of the right hand" than hailed as bold as a bear and said I'd like to be known by the other name that I and my father shared—as "Benjamin" or, better yet, just as Ben.

My mother endorsed my request, and I might have gotten my way if my father's family hadn't, as if resisting some maternally contrived genealogical coup, remained inflexibly stuck on

"Bernie Junior," leaving me with four or five twisting and turning decades to come as I fashioned an official self as Bernie into a paragon of prizewinning conformity while keeping my alter ego—the taller, wittier, handsomer Ben—surreptitiously under wraps unless I was far from home. But finally, it seems, after many years, I've succeeded in becoming Ben almost everywhere other than in my native state, where I'm still obliged by those who knew me early on to remain who I was back then as opposed to who I'd intended to become. It's something Tristram Shandy would understand.

All of which is a roundabout way of explaining why, rather than launching me like a rocket towards a single momentous goal, my childhood set me instead on a circuitous path with many close calls and narrow escapes as well as headlong blunders and successes of a sporadic sort that, though never resulting in glory or fame, would take me to lots of interesting places.

So it should come as no surprise that, as far as totems might go, I've felt an affinity with foxes almost from my earliest awareness of their existence—and that's despite the negative rap they get in most fables and children's stories compared to animals deemed more likeable or cuddly if not nearly so swift in any sense. . . which is to say, much closer to Little Beaver.

By way of contrast, foxes aren't remotely cuddlesome and are often regarded with some suspicion as the very opposite of any number of diligent single-minded rodent-like creatures. Furthermore, in addition to their penchant for twisting and turning, foxes are wily and resourceful, and though they're energetic omnivores, they only hunt and forage in order to survive—survival being the crucial point because they spend so much of their time eluding snares and pursuit, thus leading to Wendell Berry's advice about adopting their crafty habit of making "more tracks than necessary."

For whatever reason, I too have spent a lot of my life making redundant tracks, often while flouting authority and, when successful at pulling it off, feeling very much like a fox masquerading as one of the hounds or even as the enthusiastic leader of their pack—a subterfuge not only in keeping with its vaunted shape-shifting knack but a ruse that, though inherently comedic, makes the additional point that, from a fox's perspective, progress isn't always the goal. Hence, the title of this foreword.

I should also point out that, though foxes live in small family groups, they prefer to hunt alone, a disposition that suited me as well even before I went to public school where, despite my state's production of mavericks in the past—including the man who'd given that term his name—I learned soon after the end of World War II that regimentation had taken hold and that the bonanzas glittering just ahead wouldn't be going to those who'd stepped out of line or otherwise failed to make the grade. A new meritocracy had arrived along with its enforcers, and as wartime scarcities ended, inducements for playing the game grew bigger and more inventive.

We gawked at a neighbor's new Studebaker, modeled it seemed on a buzz bomb while pointing in two directions at once, and we drove uptown at night in our boxy old four-door sedan to gawk at the window of Krell's—whose slogan was "U-Know-We-Know-Radio"—where, in a video blizzard beamed down towards us from Charlotte, we saw images on a television screen, the only one in our city. . . though, in no time after that, not only were TVs plentiful but jet planes were swarming like bumblebees and people acquired refrigerators for which no iceman need ever come. New appliances of every sort began to proliferate, and there'd soon appear in our pantry at home a Bendix upright washing machine with a hand-cranked wringer attachment through which, as an experiment, I tried to feed my younger brother's arm.

That had been a bad idea as I grudgingly had to admit after he'd re-inflated, but it echoed some second thoughts that I'd instinctively started to have about our brave new postwar world as, amid repeated classroom screenings of a helmeted Bert the Turtle, we ducked and covered beneath our desks in readiness for an A-bomb attack. Even at nine or ten, some few of us questioned the film's advice to seek refuge under a tablecloth at a picnic near ground zero, and we doubted the wisdom and candor of those in charge of the show. . . *any* show, we told ourselves, including the one we were in.

Of course, at that early phase of our rebellion, we couldn't have put our grievances into words. But, after rationing and paper drives and seeing our fathers off to war, it had started to rankle with a few that our schooling was more about learning the rules than enlivening our minds and many were getting pigeonholed from the start—for being too slow or talking too much or lacking good penmanship—always, it seemed, the fidgety boys but never the more amenable girls and, almost as if by default, the kids who lived in the clapboard shacks along or across Rosewood Drive— not mill-village kids who had their own neighborhood schools or those from what was called colored town, but mostly poor white kids whose parents nobody had met.

So, in a tentative circumspect way without any noble agenda other than feeling it wasn't fair, I and a handful of others were beginning to demur and, though vaguely aware of I.Q. tests and how they were being used (one schoolyard bully kept boasting of having scored 100!), what we wanted our warders to hear along with the juvenile Robespierres staffing our safety patrols was, "Quit writing kids off as losers without giving them half a chance."

Still, nearly a decade would pass before the civil rights movement geared up and twice that long until the Sixties erupted, and, obvious though it ought to have been, it didn't occur to many of us that forty per cent of those in our state got written off anyhow simply because of their color—or that few of the girls would choose to dissent because the little they had to lose was all they were ever likely to get. Even on reaching junior high on the brink of a smugly complacent decade, we were aimless in our muted revolt and only just starting to question such things— though it's nonetheless true, I think, that, if we behaved like loners, we weren't just out for ourselves. We wanted the better postwar world that our country had been fighting for.

Admittedly, in folkloric terms, that sort of concern doesn't sound very foxlike. But after another eight or nine years when I started to study Japanese, I'd learn that, in its very different tradition, *inari* foxes aren't regarded as merely sly and amoral like their western counterparts but as bringers of good fortune, often assuming human form and acting in benevolent ways. Though I adopted it as my talisman, that wouldn't have meant a lot to most of my countrymen, either during or after the war in the Pacific—and yet, two doors down from us throughout those years was a greenhouse owned by Mitsuo Tokunaga who'd been born in Nagasaki and whose son was a friendly neighbor of ours.

Not only that, but much later in life when I was living in Tokyo, I'd meet a celebrated sculptor by the name of Minami Tada who, on learning where I was from, asked if by any chance I'd heard of an uncle of hers who, in 1908, had suddenly bolted from Japan and gone to the U.S. She told me that, several months after arriving in South Carolina, he'd traveled more than a hundred miles on foot from Charleston to my hometown of Columbia where in short order he'd gotten a job, married a young woman named Myrtle Wagstaff, and tried to get a bank loan in order to buy the greenhouse.

When informed that they'd need collateral, he wasn't familiar with the term but, on learning it meant he'd have to risk the loss of something of equal value if he failed to repay the loan, he'd pointed to his wife—not as some sort of chattel, but as what he held most precious and an iron-clad guarantee. That was, I instantly recognized, an *inari* foxlike move, and I knew as soon as I heard the tale that his name must have been Tokunaga—as indeed it actually was—and that, to the credit of all involved, he'd both gotten the loan and quickly repaid it in full.

In other words, as irregular as that was, my ultraconservative town had seen fit to make room for him—though I was also aware that, even long after the war, vandals would shatter panes at night while yelling out *"Banzai!"* or raging about somebody they knew who'd been on the march at Bataan. My mother was always indignant on those occasions, reminding me of such figures from the past as Charleston's James L. Petigru, a judge and ardent unionist who'd quipped on the eve of the Civil War that our state, for all its bluster and swagger, was "too small for a republic but too large for an insane asylum." Though I'd later come to realize that, because of his insider status, he'd been dismissed as an eccentric rather than pilloried as a traitor, that sort of accommodation would rarely be extended during my high school years when those who failed to toe the segregationist line, especially in smaller towns, were threatened, bombed, and awakened at night to crosses ablaze in their yards. . . as happened to kinfolk of mine.

That having been said, I don't mean to exaggerate the level of social ferment back then—for after nearly a generation of hardship and war what most people seemed to want wasn't radical change of any sort but an orderly path to prosperity in what they liked to call a traditional way of life. It may have been that such a reluctance to rock a storm-wracked patched-up boat resulted from post-traumatic exhaustion rather than selfish indifference to what was clearly wrong, but it served as a ready inducement for kids like me to rebel without a larger cause in mind, even causing me in time to challenge such wartime nostalgia as that of a much admired journalist named Ben Robertson who'd written in the midst of World War II that, though many South Carolinians had "wandered far off the track. . . instinct has never deserted us" and that therefore "we are not lost."

In his personal case that was probably true, but with tragic irony, he'd be killed in less than a year when his plane was blown off course while trying to land in Portugal—something I'd only learn on reading his book a second time at the age of thirty-one when, having returned from three years in England and a few months in San Francisco, I was living in Massachusetts and trying to decide whether to stay there or not. It was during a time of protests and turmoil concerning a far more dubious war and the height of the Civil Rights Movement back at home. I was then teaching a course at Harvard on "The Poor White and the Negro in the American South" and, along with standard works by Faulkner, Agee, Du Bois, and others of the sort, Ben Robertson's *Red Hills and Cotton* was totally unknown to virtually all my students—though, in the midst of my own uncertainty about whether I might have wandered too far off track myself, parts of it spoke directly to me in a very powerful way.

Foxes would once more come to mind during that inner debate, though I was at that stage of my life more inclined to reflect that, if foxes are seldom lost, that may well result from the fact that, depending on access to forage, their usual range of activity is about thirty acres or so—much less than I'm sharing at this moment with at least one vulpine tenant. It further occurs to me now while musing on the past that, for foxes and humans alike, survival might often depend on whom and what they trust in getting to where they're going—and more specifically to that point, if more of either rode motorcycles, there'd be fewer of us around. . . something I wish I'd known before finding that out for myself.

But a crucial truth for me—as I think it was for my fellow Ben whose heart had remained in the upstate—is that, if foxes know many things as they're reputed to do, it must be largely because in the course of their twisting and turning they encounter so many different sorts—the generous and staunchly brave as well as the wheedling and inane—and, as I've already said, it's my meetings with just such an array, from those who welcomed my crossing their paths to those who mildly resented it, that'll play a major part in this book. I'll bear witness to them as I do to myself if only to gainsay the thought that, as Wallace Stevens once wrote in words that, for reasons I hope to convey, now touch me to the quick:

> Children picking up our bones
> Will never know that these were once
> As quick as foxes on the hill. . .

—though none of us, in the end, can be quite quick enough. For all our cunning and wit, what we too will leave behind when we go under the hill are merely the tracks that took us there, like fossilized footsteps in mud or handprints on the walls of a cave.

1

Primordial Soup

As a rule of thumb for writing a memoir, I should probably follow the King's advice in *Alice in Wonderland*. "Begin at the beginning," he gravely advises, "and go on till you come to the end: then stop." Except, of course, even leaving aside so many regretted omissions, there's no way of truly knowing the end—not yet at least—and, even about the beginning, it's not as simple as that might seem. . . a point on which I need to elaborate.

As a student at Oxford in 1960 along with Alan Coren, who'd go on to become a famously hyper-verbal wit, and Kris Kristofferson, who wasn't yet Kris Kristofferson, I was obliged to study paleography precisely because, as prospective scholars more interested in the modern era, we would never have occasion to use what they wanted us to master—otherwise, we'd have been exempted. Reggie Alton was our teacher, of later renown as the handwriting expert who'd confirm the authenticity of both C.S. Lewis's notebooks and the suicide note of Kurt Cobain. Reggie struck us as a geek, and we joked about his terminology— "printers' balls" turned up repeatedly—and we thought of him as elderly. He was forty-one at the time and, though we didn't know it, an avid cricketer.

Many of the 15th-century screeds we were given to decipher were last wills and testaments written in a dying man's hand, scribbles that turned increasingly erratic and, in one that I well remember, ended in the middle of a word by plunging down the page as if transcribing a death rattle. Had it been an autobiography, it would indeed have come to the end and stopped.

But even playing in penalty time as I clearly am at my present age, I intend to complete this partial account before that sort of final whistle. This volume will only get us to halftime, as it were, though that still leaves the unanswered question of where exactly I ought to begin. According to my birth certificate, I was born at 5:15 on a rainy Friday afternoon, December 3rd, 1937, in the capital city of Columbia, South Carolina. My mother believed my actual debut was at 5:05, a dispute for which I was at the time no better equipped to resolve than I was to pay the hospital bill for a three-day stay that came to precisely $32.90 which, even in today's dollars, would be an incredible bargain. But such details are really beside the point for my mnemonic purposes because, despite the near certainty that what I'm about to confide will be disbelieved by many, my earliest recollection is from the womb.

Some sixty years ago, when I had done with paleography and was in my third and final year as a sometime beatnik Rhodes Scholar living in a dead-end Oxfordshire village along with a dog and a great grandnephew of Teddy Roosevelt, I smoked a little pot bestowed on me some months before by a former traveling companion who said she'd brought it back from Morocco tucked into her bra. I recall listening to the Gloria from the Klemperer recording of Beethoven's *Missa Solemnis* and discovering that a floor lamp in the corner of the room was sending forth immensely pleasurable cosmic vibrations. As I moved closer and closer to the light, I suddenly dredged up from the bottommost layer of my unconscious mind a recollection of drifting in an amniotic sea with the entirety of what nascent being I'd developed to that point focused on a throbbing insistent impulse urging me ecstatically to "Live! Live! Live! Live!"

I remember thinking at the time how extraordinary it was, at the age of 24, to have recalled such a distant prenatal sentience, like capturing light from the moment of creation, and wondering as I did so whether Beethoven too had been inspired by smoking something similar. I'd been given to understand that we contain within our bodies carbon atoms that date from nearly the beginning of time—star-stuff, in effect, as Carl Sagan would later say—which, if some form of memory might be somehow encoded within it, we should all be able to retrieve through endless incarnations what it truly was like when "Let there be light!" was first proclaimed. In any case, at my moment of revelation I had no doubt that what I'd summoned from my sojourn in the womb was absolutely authentic.

But then, assailed by an equally intense desire to feed on something in the kitchen and followed by choral strains of *Et incarnatus est*, I left the lamp behind for the Buddha-like fridge and opened it to reveal an incredibly beautiful stash of left-over food.

"Soup of the evening, beautiful Soup!" then supplanted the *Credo* in my mind as I pictured Lewis Carroll scribbling away in his Christ Church rooms for the daughter of its dean—whereas I myself, I reflected, was merely a member of Wadham College, often referred to as "Wadham-O" because it was said that, when any knowing snob inquired about which local college was yours and you confessed it was Wadham, he or she was likely to respond with a condescending "Oh!"

Nevertheless, as a Yank at Oxford, I was happily ensconced with Coren and Melvyn Bragg and others of our largely marginal social ilk who had a lot in common with each other and the freedom to pursue it—the latter all the way to a peerage and the former, though the offspring of a hairdresser and a plumber, to the Rectorship of St. Andrews. Often as twilight was falling during my first year in my seventeenth-century rooms, I'd gaze out over the well-clipped lawn, as they too must have done, asking myself what I was doing there. It's a question that I still pose in my more reflective moments, finding myself in places I once only dreamed about and remembering where I came from and how my family had gotten there.

Actually, I've been supplied with a lot of semi-credible information about my origins. My mother's family in the antebellum South had hired an itinerant genealogist to trace its lineage back not merely to Alfred the Great and William the Conqueror, whose descendants seemed to litter the farmsteads in that part of Virginia, but more inventively to semi-mythical figures like the bit-parts in *Macbeth*—Malcolm, Siward, and the haplessly ill-fated King Duncan himself—not to mention the non-Shakespearian but almost equally fictive Kenneth MacAlpin, Hugh Capet, and Rollo of Normandy.

Contemplating such lines of descent, I felt at times so much like Mark Twain's lost dauphin that at Oxford I took to signing myself "The Royal Nonesuch" in waggish notes to Coren and one or two other friends. But the burden of such a pedigree had seemingly taken a heavy toll as, except for Anne Boleyn's sister Mary—otherwise known as "the great and infamous whore"—few such resonant names had bedecked the family tree for the past five centuries or so, so I deemed it only prudent to drop all claims to the throne.

Meanwhile, back in South Carolina, my father's Scots-Irish family had traced its part of my lineage back to less fanciful origins like Robert the Bruce and the comparably combative John Knox after whom my forebears seem for the most part to have hied themselves to Glasgow or doodled their lives away in the backwater Ayrshire village of Dunlop—"the Fort at the Bend of the River"—though, for want of any invaders, the fortress had long since been reduced to no more than a featureless hillock.

I did, in fact, while studying in Britain, make a minor sort of pilgrimage to my ancestral hills and glens where I quickly discovered that, for a good long while, the marketers of our eponymous cattle and cheese had deleted the Dunlop name from their brands—in the case of the cheese, it appears, to fend off consumer complaints that it tasted "rubbery" as if confounding it in their minds with John Boyd Dunlop's more successful pneumatic tires. As a somewhat reluctant entrepreneur, cousin John had hailed from Ayrshire too but soon headed off to Ireland as would so many who shared our name, often en route to America—the earliest of whom had been my great progenitor, the Reverend William Dunlop whose adventurous nature had led him forth in 1684 with Henry Erskine, 3rd Lord Cardross, and hundreds of trusting Scots Covenanters to found a colony on the Carolina coast some fifty miles south of Charles Town. The outcome had been cautionary.

After ten awful weeks at sea, with only a third of their original number left alive, they'd established the rival settlement of Stuart's Town and, under Dunlop's direction, succeeded so well at both cornering the inland fur trade and alienating their neighbors that, when the Spaniards sailed northwards in response to an ill-considered raid on their colonies in Florida, everyone in the vicinity, most especially the English along with resentful Huguenots, eagerly pointed the way to where the Scots were holing up. The Spaniards made easy work of demolishing Stuart's Town—not only because they were guided to their target, but because the perfidious English in Charles Town had impounded a cargo of cannon intended for the Scots, thus assuring the latter would be outgunned.

But through luck or resourcefulness, my noble precursor had survived and redirected his career in ways that would postpone our family's next emigration for several generations by scurrying back to his native soil, where he'd eventually become not only Principal of the University of Glasgow but Historiographer Royal of Scotland.

Thus it was that during my time at Oxford, dimly perceiving an impending parallel with my own hopes of converting academic oblivion into something more viable, I decided to track Great William's origins in person—from his birthplace in Paisley, some twelve miles closer to Glasgow, to our ain folk's home in Dunlop—and quickly found that my pilgrimage had become what I could only describe as a Mister-Potato-Head family reunion. For I discovered that virtually everyone in the town had individual features I could instantly recognize as either Uncle George's comically bulbous nose, Uncle Spoony's emphatically philtrumed upper lip, or my father's and my own cleft chins—but mixed and scrambled in different combinations, causing me to reflect that, though we're not a handsome tribe, our genes apparently breed true. . . either that, or, on an even wider stage, we tend to intermarry.

In that latter respect, it was only in our fifty-fifth year of marriage that I learned my wife's forebears and my own were closely connected neighbors in 1439 when a man from whom she was descended had been ambushed and killed by yet another neighbor not far from my family's house where a survivor of that attack had been given refuge, and, furthermore, that, if I was indeed in the lineage of Robert the Bruce, one Robert Boyd of Cunninghame, bearing two of my wife's family names, had been among his most trusted allies. So who knows what elective affinity might have been at work when I, before we were out of grammar school and despite our difference in age (she was older by more than a year, which seemed an unbridgeable gap until I'd returned like Heathcliff from seasoning abroad) had felt so strangely drawn to her?

In any case, because I love the Old Norse sagas and in view of my own persistent wanderlust, I've long been convinced that, leaving the Orkneys behind, some Viking marauder, in or about the Eleventh Century, must have scuttled his longship at that nondescript bend in the river and impregnated one of my less travel-prone Celtic kin, a notion tenuously confirmed by my recent DNA sequencing—which, in addition to uncorroborated claims to Rollo & company on my mother's side, does indeed confirm some unidentified Nordic raiders on the other. And I feel absolutely certain that I and my left-handed daughter have inherited some portion of the genes of Bessie Dunlop, a midwife and so-called "wise woman" who, in 1576, was strangled and burned in Dalry for being an unregenerate witch.

Her offense had been saving the lives of people and livestock so consistently that her neighbors concluded no woman could be that clever except in league with the Devil—and, sure enough, when they'd tortured her sufficiently, she confessed and, for her own eternal good, they did what they thought they had to do. Though I hope to make a less stressful exit than hers, I like to think she'd approve of my more evasive response to such neighborly concerns.

Such hereditary lore may also help explain why I've taken Wendell Berry's advice to be like the fox so much to heart—that, and the fact that foxes are basically untamable, something confirmed in a harrowing way during my high school years. Though my younger brother was an avid hunter and though there was still a fifty-dollar bounty on foxes, he brought a fox kit home one weekend as the sole survivor of a den that he and a friend had discovered in the Congaree Swamp. It was only a day or two old, and he persuaded our parents to let him raise it as a pet in a pen that was quickly built behind our house under the dining room windows.

The only real dissent came from our two fox terriers and an orphaned cat named Tom who, having arrived under circumstances very much like the fox's, had imprinted on the terriers when they took mercy on it and, believing himself to be a dog, had behaved accordingly even to joining in when they were chasing cars. But nothing of that sort would be in the cards for the fox, and every book we consulted warned us emphatically that foxes couldn't be domesticated and that, even if it pretended otherwise, we shouldn't assume it was.

But inevitably, I suppose, we proceeded as if it couldn't hurt to try. When we held it in our arms, it would tremble incessantly, and we all knew better than to nuzzle it—though one warm afternoon when it was roughly six months old, my mother's maternal instincts caused her to lean down over it as it lay curled in her lap. And quick as a rattlesnake's bite, it slashed its razor-like teeth across my mother's nose, nearly severing it from her face and persuading us in an instant that the books—along with our dogs and cat—had been irrefutably right.

The following noon, as we sat for dinner around the table looking askance at my mother, we heard the fox in its pen beginning to convulse, and, in a matter of minutes, it was dead. I thought its death was a mystery, though I now realize that my father must have poisoned it in order to have it examined for rabies—a deed that in retrospect seems like something out of *Macbeth*.

It wasn't rabid, though. It was just a fox.

2

Initial Tracks

I began to wander at an early age. My first getaway on my own took place in the summer of 1941 when I was less than four years old and living in the state's oldest inland city of Camden, where five of my first cousins also lived—three of them older and two younger with two more in the offing. Fussed over still as an only child, content with all my arrangements at home and lacking even a vague idea of what might lie beyond, I decided to set forth nonetheless to see a bit more of the world. . . knowing as I did that it was full of relatives who, if I needed help along the way, would gladly provide it.

Still, based on my previous experience with mobility, I might have hesitated. I'd begun to talk at a very early age and, in fact, my mother boastfully recorded in my beribboned baby book that I was speaking in complete sentences before I was one—though she deemed it less worthy of note that, having taken a few tottering steps at about the same time, I sat down with the resolve of a union worker going on strike (few of whom could be found in our rigidly "right to work" state) and couldn't be induced to walk again for another six months or so. In retrospect, she ascribed that delayed development to a device fairly common at the time, a sort of circular chair on wheels with a seat through which I could stick my legs, propelling myself at fairly high speeds wherever I wanted to go.

Compared to such facile locomotion, walking had little to recommend it. But premature mobility had its hazards, and, at just about the age of one, I was zipping around the kitchen one day—presumably muttering to myself in complex sentences—when I found a dangling cord and gave it a tug.

As chance would have it, the cord was attached to a percolator and, when I yanked, it toppled over, pouring scalding coffee down my arm. Our pediatrician was an old friend of my grandfather's—a physician more revered for his folksy bedside manner than for his scientific knowledge at a time when the treatment of third-degree burns was hardly scientific to begin with—and it was his conviction that nothing would heal me faster than Vitamin D, which we get naturally from the sun. So he had a miniature cross devised with straps to hold my arms in place and, equipping me with diminutive dark-tinted goggles to protect my eyes, instructed my mother to slather me with cod liver oil and set me out each day in the midday Southern sun like a loaf of un-risen bread. As a consequence, I've never willingly taken a sunbath in my life, and, had I thought things through more carefully, I might well have responded like some character in an offbeat Russian novel and declined to leave my bed in daylight ever again, especially when slathered with cod liver oil.

Nevertheless, once deprived of my wheeled conveyance, I did elect to take up walking but, though I soon was getting the hang of it, had no place special to go. Inasmuch as I had any plans at all, it was for things to remain more or less as they'd been for as long as I could remember which gradually became two years and then nearly three. During that time we'd moved to another house not far removed from the long dusty road that we'd been living on before. The roads were dusty because they'd been left unpaved to accommodate the horses which some of our neighbors stabled in their yards, including the spinster next door who would join the Navy during World War II and a relative of hers who lived two houses down from her with tombstones for the former mounts she'd buried where she could see them. Both of those neighbors were eccentric, and, though I didn't know it at the time, they were aunts of the woman whom I'd eventually marry.

Actually, Camden was full of the kinfolk of my future wife, and they were all eccentric. One was an antiquarian called Duster who lived in a dilapidated house amid ancient leather-bound books and rusty cannonballs, and another was an inveterate bon vivant who'd bought two elephants from a bankrupt traveling circus and tried to train them for planting cotton. He hadn't succeeded—but then, none of my future wife's relatives seemed to make a success of anything much, perhaps in part because they tended to marry each other, though everyone agreed that almost all of them had mastered the art of living. They could shoot straight, tell a good story and hold their liquor—and, in a place yet to recover fully from the War Between the States, much less the Great Depression, those were pretty much all that mattered. And they took care of each other, as did my mother and her sister.

The name of the street we lived on, according to my mother when she was well into her nineties, was Lakeview Terrace, though I can't recall any evidence of either a lake or a terrace—and, in fact, on current maps I can only find a Lakeview Avenue, which is indeed a short distance from a lake. Details of that sort are murky now, but what I do remember vividly is that, in the driveway of our second house, I had a carpenter's bench that served as the center of my existence, something that must have been left behind when the house had been built or renovated.

I would straddle the bench for much of a typical day, pretending to hammer and saw with no discernible purpose until the big event occurred that was the other main facet of my day. Schoolchildren in knickers and skirts would return on foot from a grammar school down the road, toting their books and satchels and I, having decided that this was a meaningful task, would run down to the fence as they went by and shout out as they passed, "Hi, boys! Hi, girls!"

Sometimes they'd smile and answer. Often they merely plodded by, but I was undeterred. "Hi, boys! Hi, girls!" I'd cry as they paraded past—until one day, an event took place that left me flabbergasted. As I was standing by the fence carrying out my usual role, a student who must have been in the fourth or fifth grade came trudging along alone. "Hi, boy!" I shouted, expecting to cheer him up. He paused for a moment by the fence, glowering in my direction, then barked out angrily, "Aw, SHUT UP!"

I was stunned as he stalked away. I'd never realized the world could be so churlish or ungrateful. I stood there in silence as he slouched around the corner. I looked at the other boys and girls going by, but something was irretrievably broken regarding not only my daily ritual but the bench and my *raison d'être*. I never again went down to the fence in mid-afternoon. My mother, who was well aware of my routine, solicitously pointed out when it was time for the girls and boys to be returning from school, but I shook my head sadly. I would have to discover another purpose in life.

In a way, I wasn't alone. As I've already indicated, the town itself had never recovered from a demoralizing rout of Continental troops on its outskirts more than a century and a half before or the further debacle of the Civil War some eighty years after that and, as if in unspoken agreement, there'd been a general resolve to steer clear of history altogether. Among other things, that strategy had resulted in the preservation of numerous piazza-girdled plantation houses amid the pine trees and the white sandy by-ways of the equine-oriented town.

We didn't inhabit one of those mansions, but my cousins did while we ourselves had initially lived in a recently-built two-story house—the departure point from which I launched my great hegira—with a large dog pen out back containing a Great Dane named Fräulein (pronounced "fraw-LEEN" according to my father, who, while headed towards an eventual law degree, had detoured for an apparently desultory two semesters of German language study) plus sixteen Dalmatians cohabiting with Frawleen, all of them fenced in by boards and chicken wire.

I don't remember why we had so many dogs, though I think all but two of the Dalmatians belonged to a single litter. Notwithstanding the fact that almost everyone we knew had horses as well as dogs, neither of my parents rode nor did either of them hunt so far as I can recall. But I've got several creased and faded black-and-white photos of my cousins on horseback and one of me on foot that was taken shortly before my notorious excursion, posed in front of a pen that's teeming with Dalmatians that are tussling unconcernedly behind me as I, with a self-possessed smirk, salute the camera. I'm wearing a sized-down soldier suit with jodhpurs and boots—or maybe cardboard puttees—along with a campaign hat and Sam Browne belt, looking like a smug though dwarfish Mussolini. In another snapshot from the time, I'm dressed instead as a nurse, wearing a sort of kerchief and dish-towel sarong, apparently untroubled by any hint of gender-bending. Again, the Dalmatians are seething behind me, though this time their attention is focused on some event inside the pen.

I have no idea who took the pictures. I would suppose it was my mother since, at that point in my much-indulged existence, I was still enjoying her more-or-less exclusive attention while my father, who would have been about thirty, was occupying himself with his construction supply company, drinking and gambling after hours with some of the money-rich Yankee horse-people who lived in most of those big plantation houses. He'd been very dashing in college, starring as I've mentioned in three or four sports a year and, once at the beach as I've been told, while wooing my future mother, he'd pointed to a gull overhead and invited her to watch as he aimed and threw a seashell, hitting it in its head and, to his surprise and my mother's dismay, watching it drop down dead.

Fortunately for me, that didn't deter my mother who, at twenty, was so utterly taken with him—he being some six years older and, after several perfunctory years in his uncle Joe Roddey's bank, then halfway towards his law degree—that her mother, who must have harbored some considerable reservations, had spirited her away in the middle of the Depression for a cooling-off tour of Europe. . . which, in any case, came to naught, as my arrival would confirm in little more than a year.

As I've noted already, I had no complaint about how things were being managed at home, especially while still an only child. But, on several occasions, when I'd walked to a park some two or three blocks away in the company of my mother or our cook-and-nursemaid Pearl, I'd noticed that the boundaries of the world were somewhat farther away than I had previously supposed. That was, of course, during an era in the south when African American servants could be taken for granted by about half the white population while the servants themselves could take nothing for granted except the likelihood that, in return for the appearance of grateful loyalty, they'd get relatively civil treatment along with meager wages without the added burden of having to vote. What I remember best about Pearl is that her feet were always hurting, encased as they were in loafer-like shoes with heels flattened out in back so that, reconfigured in this fashion, they'd slide along like carpet slippers. When Pearl grumbled—as she did, I believe, incessantly—it was always about her feet in particular, however worthy of such complaints the world in general may have been.

But it was precisely the world in general that I was so curious about. I had no idea where Pearl had come from when she appeared each morning almost as soon as I woke up—and I was similarly oblivious about the park we visited, which had a bandstand at its center ringed by a half-dozen ancient cannon with their muzzles stuffed with cement aiming their impotent threats in all directions, though at what and at whom I couldn't begin to fathom. All I understood was the tantalizing insinuation that somewhere beyond what struck me as the considerable distance I'd traversed in order to get there—though well within the range of a cannonball's trajectory—was a realm of experience about which I knew nothing but for which I blandly assumed my uniform had equipped me. After all, though we weren't yet part of it, much of the rest of the world had been at war since before I'd even turned two.

So it happened that the impulse impelling me to set out alone was nothing more or less than a conviction that the time had arrived for me to explore a bit farther on my own. I can even recall the logic of my decision to let the dogs out to accompany me. It was clear that they were just as eager to see the world, and I intuitively understood that, if any trouble should arise, having a group of toothy friends could prove more useful to me than a battery of spiked cannons.

Having reached that conclusion, I slipped the hasp that opened the gate that I'd been told must always stay closed and was instantly enveloped by my grateful entourage. Replaying that moment in my mind, I picture myself decked out in military attire, though because there was no one there to record the event, I can't be certain of such details. What I do remember is my determination to travel down the long white ribbon of sand in a direction I'd never gone before, towards what I now suppose must have seemed where the rest of the world began—just past the point, some three hundred yards away, where the road curved back through a grove of trees and anyone traveling on foot would be effectively out of sight from the house I'd left behind and conceivably within view of either the lake or the terrace.

As if watching it in a movie, I can see myself making slow but painfully dogged progress towards that curve. Partly because the Dalmatians, with their heads at about my shoulder height, kept jostling me about and because, in their exuberance, they kept yelping to each other, I also remember thinking I might have made a mistake in recruiting them after all. Frawleen was mostly aloof, trotting in a silent straight line along the side of the road while the others were aimlessly milling about, turning back at times to check on me, then conferring with each other while bolstering my perception that a single serious-minded escort was all I'd really needed.

Such concerns were soon mooted, however, because, to my dismay when I was still some twenty or thirty yards from the curve, I heard Pearl's plaintive wail and, looking back over my shoulder, spied her in hot pursuit—or, at least, in a lukewarm walking-on-coals pursuit that, despite its lack of speed, would inevitably overtake me. I stubbornly plowed ahead while she just as stubbornly pursued, and, in a matter of minutes, my great adventure was over.

When my mother had returned from wherever she'd gone and been told of my defection, she was greatly distressed by the news, and I distinctly remember wanting to reassure her by what I would later recall as a know-ye-not-that-I-must-be-about-my-father's-business sort of explanation. With our neighbors' help, the dogs were quickly rounded up, and several months later we moved to that other house only a block or two away—but with a fenced-in front yard and without a tantalizing view of the long inviting ribbon of road tempting me to abscond again. Besides, I had at some point realized the basic flaws in my plan, having never considered what I would do at suppertime, where I would sleep, or any such practical matters.

That I'd been so carelessly impulsive was something I'd think about quite a lot, though at no time did I truly repent, and from that point on, my wanderlust was an indelible trait—encouraged, no doubt, by the penchant my family had displayed for moving about so much. Before I'd reached the second grade, we'd have lived in at least seven houses, and, to this very day, I've yet to see that purported lake view in Camden.

On the other hand, when a few months after my thwarted breakout, as I was racing about the house bumping into various things and heard my favorite aunt, Dee Savage, suggest that I ought to watch where I was going, I answered to her amusement, "But how can I watch where I'm going when I don't *know* where I'm going?"

Actually, though it strikes me now as an almost Zen-like riddle and reply, I can remember the vague indignation I felt at such a facile reprimand, just as I recall being mildly affronted when the same admired aunt, my mother's older sister, took to calling me "Big Business" as if in mock reproach of how I went about doing things. Were I to defend myself today, I'd argue that, despite those early snapshots of me tricked out like a would-be Il Duce, it was never about my being so full of myself—it was about my project of the moment, whatever that happened to be, big busyness in effect. . . and I can say that with such confidence because, more than eight decades later, it's still my basic default mode even for writing a memoir.

I should add that, in time, I'd come to love my aunt almost as much as my mother and my cousins as well, especially the girls who so applauded me as a daredevil that, to corroborate their flattering supposition, I quickly became a pint-sized Douglas Fairbanks—which would lead me in turn to several close calls and one roundtrip to extinction.

3

The Lover

Like most of us with blissful early childhoods, I think I was a lover from the start, though relating that to a career path was something else again. For what seems to have been a very long while—up until the actual moment that Robert Lowell cast doubts on my intention—I'd harbored the hazy notion of becoming a vagabond poet. It must have originated in wanting to please my mother because, even some years later, my sensibility clung to her youthful predilection for the verse of Edna St. Vincent Millay and E.A. Robinson's *Tristram* which she'd read to me instead of Mother Goose in a huskily rhythmic voice that I'd later recognize as close to that of Millay herself ("'Son,' said my mother, / When I was knee-high. . ."). She liked Robert L. Stevenson too. So, long before I'd heard that roses were red and violets blue, I was chanting to myself that "Whenever the moon and stars are set, Whenever the wind is high,

> All night long in the dark and wet
> A man goes riding by

with hoofbeats in the cadences of the words.

When I was in junior high, I discovered her volume of Rupert Brooke and found the *Rubáiyát* on my own and Shelley and Keats and early Yeats. Then Swinburne and Dowson during my high school years and, in my last summer at home before going off to college, I'd lie at night on the sleeping porch of my grandfather's house, up among the rustling birds in the branches of water oaks, listening to recordings and perusing stacks of library books—in particular a volume of Aubrey Beardsley's prints and the album's liner notes for Carl Orff's *Carmina Burana.*

"She stood in her scarlet gown," I read from its libretto, aware of what I felt but couldn't express or explain:

> If anyone touched it,
> It rustled.

Yes, I silently said to myself, and "Eia!" sang the soprano.

> She stood in her scarlet gown,
> Her face was like a rose,
> And her mouth was a flower in bloom. . .

"Eia!" the soprano sang again as if she knew what I wanted to say.

It had, in fact, been the rustling of a dress that, late in 1943 when I was only five (the same year during which, while my father was overseas and I and my mother were living in Atlanta along with my two-year-old brother and baby sister) would lead me to cross a boundary that I didn't know existed. It was also at about the time my mother took me to the lavishly ornate Fox Theater to see my very first movie, a rerun of *The Invisible Man* which, though it seemed a curious choice, was ironically apt in a way because I myself, having begun attending school at Williams Street Elementary two or three months before, would become a ghostly presence there as a consequence of chronic tonsilitis. . . not quite invisible perhaps, but absent more often than not.

Looking back on that year, I don't know how my mother was able to manage. Because of a wartime housing shortage, the five of us—quickly reduced to four when my father got shipped out—had been obliged to take whatever could be found, which turned out to be a cramped and dingy row house in a housing project called Techwood. The neighborhood, such as it was, was ruled by a bunch of older kids who, prompted by my debility or a class-conscious indignation at my Camden-bred air of gentility, used to waylay me on my way home from school, threatening to beat me up. I invariably fought back, returning home battered and pummeled until one day I discovered The Scissors—a smackdown sort of maneuver by which, from a supine position, I locked my legs about my assailant's waist and squeezed him like a python. After I'd won a couple of bouts in this improbable fashion, they decided to leave me alone, and, during a month or so of reasonable health, I began to feel more expansive.

At that point, I'd just begun to overcome an incident that had shadowed me since the first half-week of school when, during a portion of the day devoted to art, we were instructed to draw a picture in Crayola of our house and our family. I complied in the way that had always earned my mother's applause, by being as imaginative as I could. I can remember thinking the assignment itself was disappointingly banal—and, though I may have been impelled by some latent subconscious need to deal with my father's absence and the loss of our previous lifestyle, my sole intent was to change my teacher's perception of me as merely an enfeebled kid in a very tough neighborhood.

One after another, we were told to hold up our pictures for the class's inspection, identifying the members of our family. I complied by drawing a house like the ones we'd lived in before—except for a series of loops stacked up along each side and a total absence of people. When my turn came to hold my picture up, I saw the teacher frown and was pleased when she objected that I'd failed to follow directions because it gave me a chance to reveal my ingenuity.

"But where's your family?" the teacher asked. "And what are the things you've drawn on the sides of the house?"

"Those are the giant's fingers," I replied. "He ate my family."

I saw the horrified consternation on her face, and, before I knew what was happening, I'd been ushered down to the principal's office where I was soon closeted with a woman I'd never met before who asked questions about my views on this and that, including whether I was afraid of being harmed or wanted to harm somebody else.

I responded by assuring her that, although I'd been beaten up for a while, I now had a secret weapon that enabled me to take care of myself. I shared that development with an aplomb that she must have diagnosed as disturbingly symptomatic because, from that day on, I was treated in a circumspect but very unflattering manner—even when, walking to school one morning, I watched a bigger boy as he raced across the street ahead of an oncoming car and concluded that, if he'd made it safely across, I could do so as well. I discovered the flaw in my logic too late, but recognizing what was about to occur, I managed, by some prodigious good luck and timing, to thrust my left arm out, converting the horizontal thrust of the rapidly braking automobile into a sort of vertical vault—over the bumper, onto the hood, and up against the windshield. I was silently applauding myself when, having come to a sudden halt, the car recoiled with a lurch, dumping me back on the pavement.

It had happened so fast that, by the time most witnesses heard the brakes, they thought I'd been hit and knocked flat in the middle of the street. I was eager to hurry on to class, but the principal's minions insisted on checking me out for possible injuries. The difficulty with this otherwise reasonable precaution was that a school nurse wasn't there, all the teachers were women, and the somewhat elderly principal must have made up his mind that it was beneath the dignity of his office. So I was inspected in the furnace room by the janitor, who obliged me to remove my shirt and trousers for what resembled the frisking of some malefactor, and, by the time I was free to reenter my class, I seemed less a lucky survivor than a bothersome sociopath who'd been up to his usual tricks.

All this is by way of background to what happened several weeks later during the time of day when, having unrolled our bathmats that were otherwise kept stored in open wooden lockers for what was euphemistically known as one of two daily "rest periods," we were compelled to lie silently and rigidly in place for twenty or thirty minutes. I'm not sure if this form of torture was deemed appropriate for six and seven-year-olds—and, in my case, even younger—or whether it was the consequence of there being no schoolyard to speak of in that bleakly urban location. But to ease the tedium, I used to turn my head, like a youthful Dante in Florence, to gaze at a self-assured blonde with pigtails who'd attracted my admiration—partly because of her blandly imperious manner and largely because of a wardrobe that could easily have passed muster for a Little Miss beauty pageant (had there been such a thing in the slums). I can't remember her name but can clearly summon an image of her on the day of my transgression.

She was wearing ankle socks and white shoes with a strap that buckled across the tops of her feet. Those were standard accessories, of course, but on this particular day they were combined with a pale-blue mid-calf dress made in all probability of rayon, the new synthetic fiber that looked and rustled like silk. Though she must have known how beguiling she looked, it wasn't she herself but what she seemed to embody that captured and held my gaze—beauty, with a capital B, like a blue flag in a bog. . . if not an authentic Beatrice, then my first brush with Calypso.

When rest period had ended, while she was still rolling up her bathmat, I approached her and kissed her on the cheek. She looked at me very strangely as the teacher rushed to her aid, shoving me roughly away. It was all the same to me—I'd paid homage to what I admired—though I was struggling to comprehend why what was cherubic in Camden would be atrocious in Atlanta, and I could only conclude that, like having to fight my way home from school, it was just another consequence of moving to a place so lamentably less genteel.

But later that afternoon, after I'd gotten home, there was a roaring noise in the street no more than a sidewalk away from our dingey row-house's door, and, peering out the front window, I saw a motorcycle policeman in jodhpurs and knee-high boots dismounting and checking the number above our door. He pounded loudly for admittance, and, when my mother had let him in, confirmed my name with her while glaring in my direction. He said an official complaint had been lodged by the victimized party's parents. . . "against your son," he added.

My mother gave him a baffled look and asked him what I'd done. When told that I'd been prevented from doing anything more than an unwanted kiss, she asked what more it was supposed I might have otherwise inflicted.

"You never know," the policeman darkly said. "One thing can lead to another."

On overhearing this exchange, I began to speculate on what he might have in mind, though I could think of nothing. Letting his words sink in, the policeman nodded and was putting his gloves back on. He was letting me off with a warning, he said, but if anything like that should happen again, there would be consequences. After he'd left, my mother instructed me to restrain my gestures of affection unless I knew they were wanted. It was on the whole like fighting she said—don't start it, just retaliate. . . but, in the case of girls, not with The Scissors she warned.

I wonder now what Dante would have done if the Portinaris had dispatched a condottiere to tell him to keep his ogling to himself—or, for that matter, what Sigmund Freud might have opined about one William Dillon, the vaudeville lyricist who in 1911 had penned the ever-popular "I Want a Girl (Just like the Girl That Married Dear Old Dad"? Dillon had already had a hit with "I'd Rather Have a Girlie than an Automobile," so he was definitely on a somewhat incestuous if apparently aimless prowl—which brings me back around to the girl who'd married my own dear old dad and to yet another example of pop psychology regarding what's been soberly discussed for three or four decades now as the potent and very personal process of "love mapping."

In order to illustrate how this concept applies to me, I'll jump forward to 1980 when the term had just appeared and I in my mid-forties, having briefly achieved a modest celebrity as an expert in visual media, was asked by an archivist at the local university to examine a cache of 16mm films recorded by what was thought to have been the state's first amateur cameraman. Dating largely from the Twenties and early Thirties, all of them were silent and, as chance would have it, they'd been made by a physician who'd been one of my grandfather's closest friends—though not the one who'd treated my scalded arm. I agreed to review the films once they'd been safely dubbed onto videotape, enabling me to assess their potential historical value.

It turned out to be an intriguing undertaking, and I watched with a sort of archaeological fascination as I saw my city and state several decades before I was born. Those most frequently photographed resembled the Russian aristocrats who, in Leo Tolstoy's day, had spent their abundant leisure time riding over to Yasnaya Polyana to hunt for a couple of weeks, sharing provincial privileges that included not only the land itself but serfs who always appeared to be lurking in the background with impassive or sullen expressions, paddling boats in the marshes or displaying the spoils of daylong shooting spree from which they'd otherwise been excluded. Though in South Carolina during those years, most of the former wealth had been irrecoverably lost, there'd still been lots of land and plenty of fish and game, and as always seems to happen on film, much that would later seem revelatory had been peripheral at the time.

One example of the latter that at least acknowledged the inroads of modernity showed a couple of teenaged flappers standing beside a rudimentary landing strip that a sign somewhat grandly proclaimed in the opening shot to be the Columbia Municipal Airport. That was followed by long slow pan of a one-prop Taylor E-2 Cub landing and taxiing to a stop and then by a fairly sophisticated set up exploiting depth of field as the flappers raced past the camera to greet the incoming plane in what I took to be a parody of Lindbergh's landing at Le Bourget.

But, as I watched, I was suddenly overcome by a sense of romantic nostalgia for, though I saw her only from behind, something about the smaller, more graceful girl had so riveted my attention that it was as if, having happened on a lost clip of Anna Pavlova, I'd been enthralled by her ineffable grace. . . but only to realize that what I'd found so captivating was someone I'd missed in time but might have loved if given the chance.

Trying to fathom my response, I paused the tape to consider what it was about the flapper racing out towards the plane that had prompted such overwrought throes of regret—her exuberant gait as she'd skipped into view, the angle at which she'd held her head, the tossing about of her bobbed hair? Whatever it was, I felt a pang, knowing that, even if she was still alive, she'd now be so much older and the outcome would be the same. Then, as I started the tape up again, she turned to smile at the camera. . . and, with a stupefied lurch, I recognized my mother.

Oh, Sigmund, thy aim is true! For it's clear to me now in retrospect that all my deep and lasting loves have coded out at one or rarely more than two degrees of separation which, since I've just been invoking Freud, is all too easy to interpret as evidence of an Oedipal fixation or the product of a slack imagination deriving, of course, from a narcissistic self-regard for which I should feel abashed. But the problem with compulsions of this sort is that they do their furtive work in our subconscious minds, assuming the guise of destiny—or, as in the case of Dante, of something numinous—when they are, in fact, mostly physical and disappointingly mundane.

Though I've gradually come to recognize the features that most attract me, that hasn't reduced their appeal. Even today at what's generally regarded as an *hors de combat* stage, I'm instantly drawn to small, slender, and supple brunettes who part their hair in the middle and especially to those among them with taut Achilles tendons who move like dancers or runners—which I now perceive to mean more like Artemis or Athena and less like Aphrodite. Nevertheless, because I was long unaware of having such predilections and girls in those last two groups were in short supply back then, my search for such an ideal was largely put on hold for the eight or nine years that ensued on my missteps in Atlanta—though it's probably worth pointing out that the object of my attention there, like almost anyone with pigtails, had in fact had a middle part.

But everything went into play again one morning in the ninth grade—which, because of a high-school classroom shortage, had remained at Hand Junior High—when I was instantly smitten after chancing to see a girl a year younger than I who, at recess in a student-run canteen, was leaning on a windowsill that opened into the schoolyard, handing somebody a Nutty Buddy.

From an inside corridor, I'd idly glanced in her direction as she was turning her gaze towards me, then back again to her customer. I can see her even now in my mind, poised with one foot in the air, wearing a short-sleeved Peter-Pan blouse with an ochre vest and black ribbon tie along with a sky-blue corduroy skirt. Though I knew who she was, she'd meant nothing to me until I'd glimpsed that antique pose, the saddle oxfords and rolled white socks, the balanced but casual arabesque and lovely stretched-out dancer's calf—and in that split-second exchange of looks, something had clicked between us. So we'd date for a while as one did at the time and come back together through the years as she studied Martha Graham technique and, at one point during her college career, was a lab partner for my future wife, dissecting pickled specimens and closing yet another loop in the interconnected cast of those who'd be recurrent in my life.

Regarding the appeal of actively fleet and graceful women, I should probably note that, however slow I'd been to walk, I matured very quickly during my early teens, achieving my full adult height of five-feet-seven shortly before I turned fourteen and thinking thereafter of myself as one of the taller kids in my grade even as others kept growing. I was agile and quick afoot, playing B-squad basketball and, somewhat later, briefly taking up boxing as a stylishly unsuccessful light-welter weight while playing varsity football and running track on through high school and college—though on the gridiron, I was for the most part running for my life and, on our ill-kept cinder tracks, specialized in semi-balletic low-hurdle events that no longer exist in competition.

Being so athletic further boosted my confidence around girls, though during that phase of my life I also discovered, as most people do, that I was less attractive than I'd supposed or was hoping to become, so I took the precautionary steps of memorizing great chunks of the *Song of Solomon* and *Rubáiyát of Omar Khayyam* as basic aids for any attempted seduction—which, in those innocent days, consisted almost entirely of "necking," meaning endeavors above the neck. In my initial trial runs, I quickly learned that, if I got more than five or six quatrains into the *Rubaiyat* without the eyes of my current interest glazing over, my chances from there were fairly good. . . at least, with the sort of young women who used to be called "bluestockings" and were very much my type. Otherwise, I was generally out of luck.

Actually, while still in the early stages of my amorous career, I protested in one of my earliest journals that what I found most alluring in those I wooed wasn't only or even primarily physical, though I described those adventures in terms I must have picked up in introductory biology, comparing myself to Darwin aboard *The Beagle* with whole chains of Galapagos islands waiting to be explored—"but in wonder rather than conquest," I was at pains to point out. By which I think I meant, in the crazed

hormonal confusion of that portion of my life, an endless variety
of newly discovered selves as well as bodies with their minds and
sensibilities as willingly open to me as mine would be to them. .
. or, in other words, how Darwin might have viewed his trip if
he'd been a poet as well. What I didn't convey in my journal was
how torn I actually was between the familiar and the exotic as if
fixated on one while tantalized by the other.

What was most familiar, of course, were my cousins, the
three daughters of Uncle Henry and Aunt Dee—with Hope a year
older than I, Virginia one year younger, and Helen much younger
still, an Emily Bronte look-alike who at the age of eleven would
declare herself a Buddhist and, in a somewhat contradictory vein,
go to work on an autobiography. Over the course of my life, I'd
love each of them in a different way, but the oldest would be the
first to break my heart. . . the beautiful elusive Hopey with
whom on the 3rd of April, 1938, despite our difference in age
and the fact that, at the time, her family lived in Camden while
mine was still in Columbia, I'd be jointly christened at the same
Trinity Episcopal Church where our mothers had been baptized
as well, mine just twenty-two years before. In keeping with my
tripartite theme, our mutual cousin Carroll DuBose was baptized
alongside us—I as a firstborn, Carroll as a second, and Hopey,
though the first of three girls, as the thirdborn in her family with
four more siblings to come.

I've never read Wordsworth's "We Are Seven" without
thinking of my Savage cousins, especially nowadays when
they're down to only two. Back then my cousins were like a small
army with me as an only child a mere camp follower in the rear.
In addition to an older half-brother known by his childhood
nickname of Bill Will, Hopey's other older brother was, like our
Columbia cousin, named for our mothers' father, Carroll Jones.
Then, after I'd been around for a year, her sister Virginia would
appear followed by Sam and Harry and finally the youngest, nine
years after me, the future Buddhist and Christian Scientist named
Helen.

But even before the last two had arrived, I was so eager for
my cousins' attention that, as reported already, I got carried away
by my derring-do—recklessly climbing and swinging about or
prancing along the edges of roofs. The older boys were less

impressed than the girls, though even among the latter, holding Hopey's interest for long was more than I could pull off. . . but, then, neither could anyone else.

When those closest to my age were young—say, six and four to my five—Hopey had a precocious array of what she called her "familiar spirits," assigning them esoteric names like Beelzebub and Ashtaroth and dispatching them hither and yon within her younger sister's earshot. With no such minions at her disposal, Virginia was both credulous and modest—though when she asked if she could join the supernatural fun, she'd been told by Hopey to conjure up her own, which she'd repeatedly tried to do to no avail.

They lived in a rambling old early 19th-century Charleston-style single house called the Greenleaf Villa, turned sideways to the street with joggling boards on long porches that ran the length of both of the two main stories, and, within its wrought-iron fence and head-high maze-like hedges, was a formal garden largely gone to seed with a broken marble fountain at its center densely circled by bushes with branches intertwining overhead. That was where Hopey liked to sit summoning her spirits in a deep oracular voice whenever Gin approached. Again and again, Gin would beg to be included, but the answer was always the same—until she'd conjured her own familiar spirits, there'd be no place for her in the garden.

When Aunt Dee, with a new toddler making demands, told the girls they'd have to play more amicably together, Hopey had glowered but complied. A few hours passed and, though Hopey's voice was calling out again, Gin was nowhere to be seen or heard. Both curious and concerned, Aunt Dee began combing throughout the house and, as she was leaving the dining room, just happened to look down and saw her beneath the table, lying rigidly on her back.

"Virginia!" she burst out. "What in the world. . .?"

"Shhh," Gin whispered placidly. "I'm the woss babe in the wagoon"—the role she'd been assigned.

That was Hopey's intransigent way. She couldn't be coerced, not then or ever. But Gin, too, had a plucky sort of persistence and, finally one day after days and weeks of trying, she managed to conjure a sort of spirit. It wasn't much, as she'd later concede—a gimpy, one-legged dwarf with a long white wispy beard and a tendency to fade in and out of his surroundings—which in this case were in the dining room again, back underneath the table. But as soon as she was sure the dwarf was really there, she rushed into the garden and up to the broken fountain.

Hopey eyed her very suspiciously as Gin arrived with the breathless news that she'd conjured up a spirit of her own.

"No, you haven't!" Hopey told her.

"Yes! Yes! I really have! He's not very big, and he's only got one leg. But he's really and truly there!"

"Where?" Hopey asked, eyes narrowing to baleful slits.

"In the dining room. . . he's under the table waiting for me to come back."

Hopey gestured with both hands over her head and muttered ferociously, "Moloch and Belial! Go quickly to the dining room! Find the little man there. . . and KILL! KILL! KILL!"

"Oh, no! Oh, no!" Gin wailed as she went rushing from the garden.

But when she got to the dining room, she saw the dwarf was already dead and starting to dissolve into the patterns of the rug. Soon he was gone altogether, and she'd never conjure up anything more.

Just recently I stumbled across a photo of Hopey as a girl, seated composedly on a horse—which I suppose to be the mare named Belle that she shared with her brother Carroll who, nearly seven decades later, would note in a book of his own that, frustrated though he was by the horse's stubborn defiance, it had "submitted to her strong will." That's evident in the photograph. The horse is still, and so is she—no turbulence of any kind. I study it with a magnifying glass, but there's no hint of what would erupt in another ten years or so when she'd more or less simultaneously write to our bishop in Columbia questioning or renouncing the faith and get herself detained at the university's library for trying to swipe a volume of Friedrich Nietzsche's work—but only because the librarian, when Hopey produced no student card, had refused to let her check it out and, in that still non-air-conditioned era, Hopey had tried to toss it from a window and afterwards retrieve it. Campus Security had arrived, and she'd been banned from the campus.

In the midst of all that turmoil and headstrong goings on, she'd visited us with her mother in our grandfather's house on Catawba Avenue to which we'd moved in 1950 after my grandmother's death.

Hope, as she now preferred to be called, had taken up chess as had I, and while Rachmaninoff's first piano concerto boomed from the low-fi speaker of my Sears-Roebuck Silvertone, we played each other a couple of games. She won the first and smiled at me dismissively, but then I won the second and waited to see how she'd react. She blamed it on Rachmaninoff, refusing to play a rubber match and shortly afterwards going home.

We'd never be that close again—not because of any antipathy, but because a psychiatrist had diagnosed schizophrenia as the cause of her behavior. Shock treatments had been administered which, according to her, "had killed her soul," and, after that, she'd spent time in New York as a protégé of Randall Jarrell, then under very different circumstances with Corso, Ginsberg, and most of their beatnik friends who afterwards followed her to India where something very bad occurred. I'd never know exactly what—though I believe, whatever it was, she'd been expelled from the country.

We'd meet once more in Camden shortly after that and talk for hours about the places she'd been—among them Yemen and Bhutan, for which there was no legal entry, and Persia, as she preferred to call it, to which she'd afterwards return and have two daughters of her own. It was there, I think, if it wasn't in Bengal, that she'd overheard some tourists talking among themselves and after approaching them said, "Oh, hi! It's so good to hear some voices from home!"—which prompted a wary response from a woman who warned her friends, "Don't talk to her! That's not an American accent."

"No, really," Hope protested. "I was born in South Carolina."

"If you're an American," came the retort, "who won the World Series last year?"

Hope had been at a total loss. "I'm terribly sorry," she said, "but I don't know anything about football," confirming her hearers' suspicions.

She herself told me that story because her peculiar accent, which was shared by all her family, including me to a lesser degree, was a recurrent source of confusion and sometimes even misgivings. Later in Boston, in my own perambulations, I'd be repeatedly told that mine wasn't a Southern accent, by which was presumably meant the way people talked in *Mayberry R.F.D.* or *Smokey and the Bandit*. So I gradually learned to say I'd just been kidding and was really from Maine. "Oh, sure," they'd generally nod. "Why didn't you say so from the start?" To some people's ears, a drawl is a drawl no matter how different the vowels might sound.

In the South, to which I returned after nearly a decade away in England and then New England, it was taken for granted by strangers when they first heard me that I was either very affected or must have come from someplace else. But my accent was merely a rough equivalent of how the whole Savage family talked, transmitted primarily through my mother who'd idolized Dee growing up and maintained that they both spoke exactly like their mother who'd grown up in Louisa County, Virginia. That much I can largely corroborate, though it was really Uncle Henry whose vocal mannerisms distinguished my cousins' way of speaking from mine. Though born in Camden because its warm dry climate was considered salubrious for those afflicted with his father's hereditary lung condition, he had a strong Boston connection and even a vaguely plausible claim to a long defunct English earldom if he'd chosen to pursue it.

Once, when an academic nun wrote about letters from Herman Melville that she believed to be in his possession, he'd ransacked a trunk brought down from the attic in which they were, in fact, discovered—though that was after the family had moved to a newer and grander antebellum house that went by the name of Bloomsbury. It had been where Mary Boykin Chestnut wrote many of the entries in her celebrated diary during the Civil War, an association that I found fascinating—as I did all of Uncle Henry's scholarly interests ranging from history, politics, and geology to the carefully catalogued trays of arrowheads and butterflies that he'd collected in the field. But none of those things had seemed of much interest to Hope who, absorbed by her own pursuits, would quickly master whatever she undertook as soon as she'd turned her hand to it and just as soon lose interest because it had been too easy.

I remember that she painted a spectacular watercolor of an ancient live oak with its intricate network of limbs draped in Spanish moss and translucently lit in various mottled hues with beams of sunlight filtering through. As I recall, it was roughly five feet tall by four feet wide and hung in their library for many years. Like my mother, I too aspired to be a painter, and, though my mother succeeded reasonably well, I didn't, whereas Hope's initial effort was not only quite remarkable but apparently effortless. When I praised her upon first seeing it, she shrugged and pointed out its flaws and, so far as I'm aware, never drew or painted again. She was restlessly looking for something, though I couldn't begin to guess what—and it's possible, I think, that she couldn't either.

In recent years as the Beats began dying out, she'd become a cult figure of sorts, especially for those who'd run across what Ginsberg and Gary Snyder had thought and said about her—that she was farther out and more boldly original than any of them had ever been. Internet groupies have seized on such declarations and wondered online if she was still alive and, if she was, where or whether she could be found.

As her family knew, she was hiding in plain sight in Amsterdam where, on February 8th, 2016, she died, still "full of many plans and projects" according to her daughters.

Uncle Henry had written a half-dozen well-received books on his many interests before dying of emphysema thirty-two years ago, and Aunt Dee died of a stroke not very long after that. Other than my mother, she'd been the closest to me of that entire generation and the most truly literate person I've ever known, an opinion shared by the great Harvard scholar and sometime mentor of mine, Walter Jackson Bate, who enjoyed a friendship with her in their later years.

Of Hope's two older brothers, Carroll was briefly a spy of sorts during his time in the Air Force, a lawyer in Washington after that, and the author of a deeply reflective book about sailing

a 45-foot ketch in stages around the world along with his family
and crew, including a gallant young son, who'd subsequently die
of cystic fibrosis on a camping trip in North Africa.

One of Hope's younger brothers for whom I felt a special
affinity, had a comparably original life. While still in his teens,
in the midst of rustication from a succession of private schools,
he briefly became a fixture on the backwoods stock-car circuit
where he was known as "Psycho Sam," though the name
emblazoned on his car was actually Cyclone Sam and, in any
case, he changed careers when Yale decided to give him free rein
on their equally challenging track, admitting him as a Scholar of
the House.

After studying Nietzsche at Heidelberg and getting his Ph.D.
from Yale, Sam was for some time a carpenter-slash-fisherman
along the South Carolina coast where, for a PBS production in
the mid-1980s, I made arrangements to deploy the last known
working shrimp-boat from the post-World War I era and, while
guiding it into camera range, found that the grizzled young
captain had stashed a copy of Pablo Neruda's poems behind the
wheel.

"How does it happen. . .?" I asked, and he replied, "Sam said
you'd ask me that."

That young captain was Billy Baldwin, who'd become an
author too. Sam had that sort of impact wherever he went and
was just as irrepressible after he moved to Wisconsin and began
to turn out a succession of offbeat novels, all of them superb. We
continued to correspond about his work and mine until his death
in 2019.

His younger brother Harry, an investor and apple farmer
who'd been very close to my mother and was well described in
his obituary as "a man of wide-ranging talents and interests," died
in Sebastopol, California, in 2013, and the oldest of the boys—
though no blood kin to me, the others' half-brother Bill—died in
2020 with a half-finished book in manuscript about the Savage
family

As for the two younger sisters Virginia and Helen, in the
spring of 1962, following my next to last term at Oxford, they
and I met in Venice to take a Yugoslav freighter down the
Dalmatian coast. By then, in courtly-love fashion, I was semi-

enamored with Helen who, though so much younger than I, was in a thoughtfully watchful way—derived from incessant reading, I supposed—seemingly wiser than her years. We three were the only passengers, and, at the very end of the voyage, while returning to the Venetian lagoon and gliding with only a purring sound, there was a golden April sunset that seemingly merged into the sea like molten glass while Helen and I, alone in the prow, were huddling together against the wind as the city's darkened silhouette with its Byzantine pinnacles and domes loomed in a strangely suspended way until, apparently out of nowhere, a frantically water-bound duck ripped a seam across our path as if unable or unwilling to get airborne.

As if prompted by that intrusion, Helen turned towards me and said in a slow sepulchral voice, "I know what's going to happen to you." She sounded vaguely portentous in a quasi-sibylline way but, knowing we'd both grow older and hoping her thought was romantic, I asked what she'd meant by that. She answered with bitter finality, "You'll go on getting happier and happier."

I took that as a prediction of lifelong banality, though thinking about the duck, I feared she might be right. Though we'd love each other in other ways and places, I failed her as the lover I might have been. Now she's dead too—at least, I think she is. I was living in Thailand in 1989 when we got the news that she'd suddenly died in Galway of a congenital heart defect.

My family tends to be lax concerning obsequies and greeting-card events, but I was later told that, some months after that, her ashes had been scattered at sea. Nevertheless, while watching a YouTube video roughly a decade ago, at the end of a performance in Australia by a dancer named Rachel Brice with a group called Tribal Fusion, I saw the camera pan beyond the stage, slowly scanning the audience for only a second or two—and there was Helen, glancing directly back at me for just that lingering moment and then away again. . . very much like my mother in that film clip from the Thirties, though without any hint of a smile.

I've run the segment over and over, like Jimmy Stewart in *Vertigo*, and it's definitely she—I'm as sure of that as he was. Because she died in such mysterious circumstances and because her husband had died as well in an equally baffling way, I've tried to persuade myself that maybe her death was a hoax and that, like her older sister for so many years before her, she'd secretly relocated. Or maybe that's where we all eventually go, to a Tribal Fusion netherworld which we can preview in advance in YouTube videos. Maybe, though I doubt it.

Dear Virginia's still up in Massachusetts, exchanging emails now and again while marveling that we've grown so old and saying I'd be hearing from Carroll soon about a book that I'd just published. But, as a final footnote to my love affair with her family, I learned from their mother, my aunt, not long before she died, that, in Hopey's early adolescence, when they were trying their best to expose her to such conventional pursuits as a month at an all-girls summer camp, the only other camper she'd really liked was the girl who'd become my future wife and who must have struck Hopey then, as she had me, as comparably intense.

I next pursued with my aunt the startling coincidence that my cousin and my wife had been born on the same day of the same year in the same Columbia hospital, and by asking if I could compare their birth certificates, I found, as I'd somehow guessed I would, that they'd officially entered the world at exactly the same minute in what I assumed must have been adjacent delivery rooms. They were, in short, astrological twins—though, as if defying the stars as well as her oncologist, my wife would outlive my cousin by nearly three years.

But for me, at least, some sixty years ago, the prognosis was true enough—there was nothing for me to do but go on getting happier.

4

The Liberator

Before I got married at 25, I'd never really dwelt on my past. I filed things away in my head—sometimes, in a very deliberate way, archiving a random moment or a trivial detail—but I rarely summoned them back to mind, preferring to be either totally in the present or thinking about the future. But once I'd settled down with a wife whom I'd literally known from the cradle, it was more or less inevitable that we'd be constantly talking, and because we knew so many of the same people and had a similar sense of humor, we'd also be laughing a lot about things we both remembered. The only real lacunae had to do with the years when we'd gone to different schools or been in different classes, resulting in memories we didn't share along with a few regrets that we preferred to keep to ourselves.

"Like what?" my wife wanted to know when I happened to mention the latter. We'd been married for more than a decade.

"Oh, you know," I said. "The usual stuff. . . like not really learning to sail or play the piano well." I'd counted on her for the latter, but after fourteen years of study, she'd given it up for good during her college years while I kept fumbling about on my own.

"What else?" she asked with a sigh as if I'd recriminated— as, in effect, I had.

"Well, broken-field running for one—I kept zigging when I ought to have zagged. And reading Homer in Greek. . . I should have tried harder at that. And even Virgil. . ."

"*Dum spiro spero*," she sniffed, knowing my Latin was fairly good but goading me with the thought that, other than hitting the gridiron again, it wasn't too late for the others.

Her Latin was no better than mine. She'd been quoting the motto of our state—"While I breathe, I hope"—which to my mind struck a note of gloomy defiance and worked just as well in reverse. But either way, I reflected, aspirations aren't the same as regrets which are harder to undo. . . a thought that caused me to add another item.

"And Reuben Singletary," I said as she queried me with a look.

"Well, not exactly a regret," I shrugged, "but a really sobering lesson—though that was before you'd transferred to our school, or we weren't in the same class back then. I wonder whatever became of him?"

When she pointed out that I'd never mentioned him before, I said I'd look for an old class photo or yearbook from later on that might jog some recollection of having seen him in the schoolyard—a thought that, after rummaging about in closets and bureau drawers with no success, sent me off to my backyard study, formerly a two-car garage, where I began to dig through boxes, books, and files in a sort of nostalgic convocation (*con* plus *vocare*, I told myself since the specter of Latin was already loose in my mind)—a "calling together," as it were, of friends and foes from my grammar school days.

The first old photo I found wasn't of Reuben, though. It was of Alice Enright, whom I'd so much admired that, using an old nib pen, I'd tried to incise her initials on my leg when the other guys in my fifth-grade class were carving Nancy Hiller's instead. That had been when, newly attentive to girls, I'd thought Alice was bewitchingly captivating—but all I could see after twenty-odd years was a homely kid with braces and zits, no more appealing in looks then than I myself at the time.

That revelation distracted me momentarily but, undeterred in my search and hoping for better luck from later more chronicled times, I opened a high school yearbook where, among the expectant faces gazing back up at me, I saw teammates from my ill-fated football squad. . . including Benny Utterback in the goggles he'd worn when he played for the Caps—he'd die of some freakish blood disease in the week he finished medical school—and guileless smiling John Argoe who, because of a needlessly broken heart, would join the army in two years' time and get himself killed in Germany, riding a borrowed motorcycle.

Those doleful recollections caused me to reflect that we'd been on a more dangerous obstacle course than any of us had realized, and I saw how naively unsuspecting we all appeared, staring out of that tattered book with the corner of its cover gnawed away by some rodent that must have completed its meal before getting to the senior class, the one that I and my friends were in.

I was on the verge of regarding that as an ominous metaphor when I remembered what had launched my search and combed through the rest of the pages, but only to find no sign of Reuben—not even in Chess & Checker Club shots, for many the Ultima Thule of those most likely to disappear. That didn't surprise me really because, in his sheepish haphazard way, Reuben was never really there. He was just enrolled year after year in some purely technical sense until one day, though I couldn't say when, he'd vanished altogether.

I'd first encountered him in 1944, after my mother had moved us back from Atlanta for a short sojourn in my grandfather's house and then to a bungalow of our own a couple of blocks away in a place called Myrtle Court. The world was still at war, of course, and my father, like a barnacle on a rock, still stuck on an island in the Azores called Santa Maria. My brother and sister were three and two, and I, in theory at least, was ready to enter the second grade—though *ready*'s not really the word because not only was I younger than nearly all the other kids but, following a tonsillectomy during the previous spring, I'd ended up missing more school than I'd attended.

My mother had often read to me aloud, but I'd been more interested in hearing her often dramatic renditions than in learning to read them myself and, though I knew the alphabet well enough, I could barely sound the letters out. Still, Atlanta was in another state, and my teacher at the Williams Street School had offered to cut us a special deal. She said she'd promote me anyhow provided we did as we'd planned and got ourselves back to South Carolina—near the bottom back then in just about everything, including education.

But moving in wartime meant delays, so, in addition to missing most of the preceding year, my education didn't resume until more than a month after my new school had begun. No sweat, I thought (how tough could it be?) assuming I'd fake it for a while until I could finish catching up with whatever was going on—though that was before I entered the realm of Eloisa Brandenburg . . . the blue-rinsed Medusa of A.C. Moore.

Nearly thirty years later as I sat there in my backyard study, it was as if her name alone had been an incantation summoning her before me, and the memory was so intense that it was like watching a movie shot unbeknownst to me on that early fall day when, having been ushered to the 2-B door, I was left alone on its threshold.

I could see my six-year-old self, standing and waiting stock-still while surveying what looked at first like a Norman Rockwell tableau for *The Saturday Evening Post*—of a teacher with chalk in her hand, pursing her lips with just a hint a frown, and three distinct groups of kids gawking back at me from their midget-sized wooden chairs with arms that protruded like desks. I saw an American flag in the corner with a portrait of George Washington on the wall and, scattered about in a few of the desks, a sprinkling of rayon dresses which, despite my contretemps in Atlanta, struck me at first as auspicious. But then I detected that something was wrong, something that smacked of fear and coercion.

"Please, close the door," the teacher said, pointing me towards an empty chair placed by itself apart from the rest. Then, turning to write two words out on the board—one of them short, the other long—she paused with a hand in the air.

"What is my name?" she asked the class as if conducting them in a chorus.

"Miss Brandenburg!" the children wailed, apparently reading it off the board.

I heard a staccato rat-tat-tat as she rapidly wrote another two words, then looked at me with a tight-lipped smile.

"Bernie. . . Dunlap," she seemed to mull as if in answer to a riddle, tapping the chalk on those two words before turning back towards me again. "I'll call you by your Christian name," she said, "but you'll call me. . ."

"Miss Brandenburg!" the children sang out.

I mumbled the words myself out loud.

"*Miss* Brandenburg," she nodded and, fixing me with a meaningful look, proceeded to ask as she pointed them out, "Now, then, you see, three circles of chairs. . . can you guess why?"

I told her I couldn't, so she explained. Those in the circle next to her desk were the very best readers in the class. "They're called bluebirds," she declared. They lifted their chins at hearing their name, beaming complacently at each other. Those in the center—the biggest group—were redbirds, said Miss Brandenburg. They were the merely average readers, but that's where the girls in rayon sat and shyly shimmered, showing their dimples as they smiled. The last group was the smallest one, a lopsided jumble in the back with shirtless boys in overalls and girls in shapeless seed-bag frocks. They were the crows, Miss Brandenburg said, the slowest readers in Christendom. They gazed like goatherds waked from sleep.

What I didn't know then but soon would learn is that, even if in some utopian scheme in Athens, Rome, or Monticello all readers had been created equal, at A.C. Moore in class 2-B the one self-evident truth was this: you were a bluebird, redbird, or crow. It was useless to offer up any excuse because, for better or much for the worse, I'd come to a place where the edict was clear. . . and it was "read, hog, or die!"

That message was rapidly sinking in as Miss Brandenburg led me back to her desk. "Now, class," she said in a surgical voice, "let's see how well little Bernie can read."

She gave me a book. I opened it up. The bluebirds, quick to detect distress, began to squirm with anticipation.

"Well?" she asked.

I started to blush. It could have been Latin for all I knew.

"He's certainly not a bluebird, is he?"

The bluebirds snickered their assent. The redbirds seemed to grin and shiver.

She took the book back and held out another with shorter words and more numerous pictures, a book I'd glimpsed one day in Atlanta concerning two kids in a quaint little town who were romping about in a yard with their dog while their mother was blithely hanging up wash and a postman came bouncing up the walk.

I tried to decipher what else I saw: two three-lettered words and one with four. The first and third words were the same. Both of them started with an R.

"Rrrrrr. . ." I began. That much I knew.

"Run," I heard Miss Brandenburg say.

"Run," I repeated. But then I stopped, stumped by the unfamiliar word. "Sssss. . ." I hissed, drawing it out.

I looked at Miss Brandenburg for a hint but only received a glacial stare. I glanced at the girls in rayon dresses. Their dimples were gone, they sat and watched as the silence stretched out. I saw there'd be no second reprieve.

"The dog," Miss Brandenburg prompted me. "What is the name of the dog?" she asked.

There wasn't much chance I could actually read it but maybe, I thought, I might get lucky. I ran through dogs' names in my mind as 2-B sat tight, and the clock ran down.

"Well?" she pressed me, calling my bluff.

"Spud!" I blurted. "His name is Spud!"

"What?" she snapped.

"'RUN, Spud! RUN!'" I cried in dismay.

One of the redbirds started to laugh, but Miss Brandenburg stifled him with a look.

"That's quite enough!" she glowered at me. "I think we've determined what you are. . ." She pointed me towards the rear of the room. "Reading is not a joke," she said.

Before me yawned the dark abyss—unthinkably, but with no way out as I, with all my aspirations, had been exiled to the cloakroom's shadow, abandoned in the oubliette, shut out forever from Dick and Jane.

"Go sit with the crows," she ordered me. "I'll get to you when I can."

So that's it, I thought. My grits were cooked. The songbirds prissily opened their books, insipid accounts of dumbbell kids cavorting with a mutt named Spot (*Spot!* Of course! I should have known—the wretched beast was covered with them!) while I and the crows got shorter texts that were printed with one word to the page, encouraging words like "go" and "up."

Then I blinked and, freed from my reverie, was no longer a mortified six-year-old but a middle-aged man surrounded by books with one of them open in my lap, wishing I could have guessed back then that, decades away in that same town, I'd be trying to see the comic side of what was so painful at the time. I remembered having looked about for a place to sit and finding a chair that was missing a slat while the rest of the crows looked on with distrust as if they suspected I didn't belong. But I'd belonged all right—for the moment, at least—and Frau Brandenburg and her songbird twits had taught me a lesson I'd never forget about the uses of knowledge and power. "Learning your place," she might have said, though in my heart the lesson was different. In my heart I was still a prince in disguise, scrubbing out pots and mocked by the queen but, knowing the wheel would someday turn—as it always did in fairy tales (my mother had read me lots of them)—I vowed that my fellow scullions and churls would share in my triumph when it came.

And the lowliest scullion of them all was Reuben Singletary. Dark, high-cheeked, and rumored to be half-Indian or maybe something else, Reuben had always been a crow. Others might hope to better their lot, but Reuben, foredoomed by his hangdog smile and tub-scrubbed Rawhide overalls, had long since been pronounced a loser, and he'd accepted that decree. I hadn't though, for him or for me. I never would, and if some teacher insisted I should, I'd show that teacher that she was wrong and so was all authority that declared whatever she said was right. So, concealing the mutiny in my heart, I'd begun to plot how I'd escape from that Devil's Island reading group where girls in rayon never went.

I learned to read in record time and, after only a couple of weeks, was lending my suspect off-key voice to the anthem the songbirds sang each day after our pledge to the flag:

> A.C. Moore, we love you.
> There's no school above you.
> Even though we do work hard,
> We love you true. . .

By Halloween, my chair had been moved, upping me to the redbird group. By Armistice Day, I sat by her desk, and Miss Brandenburg all but seemed to forget she'd ever mistaken me for a crow. But I hadn't, and maybe she somehow guessed I wasn't the type to come to heel, for I had to wait much longer than most for that ultimate seal of her approval—being tapped to serve our class for the day as. . . a secret cafeteria monitor.

It was, for the crows, a ritual from hell. Each morning at noon we'd line up in the hall and march down to the cafeteria, and, clandestinely, every day, a different duo—a girl and a boy—would assume the roles of covert spies, watching the manners of all the kids who sat at our long dark trestle table. When lunch was done but before our recess, we'd march in formation to our room where the monitors' names would be revealed and each would issue a report—who'd put an elbow down on the table, who'd reached for the salt across her plate, who'd sneezed while eating his succotash.

The risk of being denounced was high, for Miss Brandenburg's code was Byzantine. If your knife had been placed on the side of your plate, its sharp edge out instead of in, if you'd slurped your soup or dribbled your milk or let your left hand stray from your lap for anything other than cutting your meat, you were sure to lose a recess or two—unless you were a leftie, of course (though, like stammers, squints, and other such tics, a persistent lack of righthandedness was taken to be a sign of emotional instability and, according to one very widely quoted physician, "an unconscious revolt against authority," precisely what I was trying to hide).

To complicate matters further, not only did I favor my left hand for quite a number of things, but I squinted and stammered too—or, more specifically, I tended to talk so fast that my sentences often collided with the ones preceding them. With issues like those in mind, it seemed prudent for me to toe the line, especially during lunchtime with our watchful informers stealthily spaced so they could keep tabs on everyone. The only escape lay in grasping the rules—which, given a head start in your home, wasn't much harder than learning to read. I never got nabbed for the slightest offense, not even by Alma "Big Stick" Boggs, Miss Brandenburg's most dreaded stooge and a regular on the Safety Patrol who, according to rumor among the Crows, had never removed her patrolman's belt, not even to bathe.

But Reuben? He'd never had a chance. He didn't know what a recess was. Each day after marching back to our room, no matter who else the monitors nabbed, the final name had always been his. Alma would nod, the songbirds titter, and Reuben would flash his miserable grin while the rest of us trooped outside to play.

I kept waiting to be appointed, but I must have been on some sort of probation because, before I finally got my shot at being a spy, Miss Brandenburg had selected virtually everyone else, some of them more than once, including a few of the more obsequious crows—though I knew it was only a matter of time. Her notion of fair play, such as it was, would oblige her to choose me sooner or later.

So I'd waited her out until December when, not long before Christmas vacation, the fateful moment arrived and, shortly before the school day began, Miss Brandenburg asked me to lend a hand in moving an easel into the room. But no sooner were we alone in the hall than she looked both ways and gravely said she had something more to ask of me. Feeling puny but seditious, I stood there as she lowered her voice to say she'd chosen me to serve as one of the secret monitors.

"Today?" I whispered back at her as she narrowed her eyes with a nod.

I knew why we were whispering—we were fighting a war all over the world to guarantee such freedoms as ours. I nodded too. I understood.

When she lined us up in a couple of hours, I maneuvered to get Reuben next to me with both of us near the end of the queue, assuring he'd have a ringside seat for something I hoped he'd never forget. My sister thug, whoever she was, would be sitting a long way off from us and, at my end of our table that day, I was going to be the law.

Everything went according to plan. Looking as casual as I could, I warmed up with some peccadilloes—leaving my napkin by my plate and letting my cornbread scatter about. Then moving on to major offenses, I spat out butterbeans as I talked and, while using my fingers for bits of the meat, was delighted that Reuben was watching me with mingled alarm and astonishment and that Alma Boggs, across from us encased in her patrolman's truss, was reeling as if about to faint. Inspired by her apparent distress, I rose to dizzying heights of invention—stuffing some green peas up my nose, then spinach too like ribbons of snot.

At first the songbirds merely froze. Then one of them laughed and someone burped, and, like an earthquake underfoot, turmoil erupted all over the place as I reveled in hectic mob-rule joy. Anarchy reigned at the trestle table, and all Miss Brandenburg could do was watch her Gestapo fall apart. Whatever the ultimate cost might be, Reuben would have a recess for once.

I clung to that thought as long as I could, which was probably less than a minute more, before Miss Brandenburg got to her feet and stiffly herded us back to our room. That was fine with me, I told myself—I'd run out of ideas anyhow.

Miss Brandenburg seethed as she stood by her desk.

"Class," she choked when we'd taken our seats. "I'm sorry to say. . ." she sputtered and stopped before she resumed, ". . . that one of our monitors let us down. I don't intend to call on him. I'll call on the one who did her job." She looked like a hangman dropping a trap as she calmly, emphatically uttered the name, "Alma Boggs, I'm calling on her."

Alma Boggs? I'd been double-crossed! She was sitting across from me all the time!

"I only caught one person today," she simpered with her vindictive lisp. "Bernie Dunlap ate like a pig!"

She pointed at me self-righteously, and a wave of derision loomed over my head, became a crescendo, and thundered down.

"PIG! PIG! HE ATE LIKE A PIG!"

I was blindly furious with myself, galled to have been so completely outwitted. Even Miss Brandenburg chuckled out loud, and from near the back where the cloak-closets were, burst forth the loudest laughter of all—from lowly Reuben Singletary, unable to see that what I'd done was for him and for all the outcast crows doomed to lose in the etiquette wars with monitors and safety patrols and the tyranny of the songbird groups.

And then I made the debacle complete. I jumped to my feet and semaphored. "Well, I got somebody! I got her too! Alma Boggs! I got her too!"

But Miss Brandenburg merely waved her hand. "We don't need a report from you today. . . and you'll stay in from recess for a month."

So the rest of the class trooped out to play, including Reuben Singletary, who must have blinked in the noonday sun like the prisoner of Chillon while leaving me with my head on my desk, scalded by chagrin.

I'd gotten that far in reliving the scene when the screen went blank and lights came on and, pitched forward again some thirty years, I was a middle-aged man once more holding an open yearbook in my lap at the very last spot where Reuben's picture would be if he hadn't apparently flown the coop when nobody bothered to notice.

As for why that story had haunted me for so long, it was, as I'd started to tell my wife, far less because of regret than as a result of what I'd learned, with the smaller, more proximate lesson being the one I owed to Reuben—that expecting gratitude for a boorishly infantile stunt isn't the best of reasons for doing what's right. The deeper takeaway—on that very small scale, at least (the one from which most foxes view the world)—was that, rather than self-destructive acts (like, say, biting your teacher's nose), it's more advisable to lie low and gradually subvert. . . and, no matter how inadvertent, that insight I learned from Miss Brandenburg.

Since arriving at that conclusion so many years ago, I've searched about for anything more regarding who she was and what became of her, though I've only been able to glean that she wasn't named Eloisa after all because, on a document that I've run across, the initials in front of her surname are listed as simply "M.O." She was probably much younger than I'd supposed, but whether she married and moved on or withered there on the 2-B vine is more than I'm ever likely to know.

In all fairness, I suppose it could be argued that her classroom methodology represented nothing worse than rewarding the manners and achievement that get one ahead in life. But her coercive birds-of-a-feather approach, especially for those an early age, is one that's been too often applied for purposes of exclusion and abuse—and nowhere more egregiously than our state. So I'm disinclined even now to cut her any slack, especially with regard to Reuben, and as far as proverbs go, there's one for every partial truth with only a few to spur the meek towards their inheritance of the earth. But the Duke of Wellington, who knew a thing or two about appraising humans as well as horseflesh, is purported to have said, "The fact that you're born in a stable doesn't mean that you're a horse." If he failed to say that, he could have.

Which brings me back to Reuben again because I've recently dug about on the internet and learned that, after his nebulous years in our city's public schools, he's lived the sort of life an Iron Duke would applaud. For, having managed to join the Navy when he was only sixteen and serving his country since then for twenty-five years and more in places as far from home as the Marshall Islands, Cyprus, and Spain, he's become in his retirement an amateur genealogist who's said to have turned up evidence that he's a distant cousin of President Obama. Not bad for a Chess & Checker Club no-show.

As for my own immediate post-secret-monitor career, I found myself once again, in Miss Brandenburg's eyes, an irredeemable pariah. But my outlook would change in the following spring when, for no reason apparent to me, I was given an I.Q. test by a woman who'd just been authorized to search for gifted children—for an Ivory-billed in the swamp, as it were. That she happened to be my mother's best friend was never considered relevant, and, though I remember few details from our lengthy afternoon session, I do recall that, midway through her questioning, I was shown a picture of pilgrims firing their God-given blunderbusses at hordes of rampaging Indians.

"What's wrong with this picture?" I was asked, and I promptly pointed out that one of the Indians in the background was wearing a Plains-Tribe bonnet, which couldn't have been the case in Massachusetts. She appeared to be quite taken aback—because, as she later confided, no one my age had ever before answered that question correctly. I felt no need to divulge that such prodigious erudition had come from perusing a Classic Comic, but I dimly understood that, like my cousins in Camden, I was suddenly in a category beyond Miss Brandenburg's reach.

And so it would be from that point on, though to some whom I'd soon encounter, that made it even more imperative to break me to bit and bridle before I'd galloped about too unrestrainedly on my own. I'd never get a report card that failed to note that I talked too much or talked too fast or needed to curb my imagination—this last from an English teacher!—but I was treated warily, like an Einstein who was flunking math or a know-it-all troublemaker.

I was closer to the latter, of course, though what comes rushing into my mind today as I'm recalling these stories is another face from my middle-school years—that of a pudgy pimply classmate from Hand Junior High who, if he got very lucky, would someday, like his father, run a drive-in hamburger joint in a seedy section of town.

His name was Doug Broome Junior, but he too had been dismissed early on as a person of little consequence, especially after he'd come to school one morning in 1952 decked out in a blood-stained windbreaker worn the night before by a Gamecock football star who'd been killed in a highway accident. The player's name was Steve Wadiak, and the jacket had been a gift from the cops to Doug Broome Senior who'd kept them well supplied through the years with whatever his curb hops could provide.

I can still see Doug Broome Junior's face when he showed up that day at Hand as if preening in the limelight. But the rest of us were aghast. Pudgy with pimples was one thing, but such crassness was another—and, besides, as we all knew, Wadiak's coach was Alice Enright's dad who'd brought Steve down from Chicago and profited mightily from his skills. "Give the ball to Wadiak," began a ditty based largely on fact, "Enright wants a Cadillac!", and the coach and his protégé were the only true celebrities that many of us had ever seen—other than James F. Byrnes, of course, who, according to some of our parents, should have become our president but hadn't because of FDR. So, out of respect for Alice's father's loss and the tragic demise of a genial local hero, Doug Broome Junior was totally written off, apparently for good.

But, despite another partial truth, there are lots of second acts in American lives—though it was only in 1992 that I'd happen to read an obituary that said our former classmate had recently died of liver cancer. It was in *The New York Times*, which noted in its

eulogy that the Hubble Space Telescope, with all the transformative knowledge that astronomers had derived from it, would never have gotten off the ground but for the sheer tenacity and skill its project manager had shown. The world of science was
mourning the loss of Douglas Broome Junior, the deputy director of the Solar System Exploration Division of NASA and the designer of its power systems for the Project Mercury spacecraft. He'd been awarded the Presidential Medal of Freedom—but hadn't run a drive-in after all.

I'm in a new house now in the foothills of North Carolina with bookstacks in virtually every room including ones down in the cellar, which is where my yearbooks have been reshelved. I've been consulting them yet again in a last-ditch effort to extract some deeper meaning from the stories I've been recounting— though all I'm able to come up with is that Holden Caulfield was right in maintaining, in effect, that there's no way you can tell who'll become a really good whistler. . . which, though I have to struggle to translate it into Latin, I suppose would be something like *Vos non scitis qui possit stridere*—though maybe *sibilare* is better, I think, after having consulted my dictionary.

So I take out an index card and print out *dum spiro sibilo* before it comes confoundingly back to mind that I can no longer share it with my wife. Instead, I stare at the card and reflect that, ornithologically speaking, crows have been proven to be a lot smarter than redbirds or bluebirds. That's something she would have applauded.

5

The Poulterergeist

I get along well with most animals, just as I do with most humans—though in the case of animals that's partly because they're so reliably what they are without much fuss about what they might become. On the other hand, because, in a curious way, my mother and I were very young together, I used to retaliate if she got crotchety or sarcastic by saying, "You're not acting like my mother," just as she, when I took off in pursuit of some wild hare, would warn me that I wasn't being myself.

With animals, as I've said, that was almost never a problem, though drawing the line at airborne maniacs with hatchets, I continue to disapprove of Pileated Woodpeckers along with dengue-bearing mosquitoes and idiotic stink bugs in the fall, all of which I've struggled against in different times and places. Of the comparatively larger and wilder species that I'm most inclined to admire, I've had little first-hand acquaintance—other than with foxes, of course, which, as noted already, are very much themselves.

But knowing foxes was like knowing myself—which is to say, I thought I did though I didn't. With the single exception mentioned already in passing, the cats I've lived with from time to time have always made it plain that any tractability on their part was only provisional because that's simply how things are while, by way of an age-old contrast, the dogs have resembled my closest kin—endowed with different gifts but bound by deep affection as well as similitude.

Not so coincidentally when I was growing up, we had a succession of dogs, usually more than one at a time—even in Columbia, where we sometimes had as many as three—though

other than an affably clumsy Weimaraner during my high school
and college years, most of our dogs were small and only one, an
English Springer Spaniel, was male. When I was offered the
chance to name it, I suggested "Atom Bomb," though that was
overruled in favor of Pax and, as its Latin name implied, it didn't
last long. Contracting jaundice after a couple of months, it
crawled underneath our house on South Saluda Avenue and died,
after which we reverted once more to short-haired female fyces.

My mother was very fond of animals, and, except for our
time in Atlanta, was never without a dog during the whole of her
96 years. As a girl of seven or eight, she'd had a fox terrier named
Mickey, and, once we were back in Columbia, she found a
similar dog for us, declaring its name to be Dolly—as in Dolley
Madison without the "e," because, as I now surmise, taking its
cues from my mother, she showed such a depth of refinement
that, when she had to make room for a tacky curly-tailed half-
breed that my brother brought home one day insisting her name
was Frisky, Dolly never wavered in either ladylike dignity or her
generous disposition.

Actually, in addition to being somewhat overbred, Dolly's
forbearance may have also derived from the fact that, prior to
Frisky's arrival, she'd narrowly survived a nearly fatal blow to
the head when I—impulsively distraught after hearing on the
radio that FDR was dead and having left the house because
everyone inside, including my mother and our on-again off-again
maid, was weeping and embracing each other—had gone
outdoors to practice swings at a baseball that I'd suspended from
a tree limb. As she invariably did, Dolly kept barking and
prancing about as I swung, but somehow or other in losing my
concentration, I whacked her head instead of the ball, knocking
her into a motionless heap. I thought she was dead and raced
inside with the breaking news that tragedy had arrived at our very
doorstep.

When I returned with my mother, Dolly was still out cold.
My mother was always resourceful in a crisis, but her nostrums
were sometimes debatable as, in this particular case, after
wrapping the dog in a blanket and taking her into the house, she
considered everything in our medicine cabinet until she'd
managed at last to revive her with something like smelling salts.

Then, while both of us stroked the groggily shellshocked Dolly, my mother recounted how, when she'd been just my age, she'd found a dead dog in a stream in nearby Maxcy Gregg Park and tried her best, with no success, to coax it onto its feet again by talking to it and blowing into its muzzle. . . after which she'd calmly told herself that, if she quietly left and went back up the hill without turning around to check on it, the dog would be okay.

Though that struck me at the time as just a fanciful effort to weave a spell for herself that wouldn't have worked for me, I'm disposed to regard it now as a precocious if naïve take on Orpheus and Eurydice whose story she would have run across in the 1907 edition of a ten-volume series called *The Children's Hour*, which she'd combed through as a girl before passing it on to me and would later repossess to use as a teacher-without-portfolio at an Episcopal grammar school, purveying the ancient Greek myths instead of Bible stories.

I loved those myths as well, but, even before I could read, I thought of myself as a highly rational person despite the all-consuming aspect of my many enthusiasms. One example of the latter that had to do with animals was that, for the longest time after seeing the movie *National Velvet*, I remained obsessed with thoroughbred horses, mainly at first as part of a plan for meeting Elizabeth Taylor. When I confided that goal to my mother—who, scarcely more than a girl herself, was devoted to reading romantic verse—she simply nodded and observed that lots of men were happily wed to considerably older women, a complication I hadn't foreseen. . . though, as an ironic matter of fact, I'd eventually marry a somewhat older woman.

"How much older?" I asked regarding Elizabeth Taylor.

"Six or seven years, I expect."

That sounded very daunting. "But at least she's not too tall," I replied—because I'd heard on the radio that Mickey Rooney was five feet two, and they'd looked about the same height in the movie which, auspiciously enough, meant just a bit taller than my mother who, though she claimed to be five feet one, was still a good deal shorter than I expected to become. On the other hand, I reflected that, in looks at least, Mickey Rooney resembled my friend Bryan Grubbs with whom I was always competing—and, if she liked Mickey Rooney so much, that didn't bode well for me.

We were living on South Saluda by then and Bryan, who'd recently moved to town, lived just a short distance away with an empty field between us which in time became a sort of battleground between his gang of younger kids and the other neighborhood guys our age whose mothers and fathers all knew each other—whereas, instead of being a lawyer or businessman, Mr. Grubbs was a Merrill Lynch stockbroker which, given the recent Depression, still reeked of fast-talking hustlers to us. Both he and his son were flashy by local standards, and though Bryan and I were roughly the same height, he acted Napoleonic while I was more like Ike—at least, in my own mind, though both of us were major generals of sorts, I mainly because my house was right next to the field.

Later, when I grew up and read about the Peloponnesian War, I'd recall our sporadic dirt-clod fights that lasted off-and-on for months or maybe years, flaring up in brief hostilities and dying down again. Bryan's gang was the larger, but ours was slightly older and, as we thought, more chivalric. . . mainly because nearly all of us—David Rembert, Bill Cain, Julian Adams, and I along with seldom mustered recruits like Julian Shand and Robert Kennedy—went to the same Episcopal church and were part of a Cub Scout den that was led by Bill Cain's mother, Miss Ann. We may not have been what Akela had had in mind, but we formed a definite pack that, by the time we got to high school together, had been allotted the name of "Hill Boys"—by whom I'd never know—at which point we were engaged in another longstanding détente with Lutherans, Baptists, and Methodists from the northern end of town.

But long before that, when Bryan and I were both fifth-graders, a titanic Armageddon had occurred, surging back and forth all over our neighborhood and, after multiple days of combat, culminating in a Waterloo-like confrontation. It ended in total victory for us—though, regrettably for posterity, I'd left the carefully composed surrender document in my desk at school overnight, and Bryan would later declare the unsigned treaty invalid. Nevertheless, his gang dispersed, and five years after that, before his family moved to Houston, Bryan and I would both suit up as undersized running backs on our high school football team, enduring its many defeats together.

But it was basically in the wake of our great showdown, when I was still in the fifth or sixth grade, that I decided once and for all to give Elizabeth Taylor up, leaving her for Bryan and Mickey to wrangle over. That was partly because I'd seen her in *Life with Father* and concluded she might be more than I could handle, "Though I still like horses anyhow," I confided to my mother despite the minor detail that, unlike my cousins in Camden, I had no more actual acquaintance with them than I had with Hollywood movie stars—although with my usual manic zeal that was something I aimed to correct.

The obvious recourse was the public library, where I found a book entitled *How to Draw Horses* and soon become fairly adept at sketching horses in profile—the drawback being that they were for the most part indistinguishable except for the names I made up and inscribed beneath each of my efforts. As for more current magazines and paperbacks, the only real outlet in town was a newsstand across from the Capitol Building, where all I could find was a racing journal called *Turf and Sport Digest* in which, amid handicapping info and parimutuel tips for those at the seasonal stables out by the fairgrounds, I read an inspiring essay on Man o' War who'd recently died of a heart attack at the elderly horse-age of thirty.

Still, my mother was so favorably impressed by my quasi-artistic persistence that she scheduled a session for me at the Webb Riding Academy out on Trenholm Road, where she herself had ridden as a girl. I don't know what I expected, but my bland assumption that whatever skill might be needed would come to me naturally would recur as a permanent character trait because a decade later I'd set out with a comparably reckless lack of preparation in a rented sailboat from Nantucket harbor, and a few years after that, I'd launch myself on skis down a nearly perpendicular slope in the Austrian Alps. So in retrospect I have little doubt that, if my mother hadn't advised Mister Webb that I'd never done anything more than sit on an motionless horse, I'd have galloped off to a similar sort of fiasco.

But, whatever my ill-advised expectations, the nag that I was allotted bore no resemblance to Man o' War or The Pie in

National Velvet and had no interest at all in bonding with me. On the contrary, as I quickly discovered, it had an obsession of its own with the feedbag in its stall as we plodded in circles around a ring with me clucking and tugging the reins each time we approached the stable, doing my best to keep it out on the track. Even before the travesty was over, I was thinking of Mr. Toad in *The Wind in the Willows,* and it didn't help at all when I learned that Elizabeth Taylor had done her own riding in the film—though I might have felt both better and worse if I'd happened to know back then that, in the course of one of its scenes, she'd had a very bad fall and fractured her spine.

But long before learning that, when we'd moved back to my grandfather's house and I was in the 7th grade, I'd heard that a classmate of mine named Carla Donen would be getting a call in two days from her much older brother Stanley, a former dancer and choreographer who was then a director in Hollywood. What made the news so exciting was that his girlfriend at the time would also be on the line—and she, to our utter astonishment, was none other than Elizabeth Taylor!

Initially, we'd all planned to join her at her Spanish-style house in my old neighborhood, ironically known back then as Hollywood-Rose Hill. But her parents decided to limit the crowd inside, so in the end only a few of Carla's closest friends—all of them girls, of course, like Sarah Hardy and Annette Berry—were able to listen in while the rest of us waited outside on the front lawn. When they repeated to us what they'd heard, it seemed disappointingly mundane except for reports that Elizabeth Taylor's accent was very English, and she'd laughed a lot and apparently spoken to Carla like a sweet-tempered older sister-in-law. That was as close as I'd ever get to meeting her, and we were all dismayed when, during the following year, she married the second of seven husbands—a fellow actor from England by the name of Michael Wilding who was nearly twenty years older. There would be no eighth, though she'd marry Richard Burton twice as if to confirm the fact that, in matters of the heart, we're all disposed to repeat our most deluded wishful thinking.

For my own part, a few months after that telephone call when I first saw Leslie Caron in *An American in Paris,* I became enamored of her instead and, for a long time after that, was implausibly convinced that, if we should ever meet, she'd feel equally drawn to me—an encounter so long delayed that, in the meantime, having heard recordings from the Broadway musical *Brigadoon*, I became totally fixated on everything Scottish from the poetry of Robert Burns and Mendelsohn's "Scottish" symphony to the royal arms of Scotland, which I duplicated in shop class with a jigsaw plus some red and yellow paint.

So it was that, for the moment at least, it seemed that my preoccupation with other species had been superseded, though it was increasingly clear that what had caused Aunt Dee to call me "Big Business" when I was scarcely more than a toddler had by then become a permanent character trait. Actually, the probable truth of the matter was that, given my mother's limitless energy and my father's easy-going but addictive personality, it was all but inevitable that I'd be what I was, a serial monomaniac who wanted to be and experience everything—though, aware of the risk of mere dabbling, I'd pursue each obsession in turn until I either ran out of gas or was ready for something else.

I suppose in retrospect that, amid her struggles with my father's self-destructive habits, my mother must have become alarmed at such compulsive behavior because, as I've briefly noted, on more than one occasion when I was off on some new tangent, she'd caution me with her version of "knowing thyself," warning me that I wasn't being myself and once, while pointing to my toy gyroscope, observing that, in the end, it was all about keeping your balance. But my impulses couldn't be curbed by what I'd come to regard as no more than a practical application of opposing mind-sets—analytical on the one hand, intuitive on the other—resorting to one or the other depending on what I was after.

That was still my vague assumption when my early interest in engineering, beginning with tinker toys and erector sets, had veered off by the time I was twelve towards pursuits both metaphysical and acquisitive—with the former prompted in part by pious stints as an acolyte at church combined with the low-key voodoo of a Ouija board at home and the latter by a semi-obsessive penchant for collecting things that began inexplicably with bottlecaps.

I think my initial motivation for the last lay at least as much in the fact that, so far as I knew, nobody else was collecting them as I did in their vast abundance if somewhat limited variety—and I soon found, in a Scrooge McDuck sort of way, that sheer accumulation was weirdly satisfying. So for weeks or maybe months, I rode my Schwinn on daily after-school rounds to a dozen or more soft-drink machines—mostly at nearby filling stations but gradually extending my range until I was spending hours each day, emptying bins of bottlecaps and storing them in my bedroom closet in oversized cardboard boxes retrieved from behind a neighborhood grocery store. In a matter of weeks, I had another five thousand or so in smaller boxes throughout my room or under my bed and spreading into the hallway.

But the living room ceiling below was in serious jeopardy, and my father, in his lawyer-like way, raised a technical objection that, since nobody wanted what I was after and all I'd ever come up with was the same old predictable stuff—Pepsi, Coke, and R.C. Cola with Nehi and NuGrape here and there and maybe now and then a TruAde or Orange Crush (which his brother, Uncle George, was bottling with only modest success in their birthplace of Rock Hill some seventy miles to the north)—I was only "collecting," he said, in the sense that a garbage man did the same.

Though stung by his argument, I resisted his final point. What if I found a bottle cap nobody had ever seen before?

"But that's what I'm trying to tell you," he said as a rebuttal. "You won't because they're mass-produced exactly like nails or screws."

"Yeah, but so are postage stamps, and you collected them." He'd given me the ledger book that he'd converted into an album just after the end of World War I. "And so did President Roosevelt!" I added for good measure. "Maybe there'll be a printing mistake or something like that I can find." I was thinking of a British Guiana one-cent magenta, which every collector dreamed about.

"Listen, son," he said, putting his hand on my shoulder. "It's not just what you collect. Stamps are fine, but the problem here is. . ." he paused for his words to sink in, as he always did for man-to-man advice, "you're not playing the odds." He was a gambler, I thought, and ought to know—though, somehow, he never seemed to win. He was very meticulous too, but his basic approach was to bet on winning the sweepstakes.

Maybe he read my thoughts because he gave my shoulder a squeeze and changed the subject to something more specific. "Get rid of your duplicates, anyhow," and there he rested his case.

I nodded okay—I would, I said. But, despite what seemed a reasonable concession, I realized that, if I complied, I'd scarcely have more than a dozen left, and almost at once, it seemed, the satisfaction that I'd derived from my ever-expanding hoard had completely evaporated. Not only that, but I began to understand how flawed my thinking had been and that what I'd overlooked was that dogged persistence isn't enough—and furthermore that, even when you played the odds, you'd also need either wherewithal or luck. . . and, given my family's means so far, I'd better depend on the latter. But I couldn't help thinking that those who appeared to be luckiest were those who didn't need it.

Economically speaking, things were still stagnant in the South. Despite a mutual assurance that we were "old Columbia," few of my family's friends had any money to speak of, and most of those who did had fathers who'd stayed at home while others went overseas. Still, being "well off" was relative, especially in matters of race, and everybody had maids—our friends were white, our "help" was not. As far as I was aware and except for Mr. Grubbs, nobody was scrambling yet to get ahead, which was why my father's advice seemed fundamentally flawed. . . the odds themselves were largely a matter of luck.

So, hoping for some positive indication, I dumped the last of my bottlecaps and, testing myself for ESP, tried rolling dice and cutting cards without much cause for optimism. Since I was my father's son, I feared it might be genetic.

But then, in 1950, when I was old enough at last to join my friends in Troop 14, a stroke of good fortune occurred that caught me as much by surprise as a message from my Ouija Board— which, in fact, had never delivered anything other than two or three random letters except on the one occasion when my grandmother, who loved all games of any sort and let me win at Authors and sometimes at gin rummy, had made it spell out "popovers," which is what she always cooked for me when I spent the night with her because my grandfather had to travel, usually to Philadelphia. We'd always split a six-ounce Coke, pouring it into orange-juice glasses, and that was largesse to me.

But what happened totally out of the blue was that I was chosen by my troop to go to the Valley Forge Jamboree, using the money we'd raised throughout the course of the year to send what we'd agreed would be our "most deserving scout." But new to the troop as I was, I'd never supposed I was even in the running, so it felt like winning a sweepstakes, the first big prize of my career—which I attributed to luck, though I now suspect it might have been rigged by an altruistic scoutmaster for reasons that had to do with my father's losing streak.

It was, in any case, a turning point for me—like finding that one-cent magenta—though, as things turned out, it was our scoutmaster himself, Pat McKinsey, a wiry sort of modern-day Natty Bumppo who'd prove to be, for everyone in the troop, the biggest windfall of all. He was a maverick vet on the GI Bill who, sick of his former spit-and-polish life, was studying math and running track at the local university while in hot pursuit of redheaded women and, on alternate weekends, slogging through swampy treks straight out of *Treasure Island* that were for him, it seemed, the essence of an adventurous life—along with his redheads, of course, who were, as we dimly understood, something other than grown-up versions of *Anne of Green Gables*, a book only our sisters had read. Devoid of condescension towards us or anyone else, he was like a kid himself, but we would have gladly followed him anywhere.

As for Valley Forge, I'd never traveled so far from home or, even at Billy Graham rallies or Gamecock football games, been part of anything that big—some forty-seven thousand kids decked out in uniforms and sashes, from every state and dozens of countries around the world. I met a pallid but friendly Scout from Lithuania, a Scout in a kilt from Scotland, and a Black Scout from Los Angeles who seemed as exotic to me as any of the others—though we ourselves were the true anomalies who, in our provincial way, thought that being from South Carolina would be of interest to everyone, a delusion quickly exposed as soon as we'd set up camp.

We'd been issued a sort of campaign tent that looked like a relic from World War I and instructed to bedizen it with something distinctively picturesque. Kirk Finlay, my older tent-mate, was of the opinion that, if we painted it with an outline of our state on one side and a Confederate flag on the other, it would be eye-catchingly *Gone-with-the-Wind*-ish. It was, but in a negative way, and we were obliged to cover it up before any famous guests arrived—among them President Truman, who spoke to us about unity and was awarded a Silver Buffalo.

Then, coupled with what would be, according to one reporter, a lavishly expensive fireworks presentation "costing over $5,000," the far more popular General Eisenhower arrived on July 4th and sternly warned us as we sat in what was then called Indian-style where Washington's men had shivered and prayed a couple of centuries before that we might soon find ourselves at war again in a place we'd hardly heard of called the peninsula of Korea.

Though the crisis there was only two-weeks old, we'd have no choice, Ike said, and a pall fell over the crowd until he told us all to get to our feet and recite the pledge to the flag, giving the event a vague and slightly disturbing Nuremberg-rally sort of feel that got reported in the national press as "massed scouts vowing allegiance. . . at rigid salute and with emotion trembling and throbbing in their voices."

After a meaningful pause, Ike signaled for the fireworks to begin, using the very same phrase he'd used for the D-Day invasion. "Let 'er rip!" he sang out, as bombs began bursting in air.

We presented him with a Silver Beaver, and a day or two later, we all went home, where I learned that a stringer for our local paper had reported on the final day—as we were presumably girding ourselves for battles yet to come—that "Bernie Dunlap has provided us with many funny stories," none of which I can now recall. What I remember most vividly is the smell of the freshly mown meadow grass that sweetened the air all through the nights and a newly awakened thought that, having lucked into one such prize, I might just win another—not so much because I deserved it but because I was on a roll. . . not exactly a matter of playing the odds but closer to my father's bent than I'd probably ever been.

So it wasn't anything either logical or obsessive that led me, on a Saturday in October, to the Reddy Kilowatt booth at the annual State Fair. I was with my friend and fellow aspirant in the sciences, Harry Scrivener, and for the first time there on our own, we were headed for the midway when, taking a shortcut through the hanger-like hall where exhibits were jumbled together, we paused to look at the booth for rural electrification.

It featured a giant incubator, lit by rows of hundred-watt light bulbs warming some five hundred eggs in vertically rotating trays like a very slow-moving amusement ride. A sign above the contraption explained that, during the ten-day course of the fair, the eggs would hatch into baby chicks, and that, in addition to taking home a six-inch glow-in-the-dark plastic figurine of Reddy Kilowatt which everyone could do, one lucky person who'd filled out a card would win a poulterer's bonanza of all the newly hatched chicks.

We were on the verge of moving on, when a woman in a calico bonnet—as if there to pose for Dorothea Lange—gestured at a boy by her side who looked to be nine or ten.

"Ain't no use yo're signin' up," she said. "My boy's go'n' win them baby chicks!"

Taking that as a challenge, I answered her with citified aplomb, "We'll see about that, madam."

"He wins at everything," Harry confided, having been my campaign manager for junior-high student council when, just after winning the scouting prize, I'd contrived a facetious slogan ("Stay Happy with Dunlap-y") for posters featuring cutouts from various magazine ads of blissful consumers of products from floor waxers to shampoo or of people miserably down in the dumps ("They Didn't Stay Happy with Dunlap-y"). For whatever reason, I'd developed a highly improbable notion that, whatever the odds might be, I was on a magical run that only my own faint-heartedness could thwart.

Maybe something of the sort was in my mind as I wrote my name on a Reddy Kilowatt entry card and dropped in the box. But I promptly forgot all about it until, one afternoon in the following week when I was alone at home and about to leave for Julian Shand's birthday party, I heard the doorbell ring.

I went to the door and saw two men in overalls. One of them grinned and asked, "You Bernie Dunlap Junior?"

I acknowledged that I was.

"Well, Reddy Kilowatt says hello. You done won yourself fo' hunnert fifty chicks!" He gestured back towards a truck with stacks of cardboard cartons. "Where you want 'em at?"

I decided to temporize. "I thought they said five hundred."

"Some of 'em didn't make it."

"Okay," I said. I was at a loss but also in a hurry to leave, so I told them to bring the boxes inside and lay them out on the floor.

"You shore?" they asked.

I said I was, so they did as I'd requested, stacking the three-by-six-foot cartons at the entrance to our living room before taking their leave with a dubious nod. I glanced at the boxes on my way out, assuming that I'd be back before anyone else got home. The only immediate problem that I could see was that the chicks, which had by then begun a distressingly pitiful cheeping, would be shut up where they were for a couple of hours at least, and I couldn't help but notice that the holes in the cartons' lids were smaller than I'd supposed, about the size of a penny. Lifting a lid to check, I saw the bottom half of each carton was partitioned very much like a Nehi Cola crate with a chick in every cubicle, barely able to move.

They looked at me despondently and redoubled their frantic cheeps. As with my previous stab at interacting with horses, I thought I could intuit what they were trying to say—"We're going to suffocate!"

"No, you're not," I tried to assure them, using my father's intonation.

"Yes, we are!" they wailed in despair, sounding like my sister and twisting their heads around to plead with me eye-to-eye. . . or with one of their eyes to both of mine. "You don't know what it's like down here," they shrilled.

I took the box lid all the way off, watching to see if they'd scramble out, but none of them could or did. "Okay," I said in effect, "if you promise to stay where you are."

Their answer wasn't entirely clear, but then, I reasoned with myself, they were barely out of the incubator—what could they possibly know? So I removed all the lids and laid the cartons out throughout the hall and living room. The chicks were still staying put, murmuring to themselves with what I took to be gratitude. Then I left for the birthday party, thinking I'd handled things well.

But sometime during the afternoon, whether from panic or perfidy, it seemed they'd changed their minds because, when my mother walked into the scene much sooner than I'd anticipated, what she found was, as she'd put it, "like something dreamed up by Salvador Dali." All over the downstairs part of the house, as if they'd tumbled down the chimney, were surreal swarms of dementedly cheeping chicks, hopping about and defecating.

After recovering from her initial shock, my mother had begun what a sensible person would do by picking them up and putting them back in their cartons—some of them more than once—then replacing the lids when the boxes were full and looking about for any she might have overlooked. By proceeding methodically, she'd managed to snare four hundred or so, but, as soon as she thought she'd gotten them all, she'd hear another cheep, mostly in places hard to reach like under the sofa or behind the refrigerator. So, as resourcefully as an Eagle Scout, she'd hauled the vacuum cleaner out and, after attaching a small round brush, hoovered the interlopers up, plucking them free from the nozzle and dropping them back in their cubicles until they'd all been found at last and, exhausted by their busy day, became as inert as tennis balls.

But when I got home, I had a lot of explaining to do. My mother wanted the whole infestation returned at once to Reddy Kilowatt, but the State Fair had come to an end and, as my father usefully pointed out, by the time we heard back from REA we'd have hundreds of dead chicks on our hands. "Or under our feet," he added. Then, to my surprise, he proceeded to reminisce— something he rarely did—about raising backyard chickens as a boy along with having to milk a cow as one of his daily chores "right there on Oakland Avenue in the middle of Rock Hill!"

As he was talking, an entrepreneurial switch was suddenly thrown in my head, and I began to compute by a factor of whatever number of eggs I guessed a chicken could lay and multiplying that result by what egg-crazed consumers might be willing pay, then again by four-hundred-fifty and adding it up in my mind to reach a conclusion that would at once placate my parents, especially if I tossed in my latest craze for racking up weirdly demanding merit badges that few kids ever earned—like Physical Development, for example, which took six months of rigorous exercise instead of the less demanding Athletics which prissily ambitious Scouts could snag in an afternoon.

Maybe, I suggested, aiming my appeal primarily at my father when he started to laugh about some mishap with his cow, especially since against all odds I'd won the chickens fair-and-square—like drawing an inside-straight—if I could just raise them to pullet stage, I'd earn myself a merit badge that would make me look really good if I ever went back to a Jamboree.

"Called what?" my skeptical mother asked, meaning the merit badge. I knew she was onto me.

"Poultry Raising," I improvised which, though I was making it up, was close enough to Poultry Keeping, the name by which it was actually known. Then I hurried to elaborate, explaining that Bird Study was one of the needed badges that most scouts chose to get if they wanted to be an eagle because all it involved was claiming you'd spotted some birds and written that down whereas for Poultry Raising you had to raise your birds from the time they'd hatched, and I'd be much prouder of taking that harder route. I was mostly inventing that too—even if what I'd said about the Bird Study badge was close enough to the truth—and nobody I knew had even considered the other.

"And here's another reason," I added to my plea, fully aware of my father's knack for making bad investments, "this is a business proposition." I'd make a lot of money, I said, sharing my calculations . . . and I'd pay them back whatever it cost to set me up a poultry farmer.

"A poulterer," said my father.

"Exactly!" I agreed, adding that word to my quiver.

I was both pleased with my performance and surprised at how easy it was—and, after a little more debate, as improbable as it seemed, they agreed to transform our largely screened-in side porch into an urban chicken coop. So the following day we drove to Assembly Street to buy some feeders, trays, and chickenfeed—regarding all of which, like the likelihood of turning a profit, I knew nothing whatsoever. It would be a gamble, my father said, causing my mother to shake her head, "But play it right," he added, "and you might hit it big."

Though that prospect had rarely panned out for him, it looked as if it might for me during the first few weeks that ensued. I got up every morning at dawn to feed my vigorous flock who seemed to grow with remarkable speed, and, except for the guano piling up like deep-dish pizza with extra cheese, I was seemingly on my naïve way to a Poultry Keeping merit badge and fun and profit as well.

But then we had our first hard freeze and, when I rushed down to check on my brood, it resembled a polar disaster—motionless chicks strewn over the porch like golf balls on a driving range. My mother heard my horrified howl.

"What's the matter?" she asked as she opened the door, expecting to find the screen door torn with some ravaging predator on the loose.

I gestured at the calamity—the birds keeled over, my start-up wrecked, all hope of a merit badge down the tube. My father, who'd showed up late on the scene, shrugged as if to a croupier, "Don't count your chickens before they're pullets."

But my mother went into action at once, collecting the frozen chicksicles up and laying them out on cookie sheets while turning the oven to low pre-heat and slipping them in for a minute or two until they twitched or started to singe. . . after which, set down on the floor, a surprising percentage would stagger about, uttering low-pitched drowsy cheeps that sounded to my over-wrought mind like, "Ohhhh, cheeep cheeeeep, what's. . . hap. . . pen. . . ing?"

But after a while they'd start to perk up and, at least for another cold day or two, it would seem I was back in business again despite my egregious oversight of having no way to heat the porch without the risk of burning it down or to avert the grim reality that, after a couple of resurrections, my flock was not only dwindling fast but displaying a growing lack of ambition. With my father's help, I constructed an insulated sort of roosting cube with heating pads at either end, but as soon as any chick ventured forth, it would slow down like a wind-up toy and creep back in to join its fellow survivors.

Then, towards the end of January, just as I'd begun to resign myself to a gallinaceous Donner Pass, the remnant appeared to toughen up. Two or three started to emerge followed by five or six more until, one day when the weather warmed up, I noticed they'd reached the pullet stage and were stalking about like Spartans.

My father talked to the friend of a friend who owned a big-time operation that sold both eggs and fertilizer—packaged as "Hendoo," I was told—and he took the hardship-toughened birds off my hands along with their feeders and water trays in exchange for a deal my father made for a lump-sum payment of twenty bucks plus two dozen eggs delivered each week for what I recall as a year.

So, we literally ate my profits—scrambled, poached, or fried but always, unmistakably, as eggs—interminably, *ad nauseum*, until I regretted the stroke of luck that had made me a poulterer and developed a lifelong aversion to lotteries of any sort or to playing the odds in general.

I got my merit badge nonetheless and wore it on my sash like a *Croix de Guerre*—a handsome red rooster in profile within a light-green circle—though I was chagrined to find that, as opposed to the unwieldy scale of my near-ruinous operation, all the merit badge had actually required was "a brood of not less than 10 chickens," which struck me as a paltry proposition. I was also disturbed by the fact that so many of my charges hadn't survived and so few of those that made it through had all their faculties intact—a reflection that caused me to conclude that, in dealing with animals going forward, there should be a division of labor: my cousins could do the riding, my brother could do the hunting (and much of the gathering too), my father would do the betting despite that getting us nowhere while I, in one way or another, would learn to do the memorializing. . . whatever that might entail.

What it entailed, as I quickly determined, was what I undertook next in the spirit of further study along with David Rembert, another old friend of mine and fellow science student with whom I jointly enrolled in the Omaha School of Taxidermy via a correspondence course advertised in the back pages of *Outdoor Life*. Part of the inducement for me was another exotic merit badge requiring nothing more than that a Scout would need to "present a satisfactory specimen of a bird or small mammal mounted by himself," though we both intended to mount and display a great deal more than that.

On the surface, at least, our arrangements with the school seemed reasonable enough. Every two weeks, from far-off Nebraska, a lesson would be mailed to my address and, in return upon receipt, we'd send five dollars back. The lessons would grow progressively in scale—from modest assignments like frogs and fish through birds and squirrels and other small mammals to deer and elk or assorted big game beyond our reach and modest means.

Regarding the latter, our wherewithal at the start consisted of fourteen dollars plus small allowances every week and the prospect of mowing neighbors' lawns to keep us on our bi-weekly schedule. That would be difficult, as we knew, especially during the winter months, but, oblivious in our single-minded way, we assumed we'd manage to work that out and launched ourselves at once on Lesson Number One in the privacy of my basement lab, relying on Old Spice and Mum to mask the noisome stench that sometimes clung to us and using whatever came to hand—like recently deceased pet turtles and smaller game fish like bream whose outer shapes were easy to maintain and then, as we progressed, an array of frozen birds, of which there were more to be found than I'd have previously supposed, and even road-killed possums and squirrels that, because of their flattened condition, were harder to reconstruct and more difficult to acquire since neither of us could drive.

In terms of my own vacillation between science and art with animals as a sort of middle ground, I thought of our undertaking as a combination of both, so I took it for granted that I'd possess a natural affinity for it. But it was Rembert whose reconstructions of birds and bigger but trickier squirrels looked persuasively recognizable while mine, to my consternation, appeared to be shapeless deep-fried lumps from some Frankenstein's nightmare kitchen.

Though surprised by my apparent lack of aptitude, I resolved to work at it harder, and there should have been time to improve. But five or six lessons into the course, our money began to run out while the installments kept arriving and piling up in my cellar along with increasingly testy notes that, though urging us on to ever bigger and better taxidermy, observed that, disappointingly, we'd fallen into arrears. When we'd failed to correct that oversight, they fired off abusive red-lettered cards threatening terrible consequences directed not only at David and me but at anyone even remotely kin.

I began to hurry home from school, hoping to intercept the mail before my parents could winnow through it and keeping that tactic up until, after consulting my fellow deadbeat, I sent a carefully printed reply reporting the scarcely credible news that Messieurs Rembert & Dunlap had met with a tragic accident, prompting another red-lettered threat, all in capital letters.

We were nearing the end of our mutual rope, hoping some miracle would occur, when—just as we'd begun to discuss absconding to the swamp near Hampton Hill where we'd often camped overnight with our Boy Scout troop—I woke to a headline in *The State*,

FLASH FLOODS HIT DOWNTOWN OMAHA

or something to that effect and prayed that a forgiving God in his infinite mercy had arranged for our School of Taxidermy to be in a ground-floor suite. . . which apparently was the case because we never heard from them again, and I gave up that field for good with a plan to concentrate instead on rocketry and explosives.

I didn't get the taxidermy merit badge which was discontinued the following year—as Physical Development would be in 1952 and Poultry Keeping in 1974—and no badges were available in my newly chosen pursuits which, luckily for everyone, would come to very little. I dabbled a bit on my own down in my secret lab using my Gilbert Chemistry Set. . . though, after some sizable detonations, one of which blew a cellar window out, I figured I shouldn't press my luck, a decision of which my parents approved.

My final shot at a comeback in science had nothing to do with animals or dangerous chemical compounds. It occurred in high school Biology, when each of us had to complete a potential Science Fair project. After much indecision, mine ended up as a tabletop tableau of modeling-clay dinosaurs prowling beneath a volcano that glowed and smoked when a battery was connected—though it failed to spew forth the molten kidney-bean lava with which I'd loaded it. It got a B+ for artistic effect, but as my teacher observed, it lacked analytical rigor.

In striking contrast with mine, David Rembert's intricate project, using resources from his father's janitorial distributorship, was a novel method for producing sulfuric acid, so ingeniously designed as an actual working model that it went on to earn a prize in the statewide competition.

Among our other friends, the creation that baffled us both as we carpooled our projects to school was Bryan Grubbs' box of gravel and dirt along with bits of metal, tar, and balsa wood which, according to an explanatory sketch, had something to do with geological strata and drilling for oil in the Southwest. When asked how the box related to his poster, he told us to wait and see.

When we pulled up in front of the school to unload one at a time, Bryan said he'd need to go last, so Rembert and I were starting up the steps when we heard a heartbreaking cry and turned to see an apparently inconsolable Bryan gazing down at a pile of debris.

"What happened?" somebody asked.

"My project!" Bryan wailed, pointing to the mess at his feet. "It fell when I took it out of the car!"

All the other kids commiserated, and, eventually, our biology teacher emerged to survey the disaster, causing Bryan to redouble his emotion. In the end he got a good grade based on his poster's claims and, not long after that, he moved with his family to Houston, where I'm told he later became a stockbroker like his father while Rembert became a botany professor and, late in life, the author of a volume of haiku in English subtitled "A Biologist View." After moving to Jacksonville, Harry Scrivener became an engineer, returned to Columbia, and died of a heart attack in early middle age. All of which proves little more than my Ouija board might have revealed—that though we do our best to make sense of it, life sometimes seems to resemble a game of musical chairs in which, when we try to sit, we sooner or later find a chair's no longer free.

As for my own continuing scramble, remembering what *The State* had said—that, at the Valley Forge jamboree, I'd provided a lot of funny stories—and drawing on a previous obsession, I decided while still in grammar school to try my hand at words, writing and then illustrating the story of a racehorse to whom, somewhat heavy-handedly, I gave the name of "Homestretch." Carefully written out in longhand in a squared-off Blue Horse notebook, it was a Seabiscuit sort of tale of an unprepossessing colt that rose to record-breaking triumphs simply because, relying on neither luck nor on merely playing the odds, it was so determined to win. In his last and greatest race, the heroic thoroughbred—with which I clearly identified—died of a fatal heart attack while thundering down the homestretch, true to his name to the last, collapsing across the finish line and winning by a nose.

It wasn't intentionally funny, and, as literary efforts go, no better than my botched re-creations of birds, but, given my increasing interest in girls, it gradually dawned on me that, if I were to prove attractive to them, it wouldn't be on the basis of taxidermy or even of merit badges. What had pleased my mother most would surely please them as well—at least, the ones towards whom I was irresistibly drawn who'd also, as I supposed, be devotees of Rupert Brooke and Edna St. Vincent Millay. . . and I had a head start there. What could possibly go wrong?

6

Expiration Dates

I don't know when or why they started, but I had night terrors as a boy. I think they may have begun before we'd moved to a new house on South Saluda Avenue sometime in 1947, which means no later than when I was eight or nine, though even that's uncertain—and their actual content is vague because in a technical sense I was neither asleep nor awake. Nonetheless, I can say with some confidence that they were less like watching a horror movie and more like the horror itself, though desolation may be a better word and, however amorphous its form, I'd find myself in its throes in the middle of the night with my mind so consumed by despair that all I could do was sob and chatter my teeth. In time I managed to program myself to stagger into my parents' bedroom where I'd tell my mother, "It's happening again!" and she'd guide me back to my room where she'd sit with me for up to an hour, doing her best to soothe me while I kept crying that nothing could ever help—though eventually it would, and I'd fall asleep again amid the emotional wreckage.

Those episodes occurred at intervals over a number of years, during which I developed some precautionary rituals such as closing my eyes as soon as I got into bed and imagining a scenario that was, in fact, very much like a movie with me standing at the base of a gentle slope in a green and hilly setting containing a number of widely spaced wooden tables behind each of which sat a seemingly pleasant but business-like woman with a notebook of some sort in front of her.

Everything about the scene was reassuringly serene, and I could see a dozen or so people, mostly kids of various ages but a few adults as well, who, having completed a short formality, were setting out in different directions across the bucolic landscape—which would soon become as familiar to me as my real-life neighborhood. When my turn came to check in, I'd tell the woman behind the nearest desk where I wanted to go that night and, having made a note of it in her book, she'd smile and wave me on with an understanding that I'd find my way to the proper location without any difficulty and that, whatever interesting or amusing adventures might lie ahead, nothing profoundly amiss could ever happen there.

Such as what? I now ask myself. And the answer, I think, is a clue as to what those alarums and excursions were almost certainly about—which would seem to have been, very broadly, a distressing awareness of mortality, and somewhat more specifically, a fear of total obliteration. . . or, in terms I might later have used after reading a bit more widely, the dilemma of "being and nothingness."

In other words, those horrific episodes were caused by a commonplace human concern as opposed to more convoluted explanations that I've considered from time to time, ranging from the plausibly neurological (like the grotesque hematoma from tripping while racing a friend up the steps of her parents' country club and slamming my forehead against the cement) to the modishly psychological (like the melodramatic scenes surrounding my father's addiction to alcohol and his self-destructive pursuits in tandem with it). So. resisting such shots in the dark, the bottom line for me is that, though scientists tend to be uncomfortable with phrases like "fear and trembling" and "a sickness unto death," we humanists don't in the least.

Therefore, I'm inclined to think the psychic disturbance started much earlier when we were still in Camden and our benignly dignified Great Dane, Frawleen, got kicked in the head by a horse and suddenly was no more—in response to which I started to reconsider what I'd been told at a Presbyterian summer day camp about death and the afterlife and how, in the midst of one of those sessions, a furious hailstorm had nearly shaken the building down, smashing a number of windows and ripping off parts of the roof.

That experience had not only led me to question the pious bromides we'd been fed but to dwell upon my own eventual demise in a way that led me to surmise that the best I could hope for if unexpectedly kicked by a horse would be either a coldly unspooling eternity or a sudden and utter extinction, both of which tied my stomach in knots and, even worse to my five-year-old mind, was the stultifying prospect of an endless unvarying bliss should our counselor be proven right despite her hysteria during the storm.

To put it in the simplest possible terms, what I think I must have been fumbling towards at that stage of my development was the basic realization that I'd been given a wonderful gift that wouldn't be mine forever. I'd not yet heard of the Venerable Bede, of course, or of his description of life as like an interval of warmth and light experienced by a sparrow blown in and out of a mead hall during a winter storm, but that was more or less where my thoughts were headed, though without his assurance of faith—the absence of which is probably why my night terrors soon began following that sequence of events. . . if that's indeed how it happened.

No doubt, my existence as an indulged and pampered first-born son had made me too happy with life as it was—too reluctant to leave the mead hall, so to speak, or even to think about it. But for simplicity's sake, when my parents pressed me about what was going on in my head, I recounted some other bad dreams I'd had which weren't night terrors at all. In one, somewhat reminiscent of "The Sorcerer's Apprentice," there'd been luminous outlines of rectangles and squares that, with metronomic regularity, kept appearing and overlapping in front of me as if on a movie screen, multiplying so rapidly that, tasked with remembering the size and location of each, I'd suddenly lose track of one of them as nothing could slow the infernal machine and panic engulfed me like a flood. In the other dream that I recounted, I'd been assigned to oversee a silken thread that was fed along a horizontal loom at increasing speed until, all at once, it snagged and became a huge and monstrously expanding knot that I could never hope to untangle.

Though both were classic frustration dreams, it's apparent to me now how related they were, after all, to the dread my night terrors caused—with the first of them imbued with a recognition that time itself, like an ever-rolling stream, was constantly sweeping away what I desperately wanted to grasp and hold (*"Verweile doch, du bist so schön!"*, had I only known Goethe at the time). The second dream, as I recall, was nonsensically set in a space behind a neighbor's garage that, roaming about like cats, I and my friends had used as a secret passageway, but endowed in my dream with a sense of irreparable loss like what I'd felt seeing photos of children younger than I minding the spindles in local mills.

As a further footnote, the setting of that second dream was fraught with such angst for me because the house and garage in Myrtle Court belonged to a couple called the Goudelocks who'd lived on the other side of a moss-ridden old horse fountain with their only son, Bill, who was recognized by everyone as a paragon of affable virtue. After college he'd become a Marine and, shortly before the unsettling event I'm about to describe in the summer of 1951, he was killed in the Korean War. His death weighed heavily on my mind, as it did for all who'd known him.

By then we'd moved twice more. My father, whose drinking had gotten worse, had been hospitalized by a nearly fatal crash while driving a company car that was afterwards left dangling from a bridge abutment. When his injuries healed, he got a new job and joined Alcoholics Anonymous and the five of us moved again to my grandfather's spacious house in Wales Garden, ostensibly giving him company following my grandmother's death.

A few weeks later, we were visited by my Uncle Witherspoon "Spoony" Dunlap, a Presbyterian pastor who, along with the rest of my father's clan, had made it painfully clear that I was on my way to becoming its first eldest son since our 16th-century forebear, the irascible John Knox, not to embrace the family faith—meaning the church of Scotland rather than that of England, a conflict very much in play throughout the history of our family and state.

They didn't blame my mother for my dereliction, but their stern disapproval of my father's apostasy in adopting her church was so palpable that it seemed to stir memories in their blood of the murderous Duke of Cumberland making his way through Ayrshire en route to dispatching kith and kin to mass graves at Culloden or to exile in the red clay hills of upstate South Carolina.

Still, as best they could, they put such issues aside when Uncle Spoony showed up from Fountain City, Tennessee, to preach at Columbia's First Presbyterian Church—whose founding pastor had, in fact, been a Dunlap—and we all turned out to hear him.

Eschatology aside and at ease in my mother's discreetly amenable church, I'd concluded on the basis of previous visits that the genial savior meek-and-mild depicted in stained glass over its altar would be far more lenient towards me and other insouciant sinners than the elders glowering from the dais where Uncle Spoony preached. I'd also learned to ignore the recurrent quip by my father's older sister, Aunt Isabel, that her son—my first cousin Bobby—was "*so* proud because he's both a Southerner *and* a Presbyterian," after which she'd look at me and sniff, "But don't worry, Little Bernie. . . you're a Southerner anyhow."

So once again, on the occasion of that particular visit, I found myself sitting with my parents and siblings in a pew with no kneeling benches or Book of Common Prayer listening to my uncle's lengthy sermon, of which I'd only recall its short non-Biblical text, "and Caesar crossed the Rubicon. . . the die was cast!" I was interested in Ancient Rome and pleasantly surprised that my uncle might find merit in such a pagan allusion—though I now suppose what he must have had in mind was the war being fought in Korea and the role that, until very recently, General MacArthur had been playing in it, a concern that was totally lost on me.

Much of what followed that day is also vague in my mind, though, after our Sunday dinner—a midday meal in the south where "lunches" were either snacks on the run or gatherings of ladies for gossip-and-chicken-salad—I and my friends took Cousin Bobby swimming at Caughman's Pond, located outside the city limits. The oldest of my friends had a beginner's driver's license, and, when we got there during the heat of the day, we had the place to ourselves for a while.

The area where we swam was like an old-fashioned swimming hole with a couple of rustic dressing rooms, a larger party shed, a dock from which to monitor kids as they splashed, and a chest-high wooden security fence topped with planks laid flush with the water to divide where wading was safe from the deeper parts of the pond. As a nonsensical temptation for those who couldn't swim, there was also a very tall and undulating sliding board that had its delivery end on one of the fence's planks so that whoever came down the slide was shot like a cannonball into the deeper water. It was strictly off-limits for little kids but a chance to show off for us—and for me in front of my cousin that day, it was all but irresistible, especially because he was largely ignoring me while joking about with my friends.

In retrospect, I wouldn't blame all that ensued on sectarian rivalry, but it must have been a factor along with sheer stupidity on my part as each of us took a turn in barreling down the slide with predictable variations—backwards, forwards, supine, prone—until we'd nearly exhausted the usual repertoire. But as I mounted the ladder for my third or fourth descent, I had such a compelling idea that I was surprised at first that nobody else had tried it. The Oslo Winter Olympics was then only months away, which was probably in the back of my mind. . . though on second thought, I knew none of my friends would dare attempt what I was about to do. Not David, Julian, or Bill. Certainly not Frank Beattie, and not my cousin Bobby.

So "Ladies and gentlemen," I declaimed in a sports announcer's voice, "now at the top of the run is Olaf Dunlapson, defending gold medalist in the ski jump!"

As I pushed off from the top of the slide, I saw all their faces upturned with Frank's looking apprehensive. In the first half-mini-second, my feet shot out from under me and, though I've tried to reconstruct what must have happened next—my making a quick half-turn in the air, my arms outstretched, my body still leaning face to the wind and plummeting towards the boundary fence—it must have happened too fast to make any sort of sense. . . and maybe the angle at which I fell was difficult to follow because nobody seems to have seen how my head bounced off the board or how I slid like a shadow into the murky depths. I'm told there were cheers and laughter—"Great, Olaf, great! Do it again!"—as they waited for me to resurface.

But in every crowd of teenage guys, there's always one who's fond of puns, who's the last to be picked when choosing up sides, who tends to miss the point when there's an inside joke or laughs too hard when he gets it. In his imperturbably geeky way, that was my friend Frank Beattie who, as I now understand in thinking back about it, had been appointed to be there on that day expressly for him to say with what everyone else would dismiss as a typical over-reaction, "My God! I think he's hurt!"

It was Frank who instantly dove down in the vicinity of where I'd last been seen and awkward non-athletic Frank who fumbled about in those watery depths, blindly grasping my hair and yanking me to the surface. When the rest of them saw I hadn't come round, they helped him drag me to the dock and did what, in theory at least, Scouts supposedly learn to do—turning me onto my stomach while trying to find a pulse and, though concluding that I was dead, proceeding with the next step, artificial respiration. . . though, never having needed that skill and uncertain how long to keep it up, they were just on the verge of abandoning it when I made a sudden gagging noise and spouted like a spigot. So they redoubled their efforts until, though entirely unconscious still, I was propped like a doll in a sitting position and repeatedly asked how I felt.

Up until then, it seems, all their efforts had gone according to the book—the *Boy Scout Handbook* that is, which for all its practical wisdom had little to nothing to say about possible side effects like blindness and delirium. Even when halfway sentient, I couldn't see at all, and, as soon as they'd gotten me to my feet, I groped about and started to babble in an incoherent way about Caesar crossing the Rubicon and the die being cast. That much, at least, my cousin might have explained, but it didn't occur to him as their agitation revived and they hustled me into the dressing room to conduct the irrelevant task of getting me properly dressed for a trip to the nearest emergency room, which was nearly ten miles away.

At that point, I've been told, things took a surreal turn as a man who'd just arrived with his wife and two small kids assumed the tranquility of their family outing was being sabotaged by a rowdy underage drunk. He demanded that I pipe down, and when my yammering failed to stop, proceeded to slap me silly. In my reconstruction of the scene, it would have been Frank who cried again, "My God! Can't you see he's hurt?" But I've got no details to share about that because none were ever provided, and all that I can recall for sure is the tail-end of my return from outer space some four or five hours later.

Nobody could say if I'd been clinically dead—our handbook was disappointingly silent on that matter—but what I'm certain about is that, when the faintest wisp of awareness returned, I was oddly untroubled by my inability to see because something far worse had befallen me, something I remember in the same way that I remember the icy vacuum of my recurrent night terrors. That's an apt comparison because, my non-stop gibbering aside, I stayed sunk in what I'd now describe as an all-encompassing amnesia—not simply regarding what had taken place that day or in any specific portion of my life or even the disconcerting fact that, as my goggle-eyed eyesight improved, there was a frantic woman I couldn't identify who kept repeating appeals that made no sense to me. My mind had simply been emptied out, not just of what you might expect—name, rank, and serial number—but of any sort of me-ness. I was nothing at all. I'm told that tears kept streaming down my face, but of that I have no recollection. What I remember is the hideous desolation, so awful and yet familiar.

The dénouement was anti-climactic. The doctors kept me awake, as I gather they always do with any bad blow to the head. After my sight was partially restored, a sense of who I was began to materialize, haltingly and bit by bit, appearing at first in my mind like a telescopic glimmer from the outer edge of nowhere and then like a photo in an acid bath slowly becoming clear. Some trivial things were seemingly lost for good, but among them were those recurrent dark nights of the soul, as if my binary way of thinking had been inarguably disproved. I even had a dream a few days later in which, having arrived at a Simple-Simon sort of crossroads signpost pointing in one direction towards eternity and in the other towards an end of everything, I simply set off overland down the middle—and my night terrors never recurred.

In that regard, I've run across an old wives' tale that, whenever we dream of falling from a great height, we always wake before hitting the ground because the subconscious mind refuses to truly contemplate its own annihilation. Further legend has it that, if and when in a dream you do in fact hit bottom, it's only because you're actually dying or dead. But since my apparent finale, I've repeatedly had a different dream in which I'm plunging in a long free-fall, hit bottom, and then get up to walk away unscathed.

"After the first death," Dylan Thomas wrote about the death of a child in the London Blitz, "there is no other." But whether I'd actually died or not, what had happened to me left such an indelible mark in my mind that I've seriously contemplated the other deaths I might have endured in parallel universes, should they happen to exist—at least four or five occasions at my last count, not including a time on the island of Java when I was, in fact, kicked in the head by a horse. It's an intriguing idea, like a Choose-Your-Own-Adventure book, if only because it would mean that, to get me to this moment, so many things would have had to be tweaked in the life I'm inhabiting now—not for any great destiny, but maybe for some tiny detail in the overall scheme of things, like the beating of a butterfly's wings that escalates to a hurricane. So it may have been with my night terrors too as presentiments of sorts for my ill-fated avatars.

One thing, at least, was certain—Olaf Dunlapson was dead. His departure had come like a thunderclap, but, even so, apart from my own survival, I was savvy enough to know that, for reasons that they themselves can't fathom or evade, some people die in slow motion, and, though he wouldn't discover for another nineteen years what might actually lie in store for lapsed Presbyterians, my father's eventual death, at the age of fifty-nine, was already underway.

With the benefit of hindsight, a lot is clearer now. My father had been a gifted athlete, but once the Depression had arrived—with Prohibition at an end and lushes with lampshades on their heads back in vogue again—he'd started to drink and couldn't stop, then started to gamble and couldn't win. He'd repeatedly tried to enlist for the war, but sky-high hypertension kept him out.

So, experienced as a contractor, he joined the Army Corps of Engineers to help them build an airfield on a rock in the mid-Atlantic that would play a crucial part in ending the U-boat threat. In traveling there by convoy, he was several times under fire and, after more than a year away, had successfully finished the job. But, when the war was over, he wasn't considered a vet when many others were who'd never even left home. That seemed basically unfair, though everybody knew that's how governments tend to work—that it's more about the uniform than what you actually do—just as they also knew that those who'd managed to stay behind had prospered while others were overseas. My father was caught in the middle when he got back and worked at a succession of jobs. . . among them, by an ironic twist, for the Veterans Administration and for the Attorney General's office.

I loved my father and admired him despite his alcoholism as if he'd been wounded in combat. He was decent, smart, and good, a man of absolute probity. On weekends around the state, well into middle age—though, as a regrettable fact, he wouldn't live much past it—he officiated at high school football games, and I noticed, when I accompanied him, that it was to him the other men deferred. It was different around the country club to which we never belonged, where out-of-shape go-getters in tasseled shoes swilled high balls mixed by resentful Blacks masquerading as Uncle Toms. In a prescient subconscious way, I perceived I'd someday have to choose between loyalty to a father who'd failed and allegiance to those others in tasseled shoes. I saw no reason to hesitate. It was time to cross the Rubicon.

That was when I told my friend Harry Scrivener that, despite my being a mere cipher in a thousand-student middle school, I'd decided to run for student council—a stilted teacher-run charade that was like a Soviet Baltic state for which, in assemblies twice a year, every candidate duly followed form by reciting vacuous platitudes to a cowed and bored electorate. The older students preceded me onstage, setting me up for what followed—really forgetting my lines at first but then as a matter of steely resolve delivering a mutinous parody, denouncing the bogus rigamarole of empty boasts and promises while laughing sardonically at myself for my own complicity in it.

From the teachers' point of view, I must have seemed what much later they might have recalled—if they'd lived to be close to a hundred—as a junior-high precursor of Donald Trump but with a sense of humor. In any case, except for them, I brought the whole house down with waves of raucous applause and, back in anarchist mode again, was elected by a landslide.

From within their impregnable teachers' lounge, our keepers must surely have disapproved, but they'd dealt with public enemies before. It was only a matter of days, they probably told themselves, before I'd overplay my hand, providing them with an excuse for putting me back in my place. I didn't, though, and having learned my lesson at A.C. Moore, I continued my populist rampage over the next two years, capturing every office in sight, becoming not only the mayor of the school but president of the honor society—the National Junior Honor Society—whose members wore a little gold torch and, in yet another school-wide assembly, stood solemnly together onstage repeating a bit of doggerel:

> Hold high the torch.
> You did not light its glow.
> 'Twas given you
> By other hands you know. . .

The teacher in charge of that self-congratulatory rite was Mrs. Christine Gaillard, a strictly no-nonsense middle-aged teacher of math who was also Assistant Principal and, like an overly zealous scoutmaster, a stickler for doing things by the book.

One day, when I was in study hall, she summoned me to her office to inform me that the latest grades were in and one of our members had made a C. It was therefore my duty as president, she sternly pointed out, to confront this miscreant and tell him he was no longer entitled to wear the little gold pin.

She said he'd already been sent for, and, when I asked who it was, she told me it was Tommy Caskey, a younger student I only knew in passing—though, like everyone else, I liked him well enough. It may have been that being liked mattered a little too much to him, but he was genuinely likeable, with freckles and sandy-colored hair and a ready and easy smile that somehow, though I couldn't say how, seemed almost apologetic.

There was a knock at the door, and Mrs. Gaillard, in a cold and peremptory voice, told whoever it was to come in. It was Tommy, of course. He stuck his head in and seemed to know in an instant what was up. Mrs. Gaillard told him to close the door behind him. He did as he was told, but his hand went up instinctively to the miniature golden torch pinned over his shirt pocket.

"No, Mrs. Gaillard!" he said.

"Bernie, you know what you're supposed to do. Tell Tommy why he's here."

But Tommy clearly knew without being told.

"No," he repeated, clutching his pin. "Don't make me do it! Please, Mrs. Gaillard!"

"Bernie, ask him for his pin."

"Please! Please!" he begged. "What will I say to my parents? I'll do better next time on my grades. . . I promise you I will!"

I was horrified, but she was adamant.

"Tommy, you know the rules. You are no longer in good standing as a member of the Society."

Academically, he was finished. He'd reached the end of the road. I wish I could report that at that moment I thought about Reuben Singletary, but each such horror seems unique, and I thought only of Tommy, who began to sob and fell to his knees.

It was, to that point in my life, the most abject humiliation I'd ever witnessed, and I was frozen in place. Mrs. Gaillard, who must have presided over other such episodes in the past, stepped forward herself to unpin the torch on Tommy's shirt. Then, looking disapprovingly at me because of my squeamishness, she placed the pin in my hand.

"Thank you, Tommy," she said. "You may go back to class."

He left, and the two of us were alone in her office. I remember the stone-like surface of the faux-granite floor and the large dark wooden door with its transom fastened shut.

"You may leave too," she said.

I turned to go—but remembered the pin in my hand and held it out to her. "Mrs. Gaillard," I said very quietly. "I don't think I can be president any longer."

She looked at me with her lips pressed together. "I was thinking the same thing," she told me.

I may not have harkened back to my grammar-school cafeteria and my brief time as a secret monitor, but it was, as I now can see, a version of the choice I thought I'd someday have to make between my father and the men in tasseled shoes. And, in fact, as with others whose paths I've briefly crossed, it was only long afterwards that I'd learn that Dr. C. Thomas Caskey, known as Tommy to his former classmates, would go on to become one of the world's most highly regarded scientists, a physician and geneticist who'd be so often at the forefront of genome technology that he'd be considered a strong contender for a future Nobel Prize. He became, in short, as far as I know, the most distinguished person from my part of the world to have ever worn the pin of the National Junior Honor Society.

"And the point of this story?" I ask myself as the first of several questions I have. Was his subsequent career impelled, at least in part, by his mortified recollection of that day in Mrs. Gaillard's office, a need to prove his worth to her and me and the rest of those who'd afterwards looked in vain for the little gold torch above his pocket? Or to put it another way, was the fear of further failure an indispensable catalyst for his eventual success?

I'm very loath to think so.

It could have been just a blip on the screen for someone whose great ability and capacity for hard work would win him prestigious prizes to come. The truth of the matter is that I have no idea what the import of that ghastly episode might have been for him. I can't recall a single conversation since that day and haven't set eyes on him in nearly seventy years—though, a decade or so ago, I ran into a brilliant young woman, herself near the top of the field in biogenetic research, who told me that Dr. Caskey was, without question, one of the most highly accomplished people she'd met in her whole career.

Probably, given such a reputation, he'd just as soon this anecdote wasn't told, and I certainly don't intend it as another public embarrassment. I recount it because it follows so naturally in my mind upon those earlier thoughts of Bede's metaphorical sparrow in our bright brief flights through a mead hall—and because it serves so well as an object lesson regarding prizes in general. They can serve as incentives, I suppose, rather than ends in themselves, but nothing in life is truly an end in itself. . . except, perhaps, what Aristotle described as εὐδαιμονία or "eudaimonia" and which Thomas Jefferson in turn, having studied the *Ethics* closely, referred to as "the pursuit of happiness"—happiness being in Jefferson's mind what Aristotle himself had been at such pains to define as not just pleasure, wealth, or acclaim but the realization by each of us of our highest natural potential.

We all have expiration dates but, as Bob Dylan wisely said, "He not busy being born is busy dying."

7

The Broken-Field Runner

When I first met Bernie Brooks, I knew he'd been a successful businessman as well as the former mayor of Teaneck, New Jersey, and that he'd recently returned to his native state. I also knew we not only shared a name but were roughly the same age, though I didn't know until we talked that he'd grown up in Camden — where I too had spent my first few years and which, when we were two or three, held barely five thousand people.

We must have brushed shoulders in the streets, but he was Black and I was white, so we never formally met until, in the early 2000s, he joined the Board of Trustees for Wofford College where I was serving as president.

That was in the city of Spartanburg located in a part of the state mostly settled in centuries past by immigrant Scots-Irish yeoman who'd rarely arrived with the wherewithal for large slave-holding plantations. That didn't mean people there were free of racial animus, though their karma was probably lighter, and they'd gotten used to cheering for African American football stars.

I knew next to nothing about Teaneck except that, though a suburb of New York, it was roughly the size of Spartanburg and that, as an undergraduate some forty-odd years before, I'd been on my college's track team with someone I thought had come from there. I asked Bernie Brooks when we met if he'd happened to know Bob Keck, who'd clocked a 9.6 hundred-yard dash with me right on his heels—having probably run, as I now believe, only 90 or 95 yards from a mismarked starting line. "My best time ever," I said, explaining that irony, but Bernie had never heard of Bob and, as I'd later discover, Bob was really from nearby Tenafly. So I followed that question up with one much closer to home.

"Well, anyhow, since you were a mayor yourself. . . did you ever happen to run across a man named Henry Savage?"

"Did I run across Henry Savage. . .?" he said in an almost rueful way that made me regret not having told him first that Henry had been my uncle as well as the mayor of Camden. "Oh, I met him, all right," he nodded, beginning to reminisce and maybe, in a subtle way, feeling me out about race. "You know, when I was a kid of eight or nine coming home after school, I used to watch the white kids on roller skates racing around a concrete rink." He rubbed his chin to reflect, and I didn't interrupt. "I could picture myself as the fastest guy on that rink, and, even without any skates of my own, I knew Christmas was coming up, and I could ask for whatever I wanted most. All the kids in my family could, assuming it didn't cost too much."

He smiled and shrugged while rolling his eyes, "One pretty good present apiece, you know." He looked away, then back again with a question. "Remember those skates you clamped on your shoes that tightened with a key?"

I said I did, and he nodded again.

"Well, on Christmas Day, I opened a box, and there they were. I couldn't wait to get out on the rink, so I asked my mother if I could go. 'Go where?' she asked, 'To the rink to skate,' I said, knowing what she would say—that the rink was only for whites. Maybe I'd somehow convinced myself that getting those skates of my own would manage to change the rules. 'So where's *our* rink?' I asked, at which she just shook her head. 'But that's not fair!' I wailed. 'So why don't you go tell the mayor?' she said as if she really meant it, and I was ready to go right then on Christmas Day. But she told me I'd need an appointment first and said she'd make it for me. . . which she did in a couple of days."

I feared the story wouldn't end well, but Bernie was clearly re-living it as he recounted how, when the day arrived, he'd been halfway out the door on his way to meet with the mayor when his mother dragged him back inside and made him put on his Sunday suit.

"Uh-huh, more rules," he'd told himself, "just to make it a little bit harder." He paused for a moment to let that sink in—he was a natural storyteller. "When I got to his office and gave them my name, Mayor Savage came out and shook my hand—which I thought was maybe just for show. Then he asked me what the problem was, so I told him and said it wasn't fair. I wanted permission to skate on that rink."

After that, he'd been led by Mayor Savage into a smaller office and asked to take a seat while the mayor sat down behind a desk, agreeing that it wasn't fair and that the law was wrong and needed to be changed. But until that was done, he'd added, it *was* the law—and he was obliged to uphold it.

"I thought I was getting the runaround," Bernie said with another wry smile, "especially when he asked if I had any skates of my own. So I told him about my Christmas present, after which he seemed to think for a minute before trying to change the subject to what I meant by a skating rink."

Bernie, who'd clearly been a much shrewder kid than I would have been at the time, had said what he meant was very simple—enough smooth flat paving without any cars for lots of kids to skate on, all at the same time. . . and it could be any shape if it was big enough.

"'Well, here's what we'll do,' Mayor Savage replied, 'when you and your friends get ready to skate, you just call me up to let me know. We'll block off a street—you choose which one—and let's see how long the council takes to change that law we're talking about.'"

Bernie looked over at me with a smile, and I felt greatly relieved.

"Did it actually work?"

"Oh, yeah," he winked. "We got ourselves a separate but equal rink—it took a bit longer to integrate. But you know what? I'd learned that even a kid like me, if he made an appointment and wore a suit, could help change things for the better. . . depending on who you're talking to. So I wanted to be a mayor too."

"He was my uncle," I confessed.

"I figured as much," he said, and I started to grasp what chasms he'd crossed in the course of achieving all that he had.

When I learned that the city of Teaneck had honored him when he retired by building a park in his name, I thought how beautifully fitting that was and hoped it included a rink

He had a brave and resourceful spirit, and I said so when I spoke at his funeral. So did my uncle, I thought—who, after the Klan was rampant again, had denounced it in bitterly scathing terms and got threatened and bombed for his trouble and had had a cross burned in his yard. When the sheriff's office had let it be known that he and his family were on their own, my aunt and cousins were moved up north while my uncle defiantly stayed where he was.

There were people like Bernie and Uncle Henry all through the South but, where I lived in my high school years, their numbers seemed few to none—with the crucial exceptions of Ernest Finney and Matthew J. Perry, two of the great civil rights attorneys, both later revered as judges and by me as personal friends.

As for the activist role that I myself might have played during my high school years, I was too caught up in my own self-serving commotion to know where to start on matters of race—though I should have found more to do than merely say what I thought and get involved in a couple of fights in which I managed to hold my own. Such outcomes were partly because my father, as a former collegiate boxer, had made a connection for me with a man whose name was Hans Wells, a trainer and physical rehab guy who got me briefly involved in Golden Gloves preliminaries, but mainly because I was playing football at the time, which generally meant I'd have some teammates around who, even if they were good ole boys, would break things up before I got pulverized. The team itself was totally white.

What was odd within our social circle was that, as in the case of Judge Petigru during the Civil War that my mother had kept reminding me of, I seemed to enjoy an immunity when I strayed, as I often did, from the prevailing orthodoxy while continuing with my winning streak through every election of any sort for which I was eligible. The climax of that anomalous combination came after my junior year of high school in an event sponsored each summer by the American Legion in each of the forty-eight states, the total number back then.

Trumpeted as an exercise for young leaders in democratic government but totally segregated—at least, in South Carolina— by gender as well as race, there was both a Boys State and a Girls State, though the latter was far less ballyhooed because, as one of the Legionnaires complacently framed the issue, who could seriously imagine electing a female candidate to a major political office? It was training in just such realpolitik that comprised the main activity during the weeklong gatherings, in the course of which a Governor and his runner-up would be chosen to represent their state at an even grander Boys Nation held in Washington, D.C.

In June of 1954, as a sort of warm-up event for our ensuing conclave, Girls State had been convened, and a friend of mine, Sarah Hardy, with whom I'd appeared in the local Children's Theatre cast for *Ali Baba and the Forty Thieves*—she being a faithful slave-girl and I the fearsome chief thief—had been elected Governor. Though it wasn't exactly a harbinger of things to come for her, she'd later become a soap-opera star and remain a close friend for years to come. In between her session and mine but still elated by what had been for her a theatrical event, she advised me that the secret of her success lay in simply acting the part—for which she thought, at my own event, "chief thief" should work out well.

As things turned out, she was right. I went, I saw, and on June 17th would conquer the hustings again by being elected as a maximum pseudo-leader, proceeding from there to Boys Nation to be photographed in the Rose Garden with President Eisenhower—whom I'd seen from a great distance at the Boy Scout Jamboree and now from only two or three feet away. . . just as nine years after my photo op, a Boys State Governor from Arkansas would share a similar moment with JFK, though the impact on our future careers would differ considerably.

In the last of my campaign speeches, I noted with earnest panache that Jefferson had been right—that consent from the governed wasn't enough for a truly robust democracy. Along with candidates fit to lead, we had to have an electorate able and willing to offer much more than merely reflexive obedience. I then declaimed with a fervor worthy of William Jennings Bryan that the key therefore was education—education for all, I emphasized, for everyone, of every race, color, gender, and creed.

Such rhetoric may sound trite today but, at that time and in that place—one month to the day after Brown v. Board of Education—even the word "education" had a resonant ring. I went on to point out that, in addition to being all male, what we were about at that moment was completely all white as well, as were our churches and public schools, our clubs, our teams, our waiting
rooms. We'd have to deal with that too, I said. Leaders would have to emerge from our midst. It was up to us to show the way. We were the hope of our state and the world!

Words come much easier than deeds, of course, but I was totally sincere. . . and sometimes even platitudes, or especially platitudes if uttered with sufficient verve, can persuade those who'd otherwise disagree by the sheer simplicity of a solution to what seems an intractable problem—for the moment at least, which is to say for long enough to cast a ballot. So once again, against all odds, I won in a cakewalk, and what I'd get for speaking those words was more than a trip to Washington.

On our final day, we'd gather at the State House in Columbia where my real-world counterpart, Governor James F. Byrnes, would speak to us as future constituents. Then I'd deliver another short speech of my own, and, after my inauguration, we'd all go back to celebrate what was called by the Legionnaires the "Governor's Ball," a dance for which they'd truck in lots of girls—though the mock-Governor's personal date had been arranged as a sort of publicity stunt when, a couple of months before, somebody had thought it a bright idea to match the newly-elected Boys Stater with a youthful local beauty queen by the name of Miriam Stevenson. . . who several weeks later had won a crown that let her compete as Miss USA and, on the night of my own election, had, at the age of barely twenty-one, become the reigning Miss Universe.

Never had politics seemed so sweet, despite the ribbing I had to take from my own teenaged constituents about how, "when the Governor's Ball came off," he'd be speaking in a much higher voice. They knew all about my improbable date, though in the meantime I was preparing remarks to make in reply to Governor

Byrnes—a former U.S. Senator, Supreme Court Judge, Secretary of State, and, as the Director of War Mobilization, "assistant president."

I decided I'd speak on leadership again and on education as the key. I'd worked it all out in my head. It wasn't ideas that threatened us, I'd say, but ignorance and bigotry and what those too often had led to which were injustice and fear. That too would sound like tepid stuff today, but in a Solid South state just after the McCarthy hearings—not to mention the hullabaloo about school desegregation—such sentiments were incendiary, if not seen as downright seditious.

At the State House on the following day, I'd scarcely assumed my make-believe eminence when Governor Byrnes and his aides appeared. He mounted the podium where I stood, and, nodding for me to stand aside, assured the Boys State delegates that, with regard to the Supreme Court's unfortunate ruling a couple of months before, he himself had looked all over the place, and nowhere had he seen or heard of blackbirds flocking with doves or anywhere in the ocean found whitefish swimming in the same schools as black fish—and he promised that our state government would protect us from what would be, as he believed, fundamentally wrong and unnatural. Then, to polite applause led by the Legionnaires and without so much as a glance at me, he stepped down from the podium.

Shades of my second-grade reading groups! I could hardly believe what I'd heard, though I can still see the backs of their heads in my mind as the Governor's entourage was sweeping him out of the room. But they were still within earshot as I stepped to the microphone and said it was a good thing that we weren't all birds or fish but morally responsible human beings. Nobody looked around, and I don't recall that the sponsors of our event were especially happy with my presumption or even took note of what I'd said.

I know I ended my speech by asking my fellow Boys Staters, as I'd been planning to do, "How does it feel to shape the world?" But, in fact, it didn't matter. I'd already made up my mind that the system, such as it was, was worthless and corrupt, and if the best leader our state had produced could do no better than that,

I'd have to try something else—like writing or preaching or raising the dead as my mother had managed to do.

Back at our barracks again, one of the counselors took me aside with bad news about Miss Universe. Her handlers had called to advise that she wouldn't be coming after all. There'd apparently been an accident—a rather sketchy one, his look and tone implied, though he said he'd been informed that her parents might have been badly hurt and perhaps were even dead. I felt terrible for her, of course, though I was reminded somewhat of the letter that I'd once written to the school of taxidermy. But I was assured that the Legionnaires had dug up another date for me: the reigning Miss Shandon Park May Queen who, though fetchingly sweet in temperament, turned out to be both short and squat with chocolate chip cookies stashed in her purse— enough of a come-down, Sarah Hardy would quip, to give a governor the bends. . . though, as I wish I'd replied, at least the Governor's Ball had been left intact.

Boys Nation was a disappointment too. I wasn't elected President, but the delegate who was—a licensed Baptist minister from the bayous and a master of platitudes in his own right— appointed me, ironically enough, to James F. Byrnes' old seat on the court, and, from that position on the bench, I'd once again foil our sponsors by rejecting their proposal for expanding the draft in peacetime. None of us took note of the fact that, just a few weeks earlier, the French had surrendered to a group known as the Viet Minh in a place called Dien Bien Phu.

But youth is ever oblivious, and, back for my senior year at Columbia High, I had other commitments to resume—one as president of the student body and the other as starting fullback on the CHS football team. My new nemesis was, in effect, my old nemesis in altered guise as the teacher in charge of Student Council, and her name once more was Christine—a primly hidebound English teacher so bent on controlling her domain that what Miss Brandenburg did for etiquette and Miss Gaillard for her notion of honor, Miss Webb would do for civics.

In her defense, she was rightly suspicious of me as an unbridled nonconformist—and yet for a moment, before my terrible gift for getting elected was fully apparent to her, she'd seemed to be slightly intrigued by my unconventional inclination when she caught me one day in study hall reading Platonic dialogues. That sounds contrived, I know, but our school was in the center of town and, though it lacked a surrounding yard, the county's main public library was literally next door. So rather than hang out at The Quarterback, a hot dog joint across the street, I spent my recesses after lunch browsing through the library's stacks—which was how I'd happened across a new translation of Plato that struck me as far more readable than others I'd tried before and, aside from worthier motivations, I'd gotten wind of "Platonic love" and thought it might prove salacious. With that at least partly in mind, I'd checked it out and taken it back to study hall where, absorbed in what I was reading, I was totally unaware of a hovering Miss Webb.

"What are you reading?" she demanded, grabbing the book and studying its cover with a frown.

Then she marched me to the principal's office. His name was Mr. Allison, a furtive man with thinning hair and fingers stained with nicotine who didn't know what was wanted of him.

"He's been reading Greek philosophy."

Her tone seemed accusatory, but then, with her, it was hard to tell—she sounded the same when reading "Crossing the Bar"—and there was always the chance that Plato would prove as risqué as I'd hoped. . . as, in a way, the *Symposium* did.

He looked at me inquiringly.

"I thought you should know," she told him.

"Thank you," he said.

He shook my hand, and following that grave but pointless exchange, Miss Webb escorted me back to class.

But after that curious episode, I ran afoul of her again when we talked about the McCarthy hearings in class. She asked us if the senator had been right in ferreting out subversives on the loose, and several of her toadies said he was. When I maintained that he'd behaved like a fascist thug, she asked if I knew what fascism was, to which I replied, in so many words, that it prized obedience above all, blindly submitting to the state instead of what you knew to be right—the theme of my Boys State address, in effect.

At that, she threw the gauntlet down, telling me with the hint of a smirk that a better way of defining it was that fascism comes about when a demagogue flouts the rules that everyone has agreed upon, substituting his own for them to follow. It's all about regimentation, she said, putting on helmets and uniforms and marching about in formations, committing crude acts of violence.

I knew where she was going, and so did most of the class, though I was the only one there to whom her scorn applied.

"In other words, like football," she snapped, prompting a couple of titters and knowing full well that, despite my elective office, I'd be spending my afternoons for several months suited up on the practice field instead of presiding at meetings she convened in the windowless third-floor Council room—which, as an ethical dilemma, would seem easy enough to resolve since both were services to the school and no duties were being neglected so long as Ann Luce, as my vice-president, filled in when I wasn't there.

But Miss Webb, as I might have guessed if I'd known the term back then, was an adamant Manichean. Her world consisted of sheep and goats, and it wasn't a vague or subtle distinction with sheep engaged in bleating on cue, attentive to *Robert's Rules of Order*, while goats were mindlessly butting heads in uniforms bought from a prison-farm team back in the days of the flying wedge—or so it would surely have seemed to her if she'd seen us aboard the battered blue bus that took us to practice after school as it sputtered and wheezed to the edge of town or watched us emerge from our cinder-block dressing room in canvas britches and clunky boots like losers without much chance of success.

That last observation, at least, was unhappily true, for, though doing our best with what we had—in coaching, equipment, and personnel—those weren't boom years for the old Red & Gold. During my sophomore year we'd lost eight games in a row before finally scratching out a win against a leaderless Eau Claire team whose quarterback, on the night before, got sick from some ribs at a barbecue shack that, according to rumors never confirmed, was managed by Benny Utterback's aunt.

But after that, the well had run dry as my junior-year season got underway with our team resuming its losing streak. Sportswriters exhausted their euphemisms, trying to hint at

gallant defeat without the use of disparaging terms like
"clobbering," "drubbing," or "rout." Still, every week it was the
same—though I got my name in headlines once for being
knocked out three times in a game. "DUNLAP STARS," the
headline said in a clipping my mother cut out from *The State* and
pasted in an album she kept because, after briefly conceding the
fact that Florence had whipped us 19 to 6, it emphasized the
positive: ". . . but it was Bernie Dunlap," it said,

> the 145-pound CHS fullback, who stole the show.
> The defeat was the sixth straight for Columbia and
> the victory the first for Florence after four straight
> losses. Dunlap blocked two successive Florence
> punts and then on the last attempted conversion
> by the Yellow Jackets, Dunlap broke through to
> block it. He was knocked cold and had to be
> carried from the field. He was reported OK by the
> Columbia bench.

The story admitted towards the end that we'd rushed for a mere
6 yards that night versus Florence's total of 203.

That account is quoted verbatim, and, unsurprisingly
perhaps, it was after that game that our doldrums appeared to
settle in for good as, despite our having some very good players,
inertia had taken over and a propensity for losing came to seem
relentless. And yet, in a "Charge of the Light Brigade" sort of
way that Miss Webb, of all people, should have endorsed, we'd
neither succumbed to discouragement nor abandoned our
solidarity as a team—both of which we definitely owed to our
coach, E.T. parenthesis "Pete" Borders, who had no place in his
personal code for mealy-mouthed whining or self-contempt.

He didn't ask Jesus to intervene or look for sanctimony in
us. He'd come to us from rural Georgia and, believing in dirt and
sweat, he saw that we got our fill of each as day after day, week
after week, we thrashed and choked in our dust-bowl hell. We
scrimmaged until the bull bats flew and, on Fridays, we staggered
onto the field like an army that's weakened by the plague. . . only
to suffer the same result—complete, abject annihilation,

followed by E.T. Borders' speech in the gloom of our dressing room after the game.

"I don't want you boys gettin' down, you hear?" he admonished us in his square-jawed way. He was a slow-footed mild-mannered man, often compared to a bulldog in the press because of his heavy jowls—though he came across in person as a very large, stolid, and slightly puzzled potato, a bit like J. Edgar Hoover's innocuous younger brother. "Another game's comin' up
next week," he told us, "an' I don't want you gettin' all down in the dumps. I know you've heard them guys are good, but try 'n' remember whut I say—they put their pants on same as you. . ." he gestured to illustrate what he meant, defying us to disagree, "one leg at a time, okay?"

I thought about hanging my trousers up and jumping in with both feet at once ("Hey, listen, Coach, I got an idea!"), but Coach Borders was deaf to innovation, mired in his endlessly joyless task of trying to comprehend defeat. He had, I think, an inquiring mind—and maybe even, in retrospect, it's not too much to call it Greek in a quirkily pre-Platonic mode forever in search of a primal cause, some overlooked underlying flaw in his intricate schemes and diagrams.

Each weekend he'd study the dismal film of our previous setback on the field, and, on Mondays, he'd call the team together.

"Boys," he'd say, "I been watchin' the films, an' I think I know whut our problem is."

"What is it, Coach?" we'd earnestly ask.

And then he'd share his latest conclusion. "Our end-play, boys. It's screwin' us up. Our ends ain't gettin' off with the ball."

That would be the start of a miserable week for each of the wide-outs on our team—one of whom, Sonny Serio, was totally blind in one eye and tended to vanish over the dirt embankment's edge whenever Coach Borders sent him out long, leaving John Argoe by himself to practice getting' off with the ball while we waited for Sonny to reappear above the drainage ditch by the road. . . and then on Friday, another shellacking—25-zip, 19-7.

It quickly became a way of life, though a moment of revelation occurred when we were nearing the end of our schedule, at which point the strain of my dual obligations was starting to tell on me—doubling up at fullback as before (at a spurious hundred-sixty-five pounds according to my program listing, clearly ignored in the clipping I've quoted) and as head of the puppet-show Student Council (absent during its afternoon meetings, but attentive to all its other needs). I still had some gridiron glory ahead, getting noticed in the paper again as one of "a pair of high-stepping backs," though nothing was lifting our team's morale and, following a string of further defeats, we could glimpse the prospect looming ahead of a season without a single win. We still had our toughest games to go, and Coach Border's postmortems were getting morose.

"Boys," he said despondently after a thumping up in Greenwood. "I been lookin' at the game films, boys, and I hate to tell you whut I seen. . ." He surveyed us with a sorrowful stare. "It's our center, boys. . . he ain't gettin' the count."

We were all relieved but for Henry Von Kolnitz, who'd suffer through a harrowing week with two or three hundred snaps a day—at the end of which we took to the field and got stomped as we had the week before.

The following Monday afternoon, we watched a haggard Coach Borders slump wearily into his screening room. We waited outside in our antique pads like unreliable samurai.

"Listen, boys," Coach Borders announced, emerging and finding us waiting there. "I'm gonna tell you whut it is. . ."

He looked each one of us in the eye.

"It's our huddle, boys. That's all there are to it. You're missin' the signals a-cause of that."

So all week long we practiced huddles—circular, choir-like, trapezoidal. Clapping and shouting, we dipped and rose while peeling off like a marching band. Our quarterback, Jesse Smarr, looked as nifty as Fred Astaire, and we lost with style, the papers said, without undue discouragement.

But after that, Coach Borders changed.

"Boys," he said in the dressing room, after the writers had come and gone. "I ain't goan lie to you this time, boys." He paused dramatically for effect. "That was truly pitiful. I mean *pathetic!* I don't know whut to tell you now. . . except I been thinkin', rackin' my brain, and this is whut finally come to me—we're goatenin' it till we win."

"What's goatenin' it, Coach?" I started to ask, but he was silent, enigmatic.

Monday, we scrimmaged in the rain. We came in muddy, wet, and cold, scraped off our gear, and stepped in the shower. We turned the knobs, but nothing came out.

"Hey, Coach!" we yelled. "We got no water!"

"That's goatenin' it, Boys," Coach Borders said. "And we're goatenin' it 'til we win."

So all that week we rode back on the bus, caked with filth and reeking of crud, dressed out next day in sweat-stiffened jocks and went back home in a scrofulous rage. That Friday, a favored and vengeful team of our cross-town rival from Eau Claire encountered eleven demented lepers. It wasn't a rout, but we finally won, and the showers came on. . . and, the following week, to close out the season, we returned to our losing ways again.

It wasn't the stuff of which champions are made, but I'd learned some lessons worth more to me than all of Miss Webb's insipid drivel. They were painful to learn and hard to express but, roughly translated, they went like this: teamwork is often worth a lot, but teams can lose as well as win; losing's no fun—and habit-forming—but a man can live with 'most anything so long as he gets a bath every week and a change of underwear now and then; and every dog *will* have his day if he hunkers down and waits it out without falling off the embankment's edge. . . and (this I concluded later on) sometimes it's better to be a goat than one of the sanctimonious sheep.

To which I'm now inclined to add that a goat's suspicion is useful too when it comes to highly organized sheep and wolves dressed up as if they were sheep, bleating their vicious platitudes demanding conformity from the flock. But, having said that, to goat it for life is not a plausible strategy—for me or Coach Borders or anyone else—which meant for me, at high school's end, a final encounter with Christine Webb.

After the end of football season, I returned to preside over Student Council meetings under her coldly watchful eye—though I never supposed she'd forget that I'd raised a black flag over her head and was surprised to find that, during my final few months at school, a sort of truce appeared to take hold that lasted until a study hall in March, when she caught me once again with a suspect book.

This time it was *Thus Spake Zarathustra*, the same book that, not long before, my cousin Hope had been so desperate to read—which offered incentive enough for me peruse it. But Miss Webb had pounced when she saw what it was and marched me back to the principal's office, implying that I should be impeached for neo-Nazi tendencies—a complaint that got no traction with him, but which must have been still on her mind when I sought her out on my final day of school.

I'd soon be on my way to a liberal arts college where, as I trusted would be the case, Plato and Nietzsche would be discussed and platitudes less insisted upon than they'd been in Miss Webb's classes even on that last day as "Grow old along with me!" she'd crooned,

> The best is yet to be,
> The last of life, for which the first was made. . .

which, with youthful disdain, I'd found impossibly sappy. But she was an aging spinster, I ungallantly told myself, and the members of Student Council stood in for children to her. I should lay old quarrels to rest.

"Miss Webb," I started off, more insufferably than I'd intended, "I know we've had our differences, and it's probably been my fault in part, and, well. . . I hope there're no hard feelings."

She looked at me with her poker face as if sucking on a persimmon.

"You've got a remarkable gift," she said.

I wondered what gift she had in mind.

"Your ability to persuade," she added.

I started to thank her, but she resumed, "But you've got to be careful, and so must we. . . because," she smiled in a bitter way, like the crusty bed of a drought-stricken pond, "you could so easily become. . . as I told Mr. Allison just last week. . . another Adolf Hitler."

She had a point, I realized. So, thanking her anyhow, I turned on my heels and left with her words still echoing in my brain. To think a midget fullback like me, a defrocked secret monitor, might hope to someday be a Führer! A crazed and dangerous demagogue, a menace not just to schools but to cities and even nations! I could hear my psychotic laughter rising above wild shrieks and howls while leading the planet to destruction.

But that wasn't for me. For the second time in less than a year, I gave up politics then and there—and bade good-bye to Christine Webb. It was safer for the world, I thought, if I became an English professor. I didn't suppose I would, but events somehow conspired, and that's what I'd actually do for fifty years while immersing myself in other things on the fly—which is how it came about that, a decade and a half into that long career, I'd find myself back in Columbia again with four degrees in hand and a fifth if I chose to request it when, out of nowhere it seemed, I got a call from none other than E.T. Borders, who'd become an administrator. He said he was planning to retire but was trying to earn a master's degree to boost what he'd get from his pension.

"Listen, Dunlap," he sniffed in an earnest but confidential way. "You were pretty good in English."

"Thanks, Coach," I answered.

"I've finished my thesis, you understand, but it needs a little going over." He sniffed again and I could see him in my mind, waving his hand dismissively. "A little proofreading should do it, I think."

"I'll be glad to, Coach!" I said, and the matter was settled.

I went by his house to pick it up and found when I got it home that, as was hardly a surprise, it was virtually illiterate. I worked it over sentence by sentence, avoiding whatever might give me away but fashioning a Borders style that was worthy, I thought, of publication—if not in the *Review of Educational Research*, at least in *Field and Stream*. I took it back to him straightaway, and, a few weeks later, he let me know his thesis had been approved.

"It was excellent, Coach."

"Thanks, Dunlap," he said. "I thought it was."

He added that, in return for my help, he'd like to give me a little something and handed me an envelope which contained, I'd find when I got home, two tickets to a Columbia High football game. I was touched by the simplicity of his gesture and thought to myself that he may have been inept as a coach but was, in his way, the salt of the earth. With that in mind, I decided to go to the game—not with my wife, who'd gone to a different high school, but with one of my former classmates and fellow taxidermist, David Rembert—and who should come up to us in the crowd but a fiftyish Christine Webb, smiling and embracing me as if we'd been fast friends.

That was okay with me by then, though I wondered if she truly thought we'd been friends or just wanted somehow to make it so. I was flush with various sorts of success, but so was she at the time, having not only taken up a fitting position as the Administrative Advisor for Discipline in the city's School District One but was verging on being appointed its first female high school principal—and, if Paris had ever been worth a mass, that promotion had clearly been worth attending a football game. . . though she must have struggled nonetheless to lend such public support to that irredeemably fascist rite, for which I bestowed on her an ironic salute.

But in the eyes of many, I'd later learn, she merited much more—so much, in fact, that I'm almost inclined to suppose that, in this very same universe, there are multiple versions of us all, not just successively but concurrently, and that, in some different alignment, we mightn't have clashed as we did. Though so far from my own experience, I've read descriptions of Miss Webb as a highly accomplished teacher, and I know that, towards the end of her career, she won an educator's award from the Freedoms Foundation at Valley Forge and, like me at a similar age, would be recognized by our state with the Order of the Palmetto.

In the spring of 2009, still orbiting on such strangely parallel tracks, I was a college president when my old antagonist died, our enmity long since over and done. It wasn't long afterwards that I entered the district's Hall of Fame where, though I haven't yet been able to check, odds are that we're there together at opposite ends of the alphabet.

But, of all the loose ends from my high school days, the most improbable resolution wouldn't occur until, after several farfetched pursuits in dance and television and well into my mid-forties, I was teaching both Browning and Nietzsche at the same university from which my cousin Hope had tried to pilfer *Zarathustra*—and, determined to stay in shape, I'd had become a fanatical cyclist with hundred-mile rides a day on the winding and steep backroads of Fairfield and Newberry Counties.

On one torrid summer afternoon, as destiny would have it, I got excruciating leg-cramps while powering up a hill at a place called Lebanon Crossroads not listed on my map. After toppling sideways into a ditch and staggering to my feet, I saw that I'd bent my bike's front wheel, and, looking about in hopes of finding a phone, I spotted a rooftop not far off with several cars in its driveway. So, shouldering my damaged bike, I staggered up to the farmhouse door, knocked two or three times and, waited until it was opened, stood face to face with the former Miriam Stevenson, Miss Universe of 1954.

"You stood me up!" I exclaimed, as if I'd been tracking her down since that long-ago Governor's Ball.

She looked startled as I laughed and tried to explain, saying I'd had an accident and needed to call my wife to come and pick me up. Cautiously, she ushered me inside where a family reunion was underway. It was her parents' house, she said. She'd been widowed just a few years before, and her teenaged children were also there. Her son looked skeptical when I confided that his mother and I had almost met a decade or so before he was born. But after I'd telephoned my wife, Miriam's parents, reassured and somewhat amused, urged me to join in as a stranger at the feast in their downhome family meal.

So I sat there for nearly an hour on a sort of chaperoned date, gnawing a piece of fried chicken beside a still lovely and very gracious—though less than apologetic—intergalactic queen.

Her parents looked slightly puzzled when I told them how glad I was to see them looking so well.

8

Flashed All Our Sabers Bare

The Scots have always been a pugnacious lot, even—or maybe especially—after leaving their native sod. My namesake, Colonel William Benjamin Dunlap, had dropped out of Princeton during the Civil War to enlist in the Lancaster Grays, and, after being promoted to the rank of brevet Captain during the Battle of the Wilderness, fought in many of the bloodiest engagements of the war, including Fredericksburg and Antietam. I was told as a boy that he was one of three brothers who'd fought—one who'd been killed, one captured, and the third, my father's-father's-father, who'd survived and come back home to marry and spawn and reminisce as long afterwards as the final year of his life when World War I was underway.

"The first real battle I was engaged in was the Battle of Seven Pines," he'd dictated just short of the age of seventy-seven so his grandchildren would have an idea of what warfare was really like.

> The sound at the opening was more like hail falling upon a tin roof than anything else I know of. You could hear the bullets whistling through the air, and when they would strike, you could distinctly hear a sound like, "Zip!" The firing on each side was terrible. We lost our colonel, the lieutenant-colonel and a lieutenant in our company besides other men. It was fearful to hear the men groan when they were hit.

He further recollected that, "We finally drove the enemy back and took possession of the battlefield," and, "I remember we halted where some of the Yankees had had their mess. The pots were on the fire boiling their dinner."

Fifty-five years had passed since those events, and he'd long been known as Pa Ben to those for whom he was writing—as I am today to some of my own children's kids. He'd held a number of worthy positions during the intervening years, but it seemed he'd mainly whittled. I used to study a hand-carved wooden dog on my grandmother's corner whatnot in Rock Hill as evidence of a life that itself had been whittled down to near-inconsequence. . . for after such tumult, what? It occurs to me now that I'm whittling too, at least in a manner of speaking.

In my mother's family in Virginia, there'd been no men of fighting age, but my grandmother's mother, Alice West Allen, had later described how, when she was a girl of eleven, their house had served for a spell as General Wade Hampton's headquarters during what would afterwards be called the Battle of Trevilian Station, the largest and bloodiest all-cavalry battle of the war. As the fighting developed that day, General Hampton had moved on, but, at some point during the afternoon, a lone horse had wandered into the yard with its rider unconscious in the saddle and his torn and bleeding scalp dangling loosely to one side.

At Alice's mother's direction, despite his Union officer's uniform, he'd been carried into the drawing room where, with threads yanked out of a silken shawl draped across their piano, she'd carefully sewn the scalp back on while Alice held out a basin to catch the gory spillage. The officer had survived and, at intervals throughout the years, wrote courtly letters to Alice as did the historian U.R. Brooks, who'd fought in that same battle on the Confederate side, though only to see his younger brother killed. Brooks once inscribed a book to her as "the little heroine of Trevillian [sic]." I grew up with the shawl in our living room, and I have that book on my shelf along with a Dante's *Inferno* presented to Alice after the war in a folio-sized edition with full-page etchings by Doré and Cary's English translation.

Such stories as hers and Pa Ben's were family anecdotage that seemed to have little to do with me—until a succession of choices that, like so many dilemmas I faced, assumed a sectarian ambience. The first had to do with where I'd apply for college. I was hoping to go to one of the best liberal arts colleges within a reasonable driving distance, a restriction ruling New England out, and I'd need a full scholarship ride—which, for all practical purposes in those days meant winning one of the awards at roughly a dozen highly regarded institutions and funded by the George F. Baker Trust.

As things turned out, of the two Baker Scholarship colleges to which I applied, one—under the auspices of the Episcopal church—determined its awards in secret and told the winners privately that, if the offer was rejected, they'd present it to somebody else who'd never need know that it was secondhand. The other school, with a Presbyterian affiliation, did everything in the open, publicizing their finalists and inviting them to the campus for a weekend of tests and interviews before announcing those who'd won.

It was at that second competition that, as part of their selection process, I happened to take the Minnesota Multiphasic Personality Inventory, which made such a deep impression on me at the time that I still remember some of the questions—as, for example, "Do you often have black tarry movements?" and "Is someone following you?"

Those were actual questions, and, because I was fairly certain that the college wasn't recruiting bright but unwary psychotics, such queries were easy enough to deal with. Though I still have no idea what "black tarry movements" might signify, they struck me as something one ought to avoid, and, as for a further question that somewhat coyly inquired, "Would you rather arrange flowers or polish metal?" I deduced that a predilection for creating floral displays as opposed to the manly activity of polishing shiny metal was probably as undesirable as having black tarry movements. So I expressed a fervent commitment to polishing things metallic along with a near certainty that I wasn't being followed.

Though I won the scholarship, which was duly announced in the papers, I didn't choose that college, partly because I'd surmised that spending four years there would probably have involved a lot of metal-polishing of one sort or another. But that college was, nevertheless, up front enough to share with me the overall assessment of my Multiphasic Inventory, which indicated in no uncertain terms that I was ideally suited for a military career.

Even given my disingenuous attitude towards the test, I was fairly astonished by that conclusion—astonished and bemused, for I'd become, by that point in my career, enough of a non-conformist to think I'd be better off with something less regimented. But there it was: a man's multiphasic inventory was his fate, and, despite my disavowals of dictatorial ambition, it seemed that I'd inherited a military gene.

Furthermore, as if truly impelled by some such obscure compulsion, midway through my sophomore year at the other college to which I'd applied and which had also seen fit to offer me a Baker Scholarship, I found myself not only enrolled in Air Force ROTC—or "Rotsy," as it was generally known with vaguely derisive intent—but enlisted as one of twelve volunteers in its Arnold Air Society chapter's first-ever Saber Drill Team.

All this was back in 1957, in the quasi-Gothic mountaintop isolation of Sewanee, also known as The University of the South. But, despite the passage of more than sixty-five years, I can vividly recall one of my fellow enlistees, Norman Ellsworth McSwain of Albertville, Alabama, who, like me, was on the college's football team and lived across the hall in a dormitory with a faintly West Point look constructed of local sandstone. As a would-be pre-med student, Norman was majoring in Biology while I, having read Thoreau and aspiring "to live deep and suck out all the marrow of life," had chosen English literature as the likeliest approach to actually pulling that off—though, true to the ethos of that time and place, we both intended to earn degrees that, whatever else we managed to glean, would endow us by a sort of osmosis with the liberal arts trifecta of a tolerance for ambiguity, an adeptness at critical thinking, and an ease in handling complex abstractions.

Such, at least, was the academic credo of the institution we'd chosen—though even so, intellectual pieties of that sort can't fully explain what might have drawn either of us to such a quixotic venture, in so many respects like polishing metal. It must have been something more than the lure of twirling razor-sharp swords while wearing slippery white cotton gloves and could well have been in part the potent subconscious appeal of our kaleidoscopic routine with its macho choreography—immaculately silent though potentially deadly too and yet faultlessly obedient to the Busby Berkeley logic of its deftly expanding but ever collapsing patterns. Not just handling or even creating abstractions but wholly enveloped within them, caught up like gnats in a furious wind or musicians in some wild orchestral surge and, goaded by that fierce geometry, slashing our perilous instruments through the air like so many Sweeney Todds in Rotsy blue.

It's precisely such overwrought language that brings it all back to me now! The martial rapture, balletic skill, and cool indifference to disaster. Riskier than skimming hurdles on our pockmarked cinder track that, following a spill near the end of a race, would leave my knees tattooed for life. Headier than rehearsing abstract-expressionist pass patterns for yet another luckless football team or plotting out daring bombing raids over Moscow for our professor and chair of air science, Lieutenant Colonel Whiteside, who'd flown missions over the Hump in World War II.

I suspect even hulking, maladroit Norman must have felt at times like a Nijinsky in brogans darting and circling about, kneeling in crisp salutes, and methodically rising again to resume our steady tread while blossoming like *fleurs du mal* in the botany of Armageddon—a paradigm of creation itself, a twenty-four-handed human clock winding precisely methodically down to a sudden unanimous stop.

As I've just suggested, it's easy enough in retrospect to detect in such rococo verbiage that, as far as higher meaning goes, we were like a dozen Monty Python knights on a semi-nonsensical quest leading us towards a fiasco that none of us would forget. But whatever our motivations, that's not entirely true, and in the end it wasn't from our instructors that I'd eventually learn the real significance of our drill, nor from the despotic Wemple Lyle, student commander of ROTC. It would be instead from Norman McSwain who, at that mountaintop Camelot, would become a local legend—not exactly *sans peur et sans reproche*, but a legend nonetheless.

He was not instinctively nimble, Airman McSwain. But Sewanee in those days was still an all-male institution stuck in the middle of nowhere, so we had lots of practice time in the humid old gymnasium with sabers glinting and puttees shining in the dim shellac of the basketball floor. By mid-spring we were looking good. Even Norman could wheel about the gym with the menacing grace of a medium-range tank. And somehow—though nobody wanted credit after the incident that would make us so notorious—word got around that something of martial note was taking place in East Tennessee.

It was then that the fateful summons came. We were invited to appear on the nation's first coast-to-coast news show, NBC's "Today" with its host Dave Garroway, a sort of early-morning Dave Letterman who sported a pair of horn rims and co-starred with a chimpanzee by the name of J. Fred Muggs. Clearly, Garroway knew a class act when he saw one. . . or happened to hear about one.

None of us had ever been to New York, and the trip alone seemed momentous for a group of student musketeers from Appalachia. We flew up in an empty Air Force cargo plane, each of us with a saber case resembling a sort of golf bag, and got to Manhattan in time for an evening to ourselves before an early-morning performance at the Fifth Avenue studio.

No sooner had we reached our hotel than the English major in me canceled out everything else, and I headed for Greenwich Village where I hoped to find large numbers of fellow bohemians, including promiscuous girls with a weakness for beatniks in uniform. Norman and Jim McKeown insisted on tagging along, which I feared might complicate my efforts to look authentically beat since, even in decked out mufti, they looked like Andy Griffith rather than Allen Ginsberg.

But I needn't have worried—the girls weren't interested in any of us, and Jim and Norman blended right in. In fact, Norman got drunker faster and more picturesquely than any bohemian I'd ever met and stubbornly stuck with it from one bar to another.

At five a.m., when we started out from MacDougal Street for the studio up at 48th, he was still entertaining the Villagers with ear-splitting whoops and blood-curdling rebel yells. Tourists and natives alike stood back as Norman at intervals threw up before resuming his whooping. Two blocks from the studio he suddenly went limp. At the studio door, he was comatose.

Inside, we got the disturbing news that the studio was too small for our routine, so we'd have to perform on the sidewalk outside. The police had put up barricades—but the signature shots of "Today" were long slow pans of people in the street who, as soon as the camera lights came on, would rush to the studio's plate-glass wall and press their hand-lettered signs up against it for one of the cameras to scan. "Hello, Omaha!" was a typical message and "Made it, Ma! Send Money!" Those people weren't going to like it when they learned they'd been cut from the show.

But the immediate problem was Airman McSwain. We got a quart of black coffee and made him gulp it down. It was like bringing the Golem to life. His eyes opened with a rag-doll stare, his feet slapped the pavement like a penguin's. Two minutes before our airtime, he was rumpled but more or less upright. He looked at me and tried to wink, but the effort caused him to lose his balance, and he had to use his saber like a makeshift walking stick in an effort to prop himself up. He got the sword back onto his shoulder just as the signal was given that in only thirty seconds our performance should begin.

We stood rigidly at attention as a resentful hush fell over the barricades where thwarted fans were restlessly maneuvering and aggressively waving their signs. Then the camera lights came on, and Cadet Commander Wemple Lyle barked out the single savage command that set us irretrievably in motion.

Like a band of desperados invading the city in wheat threshers, our intricate dangerous machine brandished its whirling blades in the light of a New York dawn. The crowd shrank back as we passed, leaning forward in our wake, still waving their look-at-me! signs.

I was so intent on remembering the counts that I didn't hear the humming begin. It was the voice of Norman McSwain setting out on his own rendition of "You ain't nothin' but a hound dog," reducing our silent drill to a sidewalk buck-and-wing.

I saw Ronnie Palmer duck as Norman's saber whizzed past his ear. "Yeaaaaa, Sewanee's right!" Norman serenely crooned, using a football cheer. I started to laugh and forgot the count. Wemple Lyle began to hiss Gestapo-like imprecations in an effort to turn the tide, but Airman McSwain was in the grip of something much bigger than Wemple Lyle—at the heart of a complex abstraction that neither he nor the Pentagon itself could hope to control, careening through our Euclidean schemes like an unstoppably runaway sputnik.

On some sort of automatic pilot, he followed the rest of us down into a Queen Anne's salute, the climax of our routine. But as we were coming up out of it, I saw him wobble and lurch, tilting shakily to one side. . . and suddenly the unthinkable occurred—he lost control of his saber. The cameras followed its terrible arc as it soared up over our heads towards the barriers where the restive mob was waiting with placards and shopping bags.

To describe what happened next risks inviting disbelief, but there were millions of witnesses as the saber fell like a javelin towards a bosomy woman in the crowd clutching a message for Des Moines. She shrieked and fell over backwards as, to all appearances, the sword-point plunged horrifically down her décolletage and, with hysterical shouts and cries, bystanders around her recoiled as if the Cossacks had arrived.

It was live TV at its best as the cameras cut back and forth from a panicky stampeding mob to shots of what the tabloids would call "the Alabama Assassin" coolly proceeding with the drill, twirling a nonexistent sword as if nothing was amiss. In strictly military terms, this might have seen as remarkable grace under pressure, exactly what we'd been instructed to do if we should lose our saber. But to viewers watching from coast-to-coast, it was merely cold-blooded indifference.

The crowd was of that opinion too as, stopping at a safe distance from us, they turned like Odessa Steps extras from the *Battleship Potemkin*, shaking their fists and reviling us as we doggedly finished our routine and stood in rigid formation, as harmless as bowling pins atop their abandoned signs.

As things turned out, the woman from Des Moines was only superficially wounded. We later heard, as we were leaving Manhattan disguised as the golf team from V.M.I., that the network had paid her off in exchange for an exclusive interview regarding what someone had dubbed the "Fifth Avenue Massacre." The longer-term consequence was that we were never invited anywhere again and were quietly disbanded shortly after our return, turning our sabers in to a humbled Wemple Lyle who saw them all locked away in a closet in the Rotsy building where they may be rusting still. . . except for Norman's, of course, which, so far as we'd ever learn, had been carried off by a scavenger as a midtown war souvenir.

What I couldn't have known at the time—and had been totally unforeseen by my Multiphasic Inventory—was how that debacle might impinge on so many subsequent lives. For it wasn't simply that our ability to handle complex abstractions had been tested and found wanting, or even that Wemple Lyle's promising service career would be under a cloud from that day on. He would overcome that setback in time and enjoy considerable success in his years as an Air Force officer. The truly astonishing ironies—ones that put me in mind of Mark Twain's mordant assurance that "Prov'dence don't fire no blank ca'tridges, boys"—derive from what happened to the rest of us.

Ronnie Palmer, whom I mentioned only in passing, became a lawyer in an adjacent state, specializing in product liability—things that malfunction or go awry causing harm to others. I myself, with my fighter-pilot aspirations, would soon learn from my ROTC physical that I couldn't pursue that goal because of a congenital eye defect that canceled binocular depth perception—a condition I'd always assumed everybody must suffer from when trying to hit a baseball or land a plane on a flight deck. But I'd spend several decades during my middle years writing and producing for Public Television as if to atone for the part I'd played in that coast-to-coast ignominy.

And, as for that former scourge of Manhattan, Norman Ellsworth McSwain, he'd go on to become one of the leading trauma surgeons in our country—an expert in emergency medicine and the much-acclaimed director of the trauma center at Tulane University where, I am almost certain, none of his former colleagues knows to this day the real beginning of his career back in the spring of 1957, when that twelve-bladed abstraction in boots was launched on the streets of New York like a dreadnought with rivets missing from in its hull.

As a footnote to this tale, let me assure you that, even if his colleagues had known, it would hardly have diminished their respect for what he could do with a knife. For, nearly a half-century later, it was none other than Norman McSwain that millions of us would see on the roof of Charity Hospital in what was left of downtown New Orleans, continuing to save lives as Hurricane Katrina raged around him. Norman, in short, was an authentic hero.

He died in 2015. I hope they buried him with his scalpel like the warrior that he was.

9

There'll Always Be a Something or Other

I arrived in England on September 30th, 1959, having sailed from New York on the SS United States—the biggest liner ever built in the U.S. and the fastest anywhere—along with twenty-nine other Rhodes Scholars out of our cohort of thirty-two, purportedly among the quickest and sleekest of our class as well. Among our number was Daryl Canfill, a classmate from Sewanee whom I hadn't known well before but who, as a fellow innocent abroad, would quickly become a close friend. We'd been assigned to two of the smaller Oxford colleges, he to Exeter to study Theology and I to Wadham for English Language and Literature, though that was as much as either of us knew about what might lie ahead.

We'd departed on the same day that Eisenhower launched extended talks with his Soviet counterpart, Nikita Khrushchev, beginning their Camp David retreat with what he'd described to the press as an "open heart and good intentions"—which was, on the whole, our frame of mind as well for what we were undertaking. I knew I wouldn't see home again for a minimum of two years and that transatlantic phone calls, though newly feasible, were still too costly and complicated to attempt more than once or twice a year and, as I'd discover to my surprise, painfully disconcerting, like conjuring ghosts you'd left behind but couldn't touch or see.

Though it hardly seems credible now, we'd also yet to adjust to casual travel by air from one continent to another, and Britain seemed nearly as far from home as it had for my forebears centuries before when headed the other way. As a measure of that perception, actually setting foot on English soil would strike me as so momentous that, to commemorate the event on the morning we reached Southampton, I impulsively brushed my hair from right to left instead of left to right and parted it on the other side. I was going to be a new person.

That newness came back to haunt me only a few months later when, during my first Oxford vac—the local slang for "vacation"—I was hitch-hiking through southeastern France with a girl I'd met in Paris who was studying in Spain. We were detained with no explanation—which, until very recently, I thought I remembered well—and, after being taken to jail, were put in separate rooms and I was interrogated. I'd been warned that, if arrested in France, you'd be guilty until you could prove that you were innocent, but in a Kafkaesque twist, I hadn't the slightest idea what the accusation was. My questioner kept firing off rapid French to which I responded as best I could while he repeatedly hectored me because of my phony accent. He said they knew I was really French.

"*Non, non,*" I insisted. "*Vraiment, je vous dis, je suis américain!*"

But they obviously knew better. Finally, they brought in a chief inspector whose manner appeared more reasonable. He held my passport in his hand.

"Well, *monsieur,*" he said in French like a harbinger of Inspector Clouseau. "You may very well be who you say you are, but perhaps. . ." he paused for the *coup de grace*, ". . . perhaps you can explain why the man in this photograph. . ." He was pointing to my passport now. ". . . has hair which, as you can see, is *parted on the other side!*"

He was proud of his ingenuity and not about to let me off the hook. But, happily, in an era before computers when identities took some time to confirm, the wealthy industrialist whose daughter had apparently eloped with a short dark ne'er-do-well Frenchman somewhat resembling me, arrived unseen by us like a *deus ex machina* to say we weren't after all the pair they were looking for.

The inspector was disappointed but let us go with a stern admonition never to do such a thing again. It still wasn't clear what that thing might be, but without any further hassle, I'd keep my hair as it was until I was back in the States resuming my previous life—which was nearly three years in the future. The girl returned to Spain, and I hurried back to England, where other such lessons would be in store.

In actuality, however, as I've learned from a rediscovered journal of that trip, the incident took place in Bern, we were never hauled off to a jail, the girl went back to Paris rather than Spain, and there was no Inspector Clouseau—but everything else, except my speculation about the industrialist's daughter, was absolutely true. . . and, in general, though I admit that particular lapse, my memory's not often so fallible and nowhere in what I'll try to recount have I knowingly exaggerated.

That's especially true about my time at Oxford because, in actuality again, aside from its history and legends and many depictions on movie screens, what I knew about England was hopelessly meager other than its literature and the fact that, in a genealogical sense, I thought I could make a case that I was coming home. The problem with that assumption was that, after the Suez Crisis, Americans weren't very popular in the eyes of many Brits as we'd not only been slow to their minds in entering World War II and swaggered about with their women when we did but had colluded when it was over in the dismantlement of their empire.

A case of sour grapes we'd tell ourselves, though we'd soon learn for ourselves that Oxford was rife with such resentment, partly because traditional privilege appeared to be under assault as a consequence of increased support for students from "lesser" schools, prompting snobbery of every sort directed at intruders from below or slipping in sideways from abroad, especially from the U.S.

Luckily for me, that wasn't so true at Wadham which, though excelling academically, was socially on a lower rung than Magdalen or Merton, say, where some four or five of our number would form a disgruntled clique. I'd benefit too from the fact that Wadham was so much smaller that I was the only Yank of any stripe then living in college rooms. So I made an inconspicuous target and, unlike some of my fellow Rhodes, was mostly out of the fray.

But all that was still to come when, having disembarked, we stood at the end of a Southampton pier with all our bags and trunks, including my cardboard box of books that had split on one side in transit and was spilling its contents out, symbolic of how I felt myself despite a show of bravado. Even the petrol fumes from our idling chartered bus smelled strangely like vomit to me, and, sitting alone by a window after we'd climbed aboard, I admitted to myself that, though nothing suggested Dickens to me or even *Lucky Jim*, there was just a hint of Dunkirk about the figure we'd cut milling about on the pier.

As if to allay such qualms, Brigadier E.T. Williams, the current Warden of Rhodes House and former intelligence chief for Field Marshal Montgomery during much of the war—most notably at El Alamein—had dispatched as a welcoming party an older Rhodes Scholar who'd been permitted to marry during his second year and, having completed his degree, had been awarded an extra year, a prospect that hadn't occurred to me but of which I duly took note.

His name was Willie Morris, a southerner from Yazoo City with four years of Austin in his past and incisively progressive views who, before another year was out, would be editor of *The Texas Observer* and a couple of years after that, of *Harper's Magazine*. He stood at the front of our bus in a modestly genial way, like a veteran back from the front with more battles yet to come.

As our cohort's most heralded member, Pete Dawkins from West Point, that year's Heisman Trophy winner, sat several seats in front of me looking Herculean, and, as I tried to imagine what tackling him might entail, the first-day rugby match in *Tom Brown's Schooldays* came vividly to mind. Though I'd thought about taking that sport up too, in such company as Pete's I realized that nobody in our group was the best at everything because all of us were so good at least something that we could relax and pursue what we most wanted to do, even in learning how to write as I was informed Willie Morris had done.

It was Bryce Nelson from our year who'd told me that. As a former editor of *The Harvard Crimson* who'd also been learning to write, he'd been very congenial on the voyage over and was headed to St. John's, where another Rhodes Scholar I knew from the previous year had gone. I knew no one who'd gone to Wadham and, in fact, had never heard of it except from a highly eccentric professor at Sewanee who'd also been a Rhodes and suggested I put it down as one of my three choices—which, having no other thoughts, I did.

I was mulling all that over as, long after night had fallen, we rolled into Oxford's early-autumnal gloom, dropping the other Rhodes off mostly in twos and threes until Willie and I were alone on the bus. No doubt eager to see his wife, he seemed friendly but reserved as he turned towards me and said, "*Your college won't be Gothic.*"

"Better plumbing?" I asked.

"Jacobean," he drawled, in a way that signaled a value judgment.

"That sounds lurid to me," I replied, thinking of Webster and Tourneur rather than architecture as we slowly creaked to a halt, and a shadowy dark façade with what appeared to be battlements loomed forebodingly ahead.

Such presentiments aside, I'd been so jaunty aboard our ship and was trying to seem so still, but, as he wished me luck, Willie's controlled demeanor cautioned me in effect to avoid the mistake I'd always made of coming on too strong at the start. As I'd soon learn, it was useful advice because it was true enough that I was a greenhorn again and, in the parlance of that time and place, it was very "non-U" to come on like a cocky "sharp-elbowed" Yank.

And yet, beyond the circle of fellow Rhodes, there was snootiness of a different sort among my own kind too, as I'd discover the very next day while standing with three recent shipmates in front of Blackwell's bookstore. We'd struck up a conversation with a graduate of Smith College named Nellie whose father was a U.S. senator and who was, as I recall, on a year-long fellowship of her own.

"Oh, God!" she'd exclaimed as soon as one of us had spoken. "Don't tell me! I know! I know! You're from Princeton," she merrily cried, gesturing at Reeve Parker. "And you're from Harvard," she said, nodding towards Jack Womack despite his being unshaven and looking deceptively scruffy. "And you," she considered, putting her hand on Steve Umin's arm. "You've got to be a Yalie, right?" She tossed her head and laughed with delight.

"So, what about me?" I asked, intending to make light of not being in on the game.

She looked me coolly up and down and said dismissively, "I don't have any idea."

For years I'd wake up at night with dazzling rejoinders. But what had surprised me at the time was not her gratuitous rudeness or the unexpected discovery that, even when labeled "Rhodes Scholars," what we'd achieved so far was less important to some than where we'd gone to college—or to put that another way, where we'd gone to college was what we'd achieved thus far, and my background didn't cut it.

That was okay with me when it came to senators' daughters—and I can't recall that I ever saw Nellie again—but I was left totally baffled by how in the world she'd done it, deciphering arcane clues of which I was oblivious. It somehow lay in the tweeds, I guessed, though I also surmised with prescient clarity that, even if I should gussy up, outfitting myself on Savile Row, the clothes would never hang right on me. I'd read *Zuleika Dobson* and realized in a flash that I was merely Oover, a provincial Rhodes Scholar in gabardine.

That assessment would change in time, not so much as a result of improvements in my wardrobe as because a group of angry young writers had begun producing novels and plays like *Saturday Night and Sunday Morning* or *Chicken Soup with Barley* or, most influentially, *Look Back in Anger* with actors on stage and screen like Albert Finney and Tom Courtenay who, at least in attitude and attire, had something in common with me. So for that brief cultural stretch prior to Liverpool mod, I found that I was dressed for success after all—along with some upstart friends from Cumbria and Golder's Green who closely resembled me.

As seemed logical in a way for a college whose founders had been commoners, few Wadham students were titled nobs and, of the handful who were, I'd get to know none even passably well. But, of course, at some level throughout the University there was a democracy of intellect—the libraries that were open to me were truly awe-inspiring, the immaculate grounds idyllic, and the company I chose to keep both gifted and convivial.

There were a few privations, and it was rumored at the time that a National Health survey had found latent scurvy widespread among those students reliant on college dining halls which, without any actual proof, sounded plausible to me given my own encounters with semi-edible fare. But the last bit of wartime rationing had only just come to an end with many items remaining in short supply—even heat, as I'd soon learn in my cavernous second-floor rooms which were warmed in their entirety by two short strands of "electric fire," too weak and remote from my bedroom to keep a glass of water from freezing overnight.

Though it wasn't so hard to adjust to that sort of inconvenience since I'd spent a year at Sewanee in a flimsy wartime barracks, my initial arrival at Wadham had dramatically undercut my previous expectations, seeming more like the opening scene of a Bela Lugosi movie. I'd seen mists swirling up from the Cherwell as we drove into the city and, after descending from the bus and hearing it rumble away with Willie's impassive half-seen face gliding off like a ghost's, I'd found myself there alone with my suitcase and steamer trunk plus a hemorrhaging box of books which I tried to shove with my foot towards the closed and apparently impenetrable fortress. Then having no other recourse, I began to thump on its massive gate.

After a very long wait with nothing stirring in sight, a tiny portal opened and a pair of eyes peered out at me, part of a small but disconcertingly cagey face.

"Yes?" it asked me testily.

I explained I was a newly arrived student.

"Not at this hour, you're not!" he cried. "Stop banging on the gate. . . and no use climbing the wall. The college is closed until Monday." The portal was shut again.

I looked more closely at what I could see of the lichen-stained three-storied wall that would have been unscalable even by an unencumbered stunt-double for Errol Flynn. So I pounded once more on the gate, and this time a door within it containing the tiny portal was opened by just a couple of inches and the cagey face reappeared, giving no indication of having seen me before.

"Yes?" he asked suspiciously.

"I'm the American student," I explained. "Warden Williams said arrangements had been made. I was told to remind the porter."

"*American?*" This registered slowly on the man I took to be the porter as, with what I hoped would be perceived as my countrymen's typical forthrightness, I extended my hand towards his while declaring that I was Bernie Dunlap. The gesture produced such dramatic results that, with seeming alarm and both hands thrust behind his back, the little man shrank away.

"Oh, no, sir! No, sir!" he exclaimed. "The lodge is closed. I'm Ted the scout!"

I had no idea what that might mean or why, if he wasn't the porter, he'd have cause to be there at all, but wheeling about for my suitcase and wedging it into the breach, I followed it into the gatehouse, still attempting to proffer my hand as one gentleman to another—though, once inside the gate, I could see he wore a short white jacket like that of a deliveryman or, as I presumed without really knowing, a waiter in Wadham's dining hall. Still, it was long after suppertime, and he'd said he was a scout.

Though no less perplexed than before, I vaguely deduced on the basis of race relations at home, that what I was encountering was a ritualized obsequiousness with layers of resentment that festered beneath the protocol. . . though it also crossed my mind that, by failing to observe the proprieties of class, I'd denied him the façade behind which he could hide his contempt for a privileged twerp like me who was less than half his age. Ted was going to be, as he explained, the scout for my roommate and me as well as for several others whose rooms would be on our staircase—which meant that, as our general factotum, he'd clean a bit and tidy up and, for a modest consideration, run errands for us on occasion or, should we commit some libidinous infraction, would presumably show a sly but more costly discretion (as would be confirmed in the spring when a friend of mine from St. Hilda's agreed to stay overnight). But the boundaries of his role would never be clearer to me than I was given to understand on the night that I arrived as he bowed me into my rooms—the same that had once been occupied by the great Sir Christopher Wren and had to all appearances remained as he might have left them some three hundred years before.

Though I'd be told that it was a honor—and believe it actually was—for me to be billeted there, their somewhat straitened condition seemed less in homage to Wren than the consequence of wars and unfortunate investments along with notorious episodes dating from 1660, nine years after Wren "went down" (i.e. left Oxford with a degree), when John Wilmot, the Earl of Rochester, had arrived at the age of 12 and proved himself, according to many reports, precociously licentious—so much so it seems that, as I was told, a scurrilous bit of doggerel describing the Wadham of that time and supposedly written by him, had begun with the much-quoted line, "Well did those amorous sons of Wadham. . ." for which the rhyming word was, of course, "Sodom."

Furthermore, it was also said but never to my knowledge substantiated that Rochester and/or many of his classmates had been expelled and "expunged" (the worst possible Oxford punishment) and the college itself been shut down for a spell—though as with a great deal of Oxford gossip, especially from centuries past, there's no real reason to think that particular detail is true because it's a matter of record that, in little more than a year and a half, Rochester himself went down with an honorary M.A.

I'd learn in time that there were similar rumors bandied about regarding the college's financial straits, including the charge that a former Warden as the owner of extensive tracts of bogland had seized on an opportunity to sell them to himself as the ultimate overseer of Wadham's investments—a transaction said to account for the fact that, while the dons at neighboring colleges were able to rest secure with shares in the London docks, the ease of Wadham's Fellows hung on the market for peat.

But even if such reports were true, the Fellows of my day appeared to cope with doggedly good humor, and high table fare in hall, presided over by the learned and expansive Sir Maurice Bowra, seemed to have suffered no decline in its gourmandise— which meant that, when dining in, we students could turn, like Oliver Twist in the workhouse, from bolting down our gruel to gazing at our bibulous dons dining in opulent splendor only a few feet away. That, like so much else, ran counter to my democratic instincts but was also, as I supposed, somehow very English.

The whole question of what in fact—as opposed to self-serving fantasy—was actually very English was hard for me to discern. There'd been populist revolts from the 14th Century onwards, though always, it seemed, after either a brutal suppression or modest accommodation, they'd basically fizzled out—a realization that caused me to wonder in hall each night, as I'd rarely done at Sewanee, if another might be in the offing led by the likes of Ted the Scout and his mates.

But why should I be surprised if the inequity and unfairness that I thought I'd left behind would be rife in England too or read that the Foreign Minister Lord Douglas-Home had declared Britain must find some way of curbing black African immigration without basing it on race alone? That sort of hypocrisy was hardly novel but, despite an extension of the social status that I and my friends had taken for granted while growing up, I was nonetheless dismayed by the bigotries of class so prevalent in England and appalled that, other than upstart playwrights and a few of the friends I'd make, those who might have spoken out—like Hugh Gaitskell, for example, the Labour Party leader, or the Archbishop of Canterbury, Geoffrey Fisher—appeared to be either indifferent or focused on other things. There'd always be an England, they seemed to agree, though with no great need for change except for who's in and who's out. . . of Parliament or heaven, whichever's your bailiwick.

I remember attending a sermon in a dingy Anglican church that would later be deconsecrated and turned into a bar. The minister was an Oxonian with a manner both earnest and self-absorbed and his sermon was on the date of an epistle by St. Paul which he believed to be later than others had supposed. His congregation appeared to consist for the most part of wearied charwomen with leg-wrappings like puttees binding their swollen calves and a handful of frail old men who might well have fought their way through Tobruk—or possibly Passchendaele—without once having asked themselves about the date of a Pauline epistles. It was a dismal embodiment of a moribund tradition.

It could easily have been that very same clergyman whom I encountered some months later when en route to see W.H. Auden, then serving a five-year term as Oxford's Professor of Poetry during which he'd written a commentary for the medieval *Play of Daniel* and was on that evensong occasion appearing as its narrator along with Russell Oberlin in the countertenor's part. It was being presented at Saint Barnabas Church in a section of Oxford with which I was still unfamiliar, so, feeling lost on an all but empty street, I hailed a passing cyclist to ask directions. He was dressed in clerical garb with gaiters.

"Can you tell me the way to the Church of Saint Barabbas?" I asked with a slip of the tongue.

"Saint *Barnabas*?" he scowled.

"Where *The Play of Daniel* is being performed. . ."

He snappishly obliged and cycled on, leaving me as taken aback by his umbrage as I was abashed at my foolish gaffe.

The performance was sparsely attended, but, in the darkening streets on my way back to Wadham on foot, I saw chalked on the wall of an alleyway something John Bunyan might have scrawled—

POOR CHILDREN
TALK TO GOD

That could have been read in a number of ways, but, in anti-establishment mode again, I took it as caustic advice intended for the meek—that they needn't expect to inherit the earth or much of
anything else until a regime change had occurred. I also had the ironic thought that, whatever else could be said of Ted and his shrewdly mutinous ilk, their never-quite-bridled irreverence was precisely what that irate man of the cloth had supposed he'd detected in me when, for the first time since my arrival, I'd seemed mistaken for a native, if of an irreverent sort.

Not that I'd ever aspire to be a counterfeit Englishman, though my mother had been an Anglophile since childhood, and one of my earliest recollections was of listening to the radio with her as, in a plea broadcast from London, a woman's oddly accented voice kept urgently repeating, "Help us, America! Help us!" I didn't know where London was or why she needed help, but I could feel my mother's emotion and knew that I ought to share it—though from roughly the age of nine or ten, when I happened on *Brigadoon* and then on *The Scottish Chiefs* and *The Lady of the Lake*, my heart would be in the highlands despite the fact that whatever ain folk I knew of from the last few hundred years had been literate kilt-free lowlanders from Ayrshire or thereabouts.

Nevertheless, such mostly fictitious enthusiasm had colored my attitude towards England and may even, in a subconscious way, have contributed to a pretentious bit of sarcasm in one of my first tutorial essays. "If what we mean by Merrie England," I read aloud to my tutor, "is merely an Ealing Studios version of loveable eccentrics and the art of muddling through, then we have to concede that George Meredith was right in pointing to sentimentality as his country's besetting sin, especially among the upper and middle classes." I went on to maintain with pseudo-Marxist indignation that the cost of maintaining that "somewhat self-serving view" had been unconscionably high among "the heretofore tractable masses bearing the weight of the system more or less like the mythical turtle that in pre-Ptolemaic cosmology was said to have supported the universe on its back."

As I recall, my tutor—whose name was John Bamborough and who was anything but a sentimentalist—had merely raised an eyebrow after having heard me out, not quizzing me in return about the huddled Black masses where I was from or what more I might have to say about pre-Ptolemaic cosmology. He knew I was still in my first term at Oxford and probably guessed that my culture shock was continuing in full swing while, abashed by my own presumption, I resolved not to tax his forbearance again in such an unseemly way.

That didn't mean I was reconciled to all that went on around me. We'd arrived in England just a couple of days before a general election, and, on the evening of the day I encountered the senator's daughter, Daryl Canfill and I had attended a Labour Party rally held in Oxford's sizable town hall. Though the university itself was generally Conservative apart from its

BEN DUNLAP

working-class menials, the massive Cowley Auto Works were only just down the road, so the hall was virtually bursting at the seams. We'd managed to grab two seats on one of the long side balconies where we found ourselves among a raucously Tory student group who'd come to heckle the speakers and, by the time the evening was over, I'd had enough of their condescending wit and self-satisfied party-line slogans ("You've never had it so good!)" It's not really an excuse, but that provocation too was probably in my mind when I wrote that tutorial essay.

In retrospect, I'm inclined to think that, in all likelihood, I was no more pretentious or shallow than most of my British counterparts though less polished in my concealments and thrown off kilter at times to find myself on the receiving end of the same sort of lofty disdain I'd witnessed at the town hall event, reminding me of how the parent of a friend at home had confided to my mother how bitterly she resented the antisemitism to which he'd been subjected. "It only takes one comment a day," she'd reported to my mother, "and, after a while, you start to believe that everyone else is thinking the same, just not expressing it."

That was very much in my mind during my first few months in Oxford and again at the start of my second year when knocking about with a new Wadham friend, Alan Coren, who'd just gone down with a first and was half-heartedly setting out towards getting another degree. I'd accompanied him on a closing-time jaunt from the King's Arms pub to the Oxford Castle jail to shout encouragement from the street to an uncle of his who was cooling his heels for a night or two there because of some minor escapade. After we'd wandered back into town, Coren had pronounced me a "true blue *mensch*," explaining that what he meant was "a fellow Jew at heart though still a bloody Yank."

"Don't call me a Yank," I replied. "I'm from South Carolina." Then I explained in turn that I'd been paraphrasing Dennis Morgan in the movie of *God is My Co-Pilot*, which was based on a World War II memoir by Colonel Robert Lee Scott of Waynesboro, Georgia, who'd been a fighter pilot for Chennault's Flying Tigers in China and whom I'd actually met when, shortly after landing in New York and before our night on the town, I'd been on a saber drill team that served as his honor guard on Governor's Island.

"Oh, yeah?" said Coren, one-upping me, "and you know who wrote that movie script? A guy named Abem Finkel!"

That's how our dialogue tended to go because Coren had that sort of mind, not just quick on the draw but loaded with arcane facts, and, as our beer-soaked errand suggests, he hadn't arrived amid the dreaming spires by the Old Etonian route—which was also part of what he'd meant about what we had in common as insider-outsiders of a sort, both fettered and free of the limits of how we were perceived.

"Freebooters," I said, "in a word"—an inside joke at the time that I didn't need to explain.

"The advantage of rooming in Wadham," he shrugged, "rather than Peckwater Quad."

That too would be clear enough to readers of Evelyn Waugh who, in *Brideshead Revisited* had depicted how the socially unassailable had not only belonged to "The House," as Christ Church college was known, but were quartered there in lavishly appointed rooms where, at that very moment, Auberon Waugh, the novelist's ultraconservative anti-American son was about to be rusticated for defiantly witless pranks—though, so far as I know, even he had steered clear of the Bullingdon Club (as the future Prime Minister, Boris Johnson, would not) perhaps because, for all their haughtiness, the Bullers, as they were called, had been described by his father as, among other repugnant things, "cretinous" and "porcine."

Purportedly founded in 1780 and limited to thirty members, it was ostensibly a dining and cricket club that had, through the years, become notorious for rowdiness and disorder even when mounted on horseback for what the wittiest of Oxford snobs, albeit a Magdalen man, had so famously dismissed as "the unspeakable
in pursuit of the uneatable"—although by the late 1950s their point-to-point pursuits had mostly declined to beagling after a drag.

Cecil Rhodes himself had been a Buller but, according to all reports, no American had ever been invited to belong, which is why Sam Holt, a fellow Rhodes assigned to The House and later a very close friend, was flattered as well as surprised when he was approached by a member about joining them for an impending event which, as it was somewhat sketchily described, would involve following a pack of hounds as they tracked a freshly laid spoor over a cross-country course. The beaglers would be on foot.

Sam was a year ahead of me, but we had a lot in common. He too was a southerner—from Birmingham, Alabama—and, though we couldn't have known it at the time, was even remotely kin to my future wife. He'd not only been first in his Princeton class but had an older brother who'd also been a Rhodes after having attended Sewanee. Sam himself was a polymath who authentically knew so much about whatever might be discussed that, after encountering him, experts of various sorts were said to feel despondent about their own shortcomings. That may or may not have been apocryphal—like reports that he'd dated Jane Fonda but failed to show sufficient deference to her egomaniacal father—though I knew for sure that there'd been a spread in *Oggi*, the Italian version of *Life*, featuring Sam and his current girlfriend as glittering young Americans abroad. If he had a vulnerability, it lay in a proud almost antebellum refusal to endure an insulting affront—which is to say, precisely the sort of snub for which the Bullers were infamous, with or without provocation.

It was only on the day of the outing that Sam was told his role was to be that of the dragger, the person who sets off minutes ahead of the dogs trailing a coarsely woven sack imbued with a pungent smell. He was handed a map of the course along with two sizable vials of wolf urine and instructions to douse the sack at regular intervals—plus an almost offhand assurance of what was airily described as an ample head start on the pack.

For reasons of his own, though indignant at this assignment, Sam elected to carry it out with high disdain, returning to his room for a long black leather overcoat he'd had custom-made in Germany. Then, adding a pair of dark glasses and tucking the vials of urine in his coat pockets, he reported to the departure point with all the insolent panache of a Wehrmacht officer at the front.

Initially, things went reasonably well, though the map was hard to follow, and, after some indecision while trying to work that out, he heard a cacophonous yelping that sounded within a mere two or three hundred yards. As the baying grew ever closer, he got more careless about the route and rapidly reached a conclusion that what was really at stake was his own self-preservation. He started searching about for stiles and fences that he could vault, and then, as he was nearing the edge of a very large open field, he caught a glimpse of apparently frenzied dogs approaching him like a canine tsunami. He looked for the tallest barrier that was plausibly within reach and, after an urgent burst of speed, clambered over a head-high wall as speedily as he could—too speedily, he discovered, as one of the vials in his pocket broke and he himself was drenched with the unmistakable spoor.

In panic he dropped to the wall's other side—but only to crash through a large expanse of *tents cloches* designed for late-season lettuce. With every step he shattered more panes until he heard a shotgun report and saw an armed farmer confronting him as the frustrated Bullingdon pack pulled up beyond the wall, snapping and leaping about.

"'Old it right there, you soddin' Nazi or whatever the 'ell you think you are!"

Sam held his hands up. "Sorry," he said.

Though at least as furious as the dogs, the Bullers arrived in time to explain, the farmer was reconciled and, for his own part, Sam, as he'd later declare whenever the subject came up, was thoroughly satisfied with how he'd comported himself which he saw—quite rightly, I think—as a personal vindication against what was soon to be a very endangered species. . . *Buller Oxoniensis*, threatened less with extinction, perhaps, than with total irrelevance, though its membership at last report had been reduced to two.

For some reason, for which I can't account, Sam now insists he'd actually been on horseback, galloping over the course like a madcap dragoon, though I have notes from the time that confirm it took place on foot and, however he was propelled, he *had* evaded the hounds, and his pride, if not his dignity, had come through fully intact.

Sam and I would subsequently travel together on four different vacs to come, and I'd learn a lot from our friendship, including how lucky I was to have ended up in Wadham where, in my initial Trinity term, I accepted an invitation to join an insouciant sort of cricket club disarmingly known as the Freebooters—the inside joke I alluded to in my conversation with Coren. Though Bowra himself had belonged as a young don, the club had no pretensions at all, athletic or otherwise. Our opponents consisted entirely of laid-back local village teams in limited-over matches during which, in between innings, beer that generally flowed as freely as tea was imbibed no less sedately, and though clearly a novice in the field, I wasn't a laughingstock.

With that happy beginning to the spring, I also volunteered to assist with a film society's nouvelle-vague-ish production featuring archly surreal tableaux in the style of René Magritte which, as confirmed by a shooting script that's still in my possession, would ironically be entitled "All Together, Boys." Neither I nor all but a few have ever seen it, however, because, though it was premiered a few months later at the Edinburgh Festival Fringe, it reportedly piled up in snippets on the floor as faulty edits snapped while passing through the projector's gate. . . in some respects, a brilliantly avant-garde touch as, during its only-ever screening, it simply self-destructed and was no more like a Banksy before its time.

According to what I was told, our director, Gavin Millar—himself a Christ Church man but an altogether genial Scot from a modest Clydebank background—had edited the only print in a frantic last-minute rush assisted by a girlfriend of the time no more adept with a splicer than I with a cricket bat. But Gavin would go on to become a highly regarded professional, directing a memorable feature film about Charles Dodgson and Alice Liddell in their halcyon days on the Cherwell and, in what must have been a redemptive act, co-authoring a new edition of Karel Reisz's classic work on *The Technique of Film Editing*.

I also spent time that spring with an actress from St. Hilda's who'd been cast in the role of Dol Common in Ben Jonson's *The Alchemist*. I'd been drawn to her vivid élan onstage and bold décolletage and, after we'd met a couple of times, to her quick and clever vivacity—and that of her circle of friends as well who, like Coren and some of my Freebooter mates, were part of a writing and acting scene that even the London papers reviewed. That prompted me to forget my tweeds and revert to a modified beatnik look based largely on my cousin's when back from India or Iran and that of ex-pat cronies of hers I'd only seen in photographs but whose verse and style evinced a rebellious verve that my new acquaintances admired.

Admittedly, my bohemian pose, adopted for good in my second year, was regarded as merely louche at first. But as that year was nearing its end, my getup was seen as avant-garde, and, once in a shop with a younger friend resoundingly named Victoria Brittain, I encountered the son of an English lord foppishly dressed as an upper-class beat but anxious about the epicene touch of a handkerchief tucked up his sleeve.

"Oh, hello, Vicky!" he burbled with a nervous sort of contortion as if she'd just come in with one of Robin Hood's men, never guessing that I was, in fact, one of his father's advisees— nor could he or I have foreseen that she'd become far more widely known than either of us as an author and human-rights journalist.

I'd developed a bit of a swagger by then, having discovered that my altered manner and appearance had rendered me more amphibian in dealing with matters of class—as on one occasion aboard a late-night bus during that second Trinity term while returning to my Iffley Road digs with a pleasant Scotch Ale buzz and the bus all to myself except for a teenaged girl somewhat in disarray. When I rose to get off at the James Street stop, I saw she was holding a shoe that belonged on her bandaged bare foot with a handkerchief as the bandage.

As if prompted by my departure, she too got up to leave and, feeling knightly but circumspect, I asked as we both touched ground, "Are you okay. . . or do you need help?"

At that point in my wardrobe's evolution, I was somewhere between Neal Cassidy and Holden Caulfield and, in any case, not conspicuously of the gown instead of town. So she explained as if to a trustworthy neighbor that she'd been jiving at the Jazz Club and climbing across the Northgate Tavern's roof which was how she'd injured her foot and, as a non-sequitur, that she was doing A-levels in school—which meant she was bright and underage— and I understood as if we were in a scene from "All Together, Boys" that just when her daring adventure had been drawing to a close, out of nowhere I'd turned up like a courtly and non-threatening Albert Finney to offer her my assistance. . . to which she replied by asking me in return with the breathless but wary tone of a novice beatnik moll, "Have you been drinking too?"

"Oh, aye," I said with what had become a weird mishmash of diction and intonation, "and a bit too much, I fear." Then I helped her off the bus and said, half-crooning the lines, "Goodnight then, lady, goodnight sweet lady, goodnight, goodnight," as she limped off on her way and I on mine as if I'd conversed with a dolphin.

What comes to mind in recalling that encounter is the relief and satisfaction I felt when, no longer consigned to the role of Oover the untouchable, I became a piece in the puzzle that, despite my droll impostures, fit convincingly into place as part of a larger picture like one of busily occupied figures in a crowd scene by Pieter Brueghel. That made me no more aware of where I was actually headed but, all fakery aside—while living an aesthete's life in a third-floor garret flat along the Iffley Road immersed in Beckett, Burgess, and Durrell as well as Orwell, Sartre, and Camus, dallying with a barmaid from The Turf, and working away obsessively on a long and turgid submission for Oxford's Newdigate Prize that wasn't even on the topic prescribed—I wasn't the rakish poet yet that I still hoped to become, though increasingly it seemed I was finding my true self.

I used to gaze at twilight from my ten-by-twelve-foot living room at the pseudo-medieval tower and roof of St. Edmund and St. Frideswide while reflecting on the martyrs for whom it had been named—one an 8th-century princess who, having founded an Oxford priory, had refused to marry a Mercian king who'd nonetheless tried to abduct her and, through divine intervention, had fallen from his horse and broken his neck, and, as her revered counterpart, an equally luckless 9th-century king about whom almost nothing is known except that he was killed by a Danish invader by the name of Ivar the Boneless and his presumably better-constructed brother called Ubba.

It also occurred to me more than once that if, as was apparently the case, like the Danes who'd stubbornly hung on in the north and east midlands or my Nordic forebears along the coast of Scotland, I'd gradually come to appear more British than not, it was nevertheless with the cavil that I'd adjusted only the rhythms of my speech while my accent remained intact. So it was generally supposed I must hail from some odd provincial outpost in Northumberland or Wales, a misperception encouraged by my wildly abundant hair which hinted at someplace remote with barbers in short supply.

Passing through Stockholm later on, after I'd sat through Schools but before my *viva voce* for a first, I was staying in the youth-hostel schooner docked there in the harbor when an Englishman roughly my age, dressed a lot like me in British Army surplus, approached me and proposed we should "look for birds" together.

"We ought to work as a team," he said. "This place is crawling with Yanks!"

I hadn't become an Englishman, but the truth of the matter was that, in ways I hadn't anticipated, it seemed the Brits had been growing a good deal more like me—for better or worse, I told myself, not being at all sure which.

Not that I hadn't tried at first to do the conventional things. On my third or fourth day in Oxford, Daryl Canfill and I had decided to buy a couple of secondhand bikes and cycle to the Vale of the White Horse in Uffington some twenty-odd miles away to visit its ancient Bronze or Iron Age site. It was where, as I dimly recalled, the hero of *Tom Brown's Schooldays* was from, though he'd wrongly supposed the enormous chalk effigy on a hill had been fashioned by Alfred the Great to memorialize a victory over the Danes at nearby Edington— which I found when I checked would have been in 878, shortly after the murderous Ubba had been killed in a warm-up battle by a Saxon leader named Odda, who must have been named expressly for that purpose.

Though as a matter of historical fact, the White Horse effigy had been created more than a thousand years before those events, probably by some unnamed Celtic people, Daryl had accepted the Alfred story because he happened to know that Alfred had been born in nearby Wantage. He also believed it would be an easy trip, and, however well informed he was about most things, he proved wrong on every count about our grueling trip—which, on a pair of single-speed clunkers, was roughly fifty miles roundtrip and consisted far more of hills than vales as quickly became apparent.

The minute we'd gotten back to town, I propped my wretched contraption against the exterior college wall and hobbled inside for a bath, vowing to never ride a bike again—little dreaming that, in another twenty-five years, I'd be pedaling through the very same countryside with my daughter on eighteen-speeds, and in any case, after breakfast in hall the following day, I was immensely relieved to find that my bike had been stolen and probably sold again by the time I'd downed my bangers, beans and greasy skillet-fried bread.

At the other end of absurdity, my tea with Princess Margaret at the end of our first term also went awry but in a totally different way—though I should first explain by way of background why, like so many from my cohort of Rhodes, I'd accepted the invitation from Miss McDonald of Sleat and the Commonwealth Fellowship Trust to attend such a formal and predictably stuffy occasion.

To begin with, it had to do with the princess herself and the notion of lining up like the would-be suitors in *Sleeping Beauty*. Significantly, in our fairy-tale-like roles as sweepstakes winners at Oxford, no aspiration seemed wholly out of reach, and, in specifically amorous terms, my sails hadn't yet been trimmed by multiple vacs in Paris during which I'd learn how impossibly hard it was for any American male to impress a native-born female there unless he was a gangster or a jazz musician. At the time of our royal tea, I still naively supposed I'd be fully equipped for such an encounter in France by following my usual prescription of memorizing great chunks of verse by Baudelaire, Verlaine, and Rimbaud—and, on top of that, by what I hoped would be a lucky coincidence, I'd discovered that, despite my persistent misgivings about my name, I'd enjoy the oblique advantage of sharing it with the hero of a steamy Louis Malle film entitled *Les Amants* in which an otherwise nondescript short dark Frenchman looking a bit like me made passionate love to Jeanne Moreau in a bathtub while the Brahms Sextet in b-flat major kept sawing away on the soundtrack—from which *succès de scandale* I surmised that, as soon as I got close to Saint-Germain, I might find success of my own with a line or two by

Prévert and a puff on a Gauloise while confiding to a receptive ear, "*Alors, moi aussi, ma cherie—je m'appelle Bernard!*"

But to no avail, of course. In my first real opportunity, I got no further than "*Je suis le ténébreux, le veuf, l'inconsolé. . .*" before my would-be inamorata burst into loud guffaws, explaining somewhat cruelly that, with very few exceptions, American men were too colorless and underdeveloped both culturally and sensually—especially, she specified, in matters of taste and smell, pointing out that our major contribution to the world other than jazz had been the underarm deodorant. When I protested that we southerners were, in fact, the exceptions, having inherited both guilt and defeat and produced as Proustian an author as William Faulkner, she said that, in any case, I didn't strike her as very Faulknerian and that, for my countrymen in general and implicitly me in particular, it was like comparing Rock Hudson to Yves Montand.

"*Mais Humphry Bogart!*" I persisted.

"*C'est un gang-stair,*" she declared, so I didn't pursue it further.

On the other hand, if I wasn't sufficiently decadent for the French, I'd begun to realize by the time I met up with Bridget, the actress from St. Hilda's, that English women of a certain sort were much easier to impress with a barrage of arty chat and uninhibited energy which, by and large, was closer to my natural style—or, if you will, the otter-most aspect of myself. That would prove a useful discovery because, over the course of time, it would help me avoid a lot of wasted effort.

But I hadn't yet learned those lessons prior to tea with Princess Margaret who, still in her late twenties at that point in a tabloid-bedeviled life, had seen her impassioned but thwarted affair with her father's former equerry and Battle-of-Britain hero, Peter Townsend, come to an end and was currently said to be having a fling with a former boxer of sorts turned man-about-town photographer, Antony Armstrong-Jones, who, if not so dashingly suave seemed engagingly energetic. Of the two, I thought in a wholly facetious way, I was closer to the second in style as well as height, so who knew what might come of that?

Some such semi-roguish curiosity was probably in the minds of most of my fellow Rhodes who chose, like me, to postpone other less structured departures for a brush with the racy young princess. A number of my friends and I—including Jack Womack and Daryl along with David Dunn and a few from the previous year like Kris Kristofferson, whom I'd later get to know well—went down to London together and put up at a bed-and-breakfast located near Russell Square.

On the day of the tea, I was fooling around on the doorstep waiting for the others and, for no particular reason as I heard their feet on the stairs, I impulsively stuck my hand through the narrow brass letter slot, waggling my fingers at their approach. But when Womack grabbed my hand, I reflexively yanked it back, slicing my middle finger to the bone.

Blood was suddenly everywhere as I tried to staunch the bleeding, but nothing I did could stop it. So, needing to catch the underground to reach Drapers' Hall on time, I improvised as best I could, wrapping my finger in a handkerchief and holding it over my head. From time to time I'd lower my hand, but only to see the bloodstains expand as I tried to imagine the consequence if, in shaking the royal mitt, I left a similar splotch of red.

When we got to the location, we discovered that the invitation list had apparently included every student in Britain from a current or former dominion—from which, with mixed emotions, I concluded that, after all, the odds were very much against a personal encounter with the Princess, and I was only mildly unnerved when a hubbub occurred at the door and, at the head of a flotilla, she swept into the hall through a sea of bobbing heads, prompting in me to my surprise a fleeting attack of royal awe.

When I managed to catch a clear view of her, I saw she was shorter than I'd supposed—about my mother's height, I guessed, putatively five feet one—and her aura was mesmerizing even though, as I'd write in my journal, "her face was lit up with a professional smile while her eyes appeared to betray either a hardened licentiousness or an ineffable sorrow bespeaking a broken heart with little hope of repair." In a more practical vein, I was relieved to note that she was dressed entirely in emerald-hued velvet with matching hat and gloves on which bloodstains would be less conspicuous. When she entered, I'd lowered my upraised arm which, with admirable discretion, the other guests had seemingly ignored. Now I furtively unwrapped my hand and quickly wrapped it back up again, plunging it into my pocket while glancing up at Kris, who was standing next to me.

"Still bleedin'?" he asked in his husky baritone—looking like Natty Bumppo in a tie, though his voice was more like Uncas.

"Not as much," I optimistically replied, noting that Princess Margaret, moving slowly through the crowd, had taken an inexplicable turn and accompanied by her minions, was making a beeline towards the two of us. She reached Kris first and stopped.

"Hello," she said with a radiant smile. "Where are you from?" she asked.

We'd been coached in courtly protocol, but, to my astonishment, Kris merely replied with a trance-like stare, apparently overcome by the same sort of awe I'd felt a few minutes before. He'd taken her hand as she extended it but simply stood there for an excruciating length of time before managing to stammer, "Ca. . . Ca. . . Ca. . ." He was trying to say California but, unable to get that out, finally blurted, "Texas!" the state where he'd been born.

In a curious way, Princess Margaret seemed reluctant to move on. "I see. . . and what's the climate like there?"

But this was too much for Kris, who merely goggled at her until, at last, she said, "How lovely. I must visit it someday," and flicked her eyes at me.

"Hello," she said, but her eyes were already moving away towards someone else, and my royal encounter was over.

"Damn!" Kris muttered to himself. His was over too—but though I was bemused by his momentary panic, I was also struck by the fact that, despite whatever route her handlers had intended, Princess Margaret—like so many whom I'd observe for many months to come—had clearly been drawn into his orbit by some mysterious power of attraction of which I hadn't a clue.

To put it in its simplest terms, Kris seemed to exude some sort of musk that women couldn't resist. During the following year, he and I and Alan Coren—who, as I've already noted, would later become a well-known wit on his own—would be kicking around together a lot while fancying that, among the plodding aspirants for BLitt degrees in English, our trio was like the Three Musketeers with each of us headed for fame. Only one of us was wrong.

For a term or two we were all but inseparable, though I remember a night in November at Rhodes House when Coren had joined Kristofferson and me to watch the U.S. election returns on a special video feed with the three of us hoping JFK would win. Though Coren had showed up as a friend, he'd really come in pursuit of a woman named Miriam May who possessed the sort of allure I'd just been reading about in Lawrence Durrell's *Justine*. He confided as we watched the early returns how obsessed with her he'd become while, seemingly ignoring us, she kept drifting through the constant chatter around us like a verse from the *Song of Solomon*.

Kris and I offered supportive advice, I in greater detail than Kris—though, based on our private appraisals of what she was looking for, little was likely to come of it. Only much later would I learn that, beginning that very night, Kris and Miriam had had an affair. I never knew the particulars, but I'm willing to bet she'd picked up his musk and thrown herself blindly under his wheels like a roe from the mountains of Bether.

The more I witnessed his appeal—and reckoned how useful such knowledge might be—the more earnestly I studied his technique. I'd enter a room with Kris, regarding myself as a little less high, wide, or handsome but a reasonable facsimile nonetheless, when suddenly and predictably every woman within fifteen or twenty feet would be helplessly drawn to him like iron filings to a magnet. To his credit, he'd generally say, "One of you girls go talk to Bernie. . . I'll do you a favor when I can," and one of them usually would.

But, as with the senator's daughter's trick, I was genuinely mystified. "How did he do it?" I wondered, impervious myself to whatever his secret was. He was taller, sure, with a deeper drawl, but neither of those was it. It was something that worked, as I surmised, on a deeper and subtler level.

And then I finally figured it out. It was all done with his eyes or, to put it more precisely, in the message that they conveyed to each and every woman flitting and circling around him like moths about a flame—a message which, if put into words, was conveying something like this: *"Baby, I'm doomed. There's nothing you can do to help—you'll only singe your wings if you try."* Simple enough, you might say, but almost without exception, they'd respond with a wavering cry however unspoken it was, "Oh, Kris, I'm sure there must be *something* that I can do!"

It was clear to me that there was something irresistible in the very nature of that message, something that worked like a powerful non-verbal aphrodisiac. So, fully aware of what I possessed, I decided to wield it first—as maybe I should have known I would—on an upcoming visit to Paris with the same dismissive young woman who'd spurned my attentions before.

When we rendezvoused along Boul'Mich, I unleashed my message almost at once. "Baby, I'm doomed," I said with a look, exactly as Kris had done.

It took her only a moment to respond, but the answer was unmistakable. *"Ah, oui! Tu me dis!"* You're telling me! she said with her eyes in reply.

Something had clearly been lost in my rendition—I'd meant *perdu* instead of *perdant*—but, as I'd once done with explosives, I renounced the awful power I'd almost had in hand and would never try to use it again. . . except in wooing my future wife who, luckily for me, had a lively sense of humor.

In my third and final year, I moved with my friend Reeve Parker—whose older brother, like Sam's, had also been a Rhodes and whose father, a medical doctor wed to a kinswoman of the Oyster Bay Roosevelts, was a hard-driving self-made man from North Carolina—to the tiny and little-frequented village of Noke where we lived in the so-called Manor Bungalow, though there was another bigger and older Manor House nearer the beginning of our dead-end road which cast some doubt on our landlord's claims. Having originated as a late Anglo-Saxon settlement that would afterwards be described as "poisoned by the vapors which arose from the moor" and long before the latter had been for the most part drained and used as a bombing range, the village, though less than ten miles from Oxford, had reportedly served members of the University as a 15th-century refuge from the plague—which was more or less the impulse driving us both as, in our mid-twenties by then, we'd had enough of the rigors of college life. Reeve was in his third year too but, having already completed his degree, he had more time on his hands and was frequently away.

As one of seven small villages on the Otmoor in between Beckley and Islip, Noke was in our day a typical not-quite-picturesque place very much in the countryside with a dozen or so small cottages, a 13th-century church, a pub called the Plough, and a genial village idiot named Stevie who gave the lie to a bit of doggerel that dated from the Enclosure Acts—"I went to Noke, but nobody spoke"—and tried over many pints of bitter to teach me the words of his signature song, a ditty called "One Meat Ball" which, in its original form, had been written by a future Harvard professor. . . a role which, unbeknownst to me, lay improbably in my future as well—though, as I'd have to learn on my own,

you gets no bread with one meat ball!

which largely accounts for what would come of that.

Reeve and I felt welcome enough at two out of three of Noke's gathering spots—the snug little pub where Stevie was one of its regulars and Mrs. George's tiny grocery shop, where our only misstep was in asking Mrs. George to add some Niblets canned corn to her inventory, a product which in her mind was suitable only for livestock and a blunder that we offset thereafter by subsisting mainly on packaged curries which, nearly alone among the items she stocked, seemed both edible and within our culinary reach. As far as we could tell, the third of the places in which to congregate, St. Giles parish church, held only sporadic services of which we never saw one underway.

According to one of Stevie's relatives, our landlord, Stuart Logsdail, had been under a cloud since the war for having brought down an RAF observation plane with his rifle one night when, still in his late thirties, he served as the village's air raid warden. With his somewhat less-than-dapper moustache, he seemed cordial in a stilted way, tweedy and, as the Brits would say, "not fearfully bright"—which appears to have been the villagers' view as well, though we were gullible mugs for our local misinformants.

But to give him his full due, Logsdail was, in fact—like Aristotle, Tolstoy, and Sir Edmund Hillary—a beekeeper on a modest scale and, in a more recent connection that I've run across on the internet, the son of a well-regarded Victorian painter named William Logsdail who, at the outset of his career, had been applauded by Ruskin and hobnobbed in Paris and Venice with the likes of Whistler and Sargent before moving his wife and children to Noke when Stuart was still a boy. I've also learned that Marjorie, Stuart's pleasantly disengaged wife, was herself from nearby Islip and would live to be a hundred, dying in Norfolk in 2005 followed some thirteen years later by her son and former Noke-ster, Edward Logsdail who'd been named for his paternal uncle, an officer in the Royal Naval Air Service, who'd died in a fatal plane crash in 1923.

Of course, such information wasn't readily available to us in 1961, and, as I've insinuated, what we picked up at the Plough was often unreliable. There was, for example, the owner of that rival "manor house" much closer to the pub—a reclusive don known as "Griff" who, despite his present standoffishness, had formerly been, according to village hearsay, sociable enough to become the natural father of the publican's nymph-like daughter—gossip I never repeated because, as I warily surmised, it was shared with us as intruders who, perhaps to even some score, might spread it further in Oxford.

It was similar with our bungalow. In an effort to be convivial on our first visit to the Plough, I told a grizzled villager where we were putting up.

"Oh, dear! Oh, dear!" he said as several regulars leaned in closer to listen in.

"What's wrong with that?" I asked.

"Well, you see. . ." our informant grimly smiled, "there's a bit of a complication."

It seemed our bungalow down the road was not in great demand because a nearby neighbor, a sort of landlocked Tugboat Annie who lived across the big adjacent field, was reputed to be a witch—her only known local counterpart having been one Benedict Winchcombe, a seventeenth-century huntsman whose mutilated effigy resided in the church but who, according to village tradition, could be heard on moonlit winter nights going by at a gallop along its only road.

In any event, the current witch was said to have put a curse on two disrespectful louts who, after their catcalls and other offenses, had been killed in a motorcar accident. After such a persuasive demonstration, we were informed, no one had ventured to mock her again—at least, not openly—but we should be forewarned that she had a regrettable habit of dropping into our bungalow unannounced and making herself a cup of tea and that, if that should occur, we'd do well to humor her.

We took that as a put-on, of course, until late one afternoon in the spring, while I was alone in the house and taking a leisurely bath, I thought I heard some noises from the kitchen. It took me a while to throw something on and good-naturedly check to see if the witch was about. But though the answer appeared to be no, the kitchen backdoor was ajar, and a half-empty cup of tea was sitting on the table—the work of Stevie, I assumed, or one of the local wags. It was also, I concluded, either a signal that I belonged or that it was time to go.

I preferred the former interpretation, but what I remember best from near the end of my last term as I was preparing to say goodbye to Oxford as well as Noke are the blissful corroborations of lines from Shelley and Keats—the startling cries of early-morning larks fired like sonic roman candles from the fields and cuckoos and nightingales exchanging nightlong trills in nearby Prattle Wood where, for several weeks in late spring, I spied a horse-drawn caravan until one day it and its occupants were gone like Arnold's Scholar Gypsy or Borrow's itinerant Romany about whom I'd been reading during my last-minute cramming. I too was about to decamp, so not long before my Examination Schools, I made several trips to town to tell old friends goodbye.

I went to visit Lord David Cecil who, along with Maurice Bowra, had been a young don at Wadham during the Twenties, inviting him for weekends at Hatfield House and hobnobbing with the last of the Bloomsbury set at nearby Garsington Manor. Lord David had overseen parts of my work over three or four different terms, and, whatever one makes of his scholarly work, he'd always been both helpful and generous to me—mainly because he truly was what Newman had meant by a gentleman but also, I suspect, because, with my accent and place of origin along with the shock of dark hair that fell across my forehead, he initially had me confused with a Rhodes from North Carolina whose BLitt he'd directed the year before my arrival—the soon to be well-known novelist Reynolds Price. After he'd managed to straighten that out, I felt my stock had fallen somewhat, but his kindness never slackened.

Being a casually disjointed dandy, he tended to twist like a flamingo and had an odd impediment when he spoke, a sort of high-pitched gobble which, like so many upper-crust stutters and lisps, seemed tailored to enhance whatever it was he'd said. Once, as a frequent panelist on a program known as *The Brains Trust*, he'd been asked a question posed by a playful listener, "Why did the chicken cross the road?" In his inimitable fashion, he'd given the only sensible reply—other than Einstein's—to that very bird-brained riddle: "Well, never having been a chicken. . . I really couldn't say."

In a somewhat similar vein, he'd listened politely to me when I confided that, for my BLitt thesis, I thought I might visit Yorkshire to see if I couldn't discover Emily Brontë's lost Gondal saga. He said that would be splendid, of course, but perhaps, before my departure, I could work on something a bit more practical, like depictions of my compatriots in the novels of Robert Bage and other forgotten authors. In the end that came to nothing as well, though in guiding me through a half-dozen drafts of a two or three-page proposal, he'd taught me how to revise as no one before him had done, and, on my final visit, we had a warm conversation during which, among other things, he showed me drawings that he possessed by Giambattista Tiepolo as if we both were connoisseurs.

I dropped in on Bamborough too, or "Bam" as we all called him, though never to his face—not because of his gravitas as Senior Tutor at Wadham but because, according to Coren and others who said the same, he'd fought behind enemy lines somewhere in Nazi-held Norway, survived, and come home with a wife with whom, in my hearing at least, he always spoke in Norwegian. More than anyone else at Oxford, he'd guided my work from start to finish through multiple changes of direction—

always in an encouraging way, though with a wry admonition that, in one way or another, the piper must always be paid. He asked what I planned to do next, and I replied by saying I hoped to go everywhere, trying my hand at everything and writing about what I learned.

As usual, Bam had a cigarette in his mouth, but he also had a peculiar way of smoking by sucking in air around instead of through it while making a gasping sound resembling an iron lung. So, with a Senior Service dangling from his mouth and an intake of breath or a sigh, he held out his hand and said, "But oh, beamish nephew, beware of the day if your Snark be a Boojum!" Then, after inhaling again, he added, "So long, Dunners," and we shook hands—and I was soon on my way, though his enigmatic goodbye continued to reverberate and would draw me back from a precipice when it suddenly leapt to mind in another six months or so and more than once since then. It was so typical of him, for whom all learning had to pass a rigorous down-to-earth test.

Finally, in making my last rounds, I went up to Jericho in North Oxford to see my Anglo-Saxon tutor, Alan Ward, who was an accomplished scholar and very likeable man but hopelessly ineffectual as a teacher. He wasn't given to perorations and tended to get discomforted as soon as what he was saying had grown to paragraph length—and, even then, in a mumble—causing his students to feel obliged to keep up a running patter when he was starting to wind down, often meeting in unlikely places involving hard cider or beer which tended to loosen his tongue a bit and sometimes his volume as well without strengthening the lesson.

He once confided to me that he suffered from synesthesia and said that, early on in maths, he'd made a lot of careless mistakes involving the number nine. He'd tried to explain to his teacher that nines had a scarlet hue, a color he couldn't abide, so reflexively and unconsciously he'd often supplanted them with either eights or noughts. When asked if I had a color, he said I was brickish red, with which I would have agreed if he'd meant my name alone as in "Bernie" rather than Ben—though if he meant Dunlap instead, I believe that's a light mahogany and, in any case, not nearly so close to scarlet. As for what color I myself am, I think I'm a deep blue-green—"like the color of E flat major," as I'd later observe in Leipzig to an eminent musicologist while discussing Bach's *Saint John Passion*, prompting a blunt "Who *are* you?" to which I should have replied, "A student of Alan Ward's."

On another occasion, over a pint of bitter, Mr. Ward had also shared with me that a major crisis during his early years had occurred when he fired a pop gun at a bed of blooming tulips which had instantly keeled over in a row. Since then, he said, he was taking no chances—though I couldn't guess what he'd meant by that except that it somehow explained his wholly mild-mannered mien. He let his students bully him, but he truly was an extremely intelligent man with a very droll sense of humor.

Admittedly, he tended to dress in a way that made me feel by contrast almost dapper, which otherwise rarely happened. He generally favored a short-sleeved dark-red shirt, fairly close to a brick-red hue but usually offset by a tattered plaid tie and weathered Harris tweed jacket with a rip at the back of one armpit. As part of this modest ensemble, he often appeared to be sporting a two-day growth of beard, though I never supposed he'd contrived it for effect—he was simply at heart, I think, a saintly tatterdemalion.

I got the impression that he played the horses a little and, when we met for tutorials at a North Oxford pub called The Rose and The Crown, we'd usually get the ball rolling by discussing the weather and sometimes the track followed by Anglo-Saxon for a bit if there was nothing else to discuss as we worked our way towards Chaucer, the ultimate end of his line.

He'd invited me to lunch on the day I went to tell him goodbye, but, as soon as I arrived, it was clear that he'd neglected to tell his wife, whose name I discovered was Peg. She was dressed in blue jeans and a sorely distressed man's shirt and seemed flamboyantly harried. In exasperation, she went to buy some cider and pork pies, though behind her façade of incipient despair, she was very pleasant towards me and, to all appearances, had managed to inject a number of practicalities into their co-existence—sufficient, at least, to account for a son named David, who was five years old at the time and had a tantrum while I was there.

We sat out in their backyard drinking potent Merrydown while basking in the sun of a late English spring. David had suspended a red ball on a cord that was tied in turn to a clothesline overhead, and he was hitting the ball with an old tennis racket that seemed to have seen past use for various modes of swatting—possibly, even, at tulip beds. While his father muttered and mumbled in his habitual mode and I kept up my prattle, David repeatedly snuck up to drink from his father's mug. So we chatted on in a mellow directionless way while the increasingly tipsy five-year-old went staggering about and flailing at a ball that grew more and more elusive while my tutor was looking on with a puzzled abstracted expression. He'd always been, as I've indicated, so diffident and considerate that, aside from its slight absurdity, it was altogether serene for me to be sitting beside him in his backyard drinking hard cider in the sun until we too began to get a buzz on.

We ate casually in the kitchen. Peg's sister was also there with their mother who was in the charming grip of an advanced senility. She was ninety-four years old and giggled and blushed like a schoolgirl. My tutor sat down and, with a tiddly sort of good humor, began to pound the table like a famished Mr. Morel in *Sons and Lovers*. But the tremors from his blows caused a miniature derrick that his son had made out of pieces from a Meccano set to collapse—which was when the boy had his tantrum, shattering his father's euphoric mood as I saw him transformed into an angry beleaguered Hrothgar with a torrent of imprecations roaring from his throat as if from a massive but ill-aimed popgun.

Nothing much came of his furor, but everyone, with the exception of Peg's mother, grew both deliberate and detached as though that sort of eruption had happened before, and they all knew how to deal with it. For her part, the girlish old woman, for no apparent reason, began to pour tomato sauce over her plate and placemat until the bottle was taken away—at which point I gathered, with no corroboration, that Peg's sister lived along with her mother and several additional children somewhere else on the premises, perhaps in a shed I'd glimpsed out back.

In the middle of this confusion, there was a knocking at the door that turned out to be a social worker who'd come to see about the children's heads. I didn't understand her concern until it was explained to me that my tutor's wife's sister's children had been sent home from school the previous week "because of their dirty heads."

Everyone tried to reassure the embarrassed social worker, who was mortified to be making such a call on the household of an Oxford don, so they acted very interested and asked her a number of questions about the issue of dirty heads. It all became quite jolly, and my tutor's wife's mother got hold of the ketchup again as David reappeared, having recovered from his tantrum with a head that was quickly inspected and found reassuringly clean. Inspired by that turn of events, I began to tell funny stories, and my tutor's wife's mother put the ketchup bottle down and, clapping her hands, smiled coyly when I offered her a cigarette.

"Ohhhh," she exclaimed, "They're French!" as if I'd offered her something illicit.

And, with that, the moment blossomed into what felt like a true epiphany, a sudden realization that, if there was always going to be an England, that's what it would be like—what I'd written off too quickly in my first term's tutorial essay. I thought of Walter Pater who, after scoring a second in Schools had returned to teach at Brasenose, urging his students to burn with hard gemlike flames amid lives of exquisite aestheticism. . . whereas what I'd found in my tutor's backyard was closer to *Cold Comfort Farm*, an Ealing Studios comedy come to life amid what, in Pater's own turns of phrase, were "variegated, dramatic lives" that were "irresistibly real and attractive"—more to me, perhaps, than they would have been to him. Near the very last hour, it seemed, I'd stumbled on what I'd been seeking, some part of it at least.

Several days later, I sat for Schools—twenty-seven full hours of proctored exams taken while wearing *sub fusc*, which was roughly like donning white tie and tails to fight a trial by combat—and, when that exhausting ordeal was done, I found myself out on High Street guzzling champagne with my friends, most of them English by then. We laughed as we always did, poked fun at each other and drank a bit more than planned because, for the first time since we'd met, there was nothing for us to do next.

Then one by one we dispersed—Bridget, Victoria, Jill, both Rosemarys whom I'd liked so much (it appeared to be a popular name) but had never approached as a swain, and Bertie from Northern Ireland who, as soon as the rope had been dropped for our initial exam and the scramble began towards our desks, had collapsed in a panic again and, disallowed from further attempts, was already headed back across the Irish Sea. Quentin was off to get married, I learned. Melvyn was with the BBC and Alan on a Harkness in the States. Roy Stuart had won the Vinerian Scholarship and would be staying on in law as Jeff Hackney would as well—and is still to this day, after nearly six decades have passed, the Clerk of the Market at Oxford. The first of my roommates, Trevor Anderson, went back to Winnipeg and David Plant to New Zealand. A couple of Peters had gone I knew not where. . . and, in short, with astonishing speed as we stood outside the Examination Schools in our preposterous attire, the tent had been struck, the merriment done, and *la commedia era finita*. Most of them I'd never see again.

I'd been through it all before, of course, and had learned the first time around that there's no easy way to say goodbye. Shortly after moving to Noke, Reeve and I had found ourselves adopted by a village dog named Laddie who'd taken up residence with us at the Manor Bungalow. As soon as I'd finished Schools and driven back there to pack, I made a quick sketch of the living room with Laddie on a rug in front of the open French doors. When we both took off for good next day, Reeve in his Austen-Healey Sprite and I on my Italian scooter, Laddie followed us to the driveway. The last thing I saw as I glided away was Laddie closing his eyes in histrionic grief and toppling over sideways. All you can do, I told myself, was "exit [as if] pursued by a bear"—the semi-comedic stage direction I'd discussed on one of my recent exams.

After several weeks touring the Lake District on my scooter with a Canadienne I'd met in Scandinavia, I returned to be viva-ed for a First, appearing before a dimly lit tribunal chaired by C.L. Wrenn, the eminent Anglo-Saxon scholar who was then, in my eyes at least, extremely old and almost totally blind. He read my name out from a list held almost flush with his nose but could come no closer than "Duncan" to which I dutifully answered.

Things went swimmingly well until, after holding forth on *The Winter's Tale* and other late plays by Shakespeare, I ran afoul of *The Two Noble Kinsmen* about which a woman I didn't recognize but who'd been smilingly nodding as I spoke began to ask me questions. Not knowing her most important research had been about that play, I breezily said I'd found it hardly worth my time and that, in any case, Shakespeare hadn't written it. She nodded at me no more, and I sensed I was on my way to garnering a high Second. Bam afterwards sent me a note assuring me that I'd earned "a very good set of marks, and well within striking distance of the 1st," adding that, "I was told how much they enjoyed talking to you—but they didn't quite manage to convince themselves. . ." nor was I convinced about that play, though I have to admit, in the sixty years since then, her opinion has prevailed, at least as far as its part-authorship.

But that was that, and there wasn't much else for me to do in Oxford. As a very self-conscious good deed, I went to see an English acquaintance who'd supposedly gone mad—or who, as I was told, had been caught in the act of stealing books from Blackwell's and was assumed to be deranged or permitted to claim he was. He'd been secreted away in a nearby sanitarium called the Warneford, which was a lovely old estate with carefully trimmed lawns and majestic copper beeches. I remember our conversation on its grounds amidst the quiet click of bowls on a shaven green and the plaintive song of another student refugee who, in a listless monotone while strumming two or three chords on a guitar, warbled a bluesy song about feeling so sad he could put his head on a railroad track and drift off to pleasant dreams.

I'd only decided to pay that visit because I'd heard that my acquaintance, whom I actually hardly knew, had been abandoned by all his other Oxford friends. But it felt like a confirmation that many things were ending all at once.

Later that afternoon, I got on my motor scooter and rode once more to the Vale of the White Horse in Uffington. I climbed up the steep hill to its equine effigy where, long before Tom Brown's fictional days, the Anglo-Saxons had worshipped—or maybe whoever was there before the Anglo-Saxons, which had probably been the case—and, as darkness began to fall and the moon to climb in the sky, I waited for something to happen. The broad chalk trench by which I stood still glimmered as it had for over a thousand years, arrested it seemed in mid-gallop. But then I heard a bark and, outlined on the high hill's crest, caught the moon-glint in a watchful fox's eye. As if at the end of a vision quest, I stood completely motionless while the two of us exchanged a lengthy lingering look, then it turned to dash along the ridge and disappear down the other side.

I returned to my motor scooter and went back to where I was staying and, the following day, having sent all my luggage ahead, I rode the sixty-odd miles to Southampton where, closing a great parenthesis in my life, I gave the scooter to a bobby on the pier in exchange for a one-pound note, which he insisted on paying in case it was stolen goods. Then, with an Oxford degree and a restored former part in my hair, I left England on the student ship *Grooterbeer* for what I knew would be a good long while to come.

10

West Is West

Though for everything there's a season, that doesn't address the problem of momentum, that things in motion tend to keep moving, and for me, all in or all out, that's sometimes been a problem—as it was after leaving England. . . not that I couldn't locate the brakes, but that I wasn't inclined to use them.

For the past three years, partly because it was cheaper than staying on in Oxford but mainly because I'm by nature a peregrinating creature, I'd spent more time on the road than I had in any one place. So when heading back home again, it was mostly willful inertia that caused me to overshoot the mark by twenty-six hundred miles, intending to pursue what I'd told my tutor I'd do—keep living my life to the fullest like my wayward cousin from Camden and write about the spillage like her friends, assuming that what I wrote would be both vivid and new while ignoring the dismal fact that, despite such aspirations, I had nothing special to say.

I'd touched down briefly in South Carolina, but telling myself that, at twenty-four with twin degrees in hand though no career plan in mind, I should gather a bit more material by squandering half my remaining net worth on a three-day cross-country bus ride, pausing only for burger-and-bathroom breaks at grubby and zombified terminals, each a replica of the other at the end of which I'd resume my freebooting ways by rejoining some Oxford friends who'd been wafted already in lotus-land—from among whom, in actual fact as my Greyhound sighed to a stop stood my former fellow Wadhamite, Alan Coren, who'd induced me to make the trek.

Coren had become at that point the same sort of vagabond expatriate on a stipend that I'd been back in England, having come to the U.S. on his Harkness Fellowship during my third and final year at Oxford and, after sampling Yale and Minnesota, continuing on to Berkeley. Provided with a car and other such conveniences omitted by Cecil Rhodes, he was also a stringer for *Punch*, the venerable though somewhat creaky publication which, during its frantic declining years, he'd continue to serve in various rejuvenizing ways—though, at that early stage of his career, he was merely looking about for whatever grist for the satirist's mill might have been overlooked by Waugh and other visiting wits. . . which was part of my reason for showing up. We thought we might collaborate.

All this was in the fall of 1962, and I, on the verge of vagrancy, was newly in the role of a truly mendicant beatnik with virtually no resources. If I'd had a precise agenda (which I hadn't), it would have included writing the draft of a novel which (if I'd gotten around to writing it, which I didn't) would probably have been the length of *War and Peace* in the style of Jack Kerouac (or, worse yet, William Saroyan) with a vaguely Faulknerian tinge. Plan B would have been to join the newly-created Peace Corps and go to Tanganyika, where I'd rendezvous with a former girlfriend of sorts named Jemima Jo Taylor who'd lived below me in my Iffley Road digs and on whose behalf I'd learned a few words in Swahili—mostly sweet nothings like *ua zuri* and *malaika* along with useful phrases like "the rat is in the granary" or "I believe my leg is broken." Plan C, which was very far from my mind, was to join my fellow Rhodes and former Nokester Reeve Parker in getting a Harvard Ph.D., though I find that option included on a list compiled at the time for pathways towards a restored respectability alongside applying to medical school or even attending seminary, assuming that A and B fell through and Harvard wasn't compliant with my whims. In other words, I was totally at loose ends and much closer than I knew to Rimbaud's netherworldly plunge in his *Season in Hell*, the Gallic precursor to Allen Ginsberg's San Francisco-begotten, peyote-inspired, Whitmanesque poem *Howl*.

One of my first stops after arriving in San Francisco was, in fact, at the City Lights bookstore in North Beach, but

Ferlinghetti, whom I'd met in Tennessee, looked older and disappointingly staid, drawing a total blank on who I was. I'd also hoped for a discount but didn't get one and concluded that most of the other beats had long since headed east instead of west, to India or Iran, still in pursuit of my cousin.

Among contemporaries from Oxford whom I'd only known in passing was yet another Rosemary whose surname was Fitzgerald. She was rooming with Janet Dawson whom I didn't know at all and had been in Lady Margaret Hall, reading English for her degree and taking part like me in David Cecil's weekly sessions conducted with John Bayley, Lord David's former pupil and Iris Murdoch's spouse. I didn't know and never asked if Janet had also been at LMH or what either of them was studying while at Berkeley, though they'd rented a nearby one-story house where Alan and I would visit from time to time.

But there were lots of other Brits, strangers as well as acquaintances, who'd settled about the Bay as well as in Los Angeles. Coren had run into quite a few, many of whom were roughly our age but others a good deal older and more productively engaged like Jessica "Decca" Mitford, Nancy's Communist sister who was nearly my mother's age, and a man named Leslie Strickland, who was married with a young daughter and served as production manager for KPFA radio, a listener-subscribed operation that featured an unpaid movie reviewer whose segments I liked to listen to by the name of Pauline Kael. It was primarily her example that had prompted Coren's notion that the station might do with comic dialogues in the manner of Bob and Ray or the far more caustic *Beyond the Fringe* which was slated to open soon in New York—except, of course, from the two of us, pairing a Brit and a Yank as transatlantic wags. . . hence his having persuaded me to make the westward move.

As for *Beyond the Fringers*, I'd met Alan Bennett in England—along with Dudley Moore, one of a pair of Oxonians who'd joined two others from Cambridge for their satirical review at the very same Edinburgh Festival at which our Oxford film had premiered and disintegrated. Not so coincidentally, John Bassett, the person who'd initially convened the soon-to-be-famous quartet had also been at Wadham and, though I scarcely knew who he was, I got dragged along in his wake for an evening at a pub with Alan Bennett and several friends. It would have been more memorable for me had I not been so starved for company in Noke while studying for exams that I talked non-stop myself and could hardly recall his squeezing in a word. Nonetheless, the Fringers' success made it seem just barely plausible that Alan and I, with a little luck, would be famous overnight.

We weren't, of course, but not entirely from want of trying. We got as far as taping a number of improvisations on an old reel-to-reel recorder, including some folksong parodies with lyrics like one of mine—"the sun goes down in the morning, the evening comes rising in me," which was warbled by me off-key in a backwoods nasal twang—and thanks to my collaborator, a few authentically clever turns like my interview with Marcel Proust's former landlady as channeled through Coren's cockney falsetto: "'Scribble, scribble, scribble, Mister Prowst,' I used to say, 'it'll be the death of you yet'. . . and it was, it *was*!"

The truth of the matter was that, in the glossolaliac manner of S.J. Perelman, Coren was the quickest and most exuberant *improvisateur* I've ever encountered, and I dearly wish he was still alive to corroborate what I'm about to say—which is, quite simply, that every detail of what I'm going to recount of my three or four misspent months in Berkeley and San Francisco is absolutely true. It was a very strange time—not just for me but, it would seem, for much of the rest of the world as if we'd reached a collective end of our tether.

But as a sort of curtain-raiser, shortly after my arrival, having traveled so far to the west that just beyond the horizon was a glimmer of the Far East and still in post-Greyhound mode oblivious of our planet's orbital wobble, I hired myself out as a babysitter for the Strickland's daughter Julie who, refusing to go to bed, had insisted I had to admire her precious pet guinea pig that, at that early nighttime hour, was skulking beneath a heaped-up pile of cedar chips and shavings. To summon it, she called its name—which my notes record as Cadwallader, presumably meaning it was Welsh—but, when it failed to appear, she began to rattle and shake its birdcage lair, quickly growing exasperated and whacking it as she shook. I tried to persuade her to stop, but she grabbed what must have been a balloon stick and began jabbing it into the pile. Before I could intervene, a tiny but hideous shriek was emitted from the cage, and a miserably blinded creature staggered into view like a rodent Oedipus Rex.

Blood was squirting everywhere as the poor beast died in agony and its murderer had a hysterical fit, bawling and throwing herself on the floor—which was, of course, when her parents walked in on the lurid chamber of horrors with which I'd traumatized their daughter. They were deaf to my explanation, and the episode cast a subsequent pall over Coren & Dunlap's comic routines at their animal-friendly network.

That was only the first of what would become for me a series of twilight-zone adventures, some as unpredictable as an earthquake but many triggered by Coren's *Punch*-driven quest for outré Americana—and as Nathaniel West had pointed out, California was full of nuts, not all of them home-grown. As the first of our jointly conducted interviews, we made an appointment to interview Peter Koch, a strung-out self-proclaimed prophet who'd shown up from post-war Germany with the secret of the Second Coming which, according to him, was imminent.

His organization—or "movement" as he described it—had a labyrinth of rooms over a Chinese restaurant with the scent of his incense sticks mingling with Sichuan-pepper fumes to lend the whole enterprise a vaguely back-kitchen ambience, though as we mounted the stairs, we heard a recorded dulcet-toned voice narrating some sort of scripture—which turned out to be a detailed account of how Koch's followers should behave before "the *Parousia*" began, or, as the soothing voice explained, "what those not yet familiar with the work of Gustav Adolf Deissmann would refer to as an advent."

A tight-lipped matronly woman was standing in the entry hall, whether guarding it or worshipping wasn't clear. Beside her was a burly Asian man whose commitment seemed to be wavering as he heard his spiritual contract in detail—no sex for now but lots of it later, after a day of reckoning. He wouldn't have long to wait, the recording promised or warned.

We were queried and escorted by the woman to a dimly lit and sparsely furnished room with little more than a badly parched snake plant in a huge ceramic urn—presumably the sort of neglect that end times tend to provoke. Koch himself was waiting for us, surprisingly young and impassive behind a pair of bifocals but weirdly euphoric about the truth that he'd been vouchsafed to convey. "It's coming soon!" were his first words, echoing what the recording had said.

Coren appeared to write that down. "Today's October the 6th," he said, launching his opening gambit. 'I know our readers will be eager to learn when they can stop paying PG&E."

Koch smiled and gravely shook his head, adopting a monotone. "Your sarcasm is irrelevant. My friends have seen the Apostle Paul. He told them we'd gotten everything wrong and needed to wholly rewrite his portions of the Bible, especially those that pertain specifically to today." We further learned that the voice we'd heard while climbing the stairs belonged to the very same woman who'd taken down Paul's dictation. The apocalypse was on its way.

We listened for quite a while as he droned on in his flat monotonous mode, citing the unmistakable clues that Paul's revision entailed. When he reached a pregnant pause, I asked if he'd meant Saint John instead of Paul.

Koch turned the same mild gaze on me. "A prophet's a prophet," he said. "You doubters are pretty much all alike. One of our friends asked Paul for proof, handing over a five-dollar bill that Paul transformed to a fifty. Would that convince you?"

"No," I said.

"Precisely," he smiled dismissively, and, after several more such exchanges, he nodded with his chin and we were led away—though he followed a few steps behind to watch us descend the stairs as if the gates of heaven were being clanged shut amid the pungent *hoisin* smells. It hadn't been much of an interview either for him or for us.

Peter Koch would die in Vienna in 1984, at the age of 57. Having become a major figure by then in the Rev. Sun Myung Moon's Unification Church, he would be eulogized by a fellow believer who said, "If Peter could be compared to a fruit, then the coconut would be a fine example."

Though that came many years too late for Coren's story in *Punch*, it was exactly the sort of thing his editors craved as opposed to yet another account of the ailing Aldous Huxley dropping acid in L.A. But the loopiness we encountered wasn't confined to cults or those getting high on peyote. One of Coren's newly-acquired Oxonian friends was a different Peter named Skinner, who looked like a former rugby player gone carelessly to seed—but then, as far as I could tell, that's what most of the Brits in San Francisco were doing one way or another. And yet, for the sheer persistence and variety of his soap-opera-like entanglements, Skinner would come to seem, as Peter Koch might have said, their utter apotheosis.

He was at most, I think, about two or three years older, and though he vehemently denied it, he was self-destructively obsessed in some mixed-up star-crossed way with a woman named Linda who, though barely nineteen, claimed no last name that I'd ever learn and—according to Skinner, at least—had slept with innumerable men over the past year alone while taking every conceivable drug and finding no joy in anything. For his part, Skinner insisted that he himself by contrast, having sampled all varieties of mind-altering substances, had settled on strictly non-addictive ones without identifying what they were but confessing that, shortly before he made that claim, he'd gone to a gay hair-dresser's salon and, after they'd both gotten high on something hallucinogenic in the salon's lavatory, had ended up dyeing his hair jet black which had dulled to a peat-boggish hue by the time I first encountered him.

Coren, who was also planning to write a novel, was making a study of Skinner whose father had apparently been an upper middle-class Brit driving himself to an early grave by putting three sons through public schools of the English sort and on through Oxford after that. Either before or after getting his degree, Skinner had spent three years as an officer in the Royal Navy followed by two years in the States in New York and San Francisco. Linda had followed him from New York, sleeping, he said, with everyone but him—drug dealers and delivery boys and even Skinner's best friend in the course of a two-day break from an archaeological expedition to Baffin Island and, in an even narrower window of opportunity, a destitute Mexican homosexual named Napo sporting an open-necked Cornel Wilde-ish shirt and a silver-plated Saint Christopher medal as his only possessions of value other than his "winning personality."

Somehow, Skinner's entourage all seemed to come with such phrases attached.

Coren wasn't sure how he'd put his research to work, nor was I clear about my role as his nominal collaborator for some of his other undertakings in exchange for getting free rent, but with Skinner he'd hit the mother lode for a degenerate updated *Cannery Row* set in the Bay Area, especially considering Skinner's slew of friends. One of the latter was an American named Willie Holst, a down-and-out Savonarola who'd become an ascetic after getting into a fight with a man who called himself Hamlett (*sic*) over an unidentified girlfriend (call her Ofeelia) and, despite being as tall and rangy as Jack Palance, he, Willie, had gotten smashed in the teeth and, in the course of some sort of orthodontic complication, had met up with Jill Jeffery and introduced her to Coren and then to me since both of us, to Willie's ear, appeared to be as authentically English as she was.

During my first encounter with Willie, he'd gone raging through a Berkeley newsstand pointing at furtive men who were pouring over the girlie mags. "Just look at the fuckers!" he yelled, slapping the magazine racks. "Stuffing their minds with pornographic filth. . . like ten-year-olds preferring shit to sex!" while the voyeurs put the magazines back and slunk away like roaches under a fridge as Willie spewed forth at passersby, "What're *you* looking at? You got a problem with me?"

It was shortly after meeting Willie that I too started to jot things down in a series of 8x5 notebooks, though less as future material than as a way of maintaining some sort of detachment from what was going on all around me. Willie himself was the subject of my first entry in which I noted that, according to Coren, he was working at the time for an insurance underwriter in a job he said he hated while intending to save enough to get himself to Japan and join a Buddhist monastery—a plan he'd recently hatched when his only compatible co-worker, an Italian violinist who'd endured his miserable job for years, had simply walked away declaring he'd rather starve. Though Willie's own style seemed far too full-tilt manic to endure any misery for long, I'd heard him declare mid-rant that he'd soon have no needs of his own other than tofu and sake which I took to be his take on monastic serenity.

Jill Jeffery, though, was something else again despite some seamy encounters of her own, including one in which she'd been propositioned by a newsboy who'd found her asleep on the docks following a wild night out and, as she recounted it, she'd been so touched by his awkward temerity that she'd lectured him on good and bad sex and the difference between the two while he continued to gawk as she offered her earnest advice until, finally, by way of reply, he'd stuck his trembling hand between her legs—at which she'd rolled her eyes while plucking his hand away and walked off giggling to herself, telling the Black man she met next who looked like Henry Fonda in *Grapes of Wrath* and gallantly took her home, "No, I'm sorry, this isn't the time" despite his decorous advances.

Later I'd hear from Jill that her way of signaling that a love affair was over was to ask the man in question to give her a child when she turned twenty-eight. . . still presumably some time away, though maybe not, I couldn't tell. She was nearly as tall as I—which was, to my way of thinking, at the low end of average height for a man or, as I'd run across somewhere, exactly that of a typical doughboy in World War I—and she wore her hair cut short like Leslie Caron's in *An American in Paris* with a dancer's knack of resembling a minaret when, as she sometimes did, adopting a motionless calm, a capacity accentuated by her quick dark eyes that matched the coloratura of her very English voice and the ebullience of her apparently reckless life.

She had a picturesque flat on North Beach's Sonoma Street of which I mainly remember her decks of tarot cards and a Helen Nevelson-like construction fashioned from scraps of wood that she'd hung over the mantelpiece with an inscription across it reading REPELLI DRAGONI. I was there one wine-soaked night when the room was suddenly filled with people from a costume party upstairs, and, to Jill's delighted approval, I greeted Richard III and his courtly entourage while bedizened with her gold-brocade table-runner and a crimson knitted cap that I'd seen her toss aside along with a purple feather duster with its handle down the back of my shirt, announcing as the feathers waved back and forth that I was the exiled Prince of Cofitachequi and more recently of Crete.

"So a cretin then?" King Richard asked, adding with mock disdain, "Just judging by your attire."

"But not a villain," I nodded, which seemed much cleverer than it was because of Jill's amusement.

She was very intense but self-contained, like the priestess of a sect devoted to solving riddles. She told me about her friend— and I presume her lover—a painter who'd made the dragon repellent. He'd fought when he was younger with the Lincoln Brigade in Spain, and he was, she said, a big gentle man with a slow wild fervor who'd suffered serious damage to his lungs during the Spanish war and, afterwards when she knew him, had been wracked in his mid-fifties by silicosis and then by cancer throughout "his beautiful brown body." He'd painted an ecstatic depiction of Elijah and the ravens in swirling shades of blue, gray, black, and green reminiscent of an El Greco, and he had a corresponding theory of life, accepting its rhythmic ups and downs but not what he regarded as the shameful intimidation of mortality, being determined to represent in himself the validity of his vision, dying and wasting away piecemeal in a hospital bed while his face grew thinner and thinner as, with a terrible fascination, Jill saw it become like that of his Elijah with everything gaunt and shriveling except his hands which lay outside on the coverlet and were the same strong painter and sculptor's hands.

She said she'd gone every day to read to him and, at his request, had recounted and laughed at every detail of what had happened to her outside while he died and fought against dying, straining with all he had left in him without ever ceding defeat while, to her immense surprise, she'd found it beautiful and exalted to see that powerful man stretched like an ancient warrior to the limits of his strength, and she changed from sadness and misery for him to a heedless exultant cheering him on. . . and he'd sensed she understood as, with a grim determination, he plunged further into his grappling with death like Jacob and the angel, refusing all offers of morphine because he was convinced he couldn't die as long as he was conscious.

She'd continued to go every day, and at times he seemed to grow stronger, and she'd urged him to "Fight it! Fight it!" until the nurses gave him morphine anyhow because he was crying out in pain in spite of himself, and he'd become groggy and in and out of consciousness, and she'd slept next to him in his hospital bed until he came to again and would fiercely demand a precise account of what she could see from the window with each exact detail until finally he lost consciousness for good and lay there like a palette with all its colors scraped away.

When she told me that—not as a self-conscious shtick, but as if she were reliving it—I loved her with all my heart, but after a few days I met her in the company of John, introduced to me as the best friend of a man back in England to whom she'd become engaged over the telephone who, having sworn he'd never marry, had found he was terribly lonely and deeply in love with her and, though she'd refused at first, he wanted to pay for her ticket anyhow and, though technically not committed, she'd been so touched, she said, that she agreed, and Coren slept with her that night. So we were all in love with her in one way or another.

And when she left the following day we plunged into each other's arms, and she kissed me feverishly through her faux-fur collar, meaning I couldn't say what except she wanted to know if I really had visions which, though not exactly true, was close enough to what I was straining to grasp which was little more, I think, than how we all relate to everything around us, the trivial and the sublime—and anyhow, she said as if she hated for it to end that the three of us had made a magically exhilarating scene, causing me to recall that once, when I'd spent the night in her flat, her Creole roommate Beryl, who'd just had a mind-numbing break-up, went stumbling nakedly through the room and Jill had whispered in my ear while pointing to the sculpture on the wall, "I knew that thing didn't work."

It crossed my mind as we said goodbye that, in any case, she was leaving that piece behind because, like us and all the others and whatever we represented, it was far too cumbersome to include in what she'd be doing next. . . which prompted me to remember in turn an afternoon when the three of us had gone from the Palace of Fine Arts to visit Coit Tower at sunset and, having it all to ourselves, had bounded about as if the world was at our disposal—but though I'd been on the verge of chanting the *Song of Solomon*, I was afterwards glad I hadn't because, in a time and place when nothing at all seemed stable, quotations came more easily than commitments—so they'd be suspect too and I'd wanted the moment to stay precisely as it was.

A week or so after she'd left, we got a typically extravagant note addressed to us both from a ship in the mid-Atlantic, invoking that same moment that she was holding close, she said, "in order to remind me that I once lived amongst those I love" and that

> One time when we stood on a hill and the world
> was covered in blue cellophane, I felt as if my
> belly and eyes were the center of the universe and
> you two the possessors of the only loins on earth.

I would have preferred that her note had been written to me alone and that, of the loins in question, mine hadn't been the ones that were held in reserve—though, at some deep level I didn't try to verbalize, it seemed somehow to ring hollow. . . like the Repelli Dragoni which, for all its whimsical verve, had proved in the end a fake.

But, as to belly, eyes, and so forth, one afternoon in Berkeley shortly after she'd left, I emerged from a secondhand bookstore on University Avenue and saw or thought I saw the souls of passersby which, somewhat to my surprise, bore no resemblance at all to the clouds of numinous auras or glowing bits of divinity I might otherwise have expected. It appeared instead that everyone on the street, dawdling or rushing along, talking or pausing to think, was encumbered by an awkward sort of bundle that shook and churned as they moved as if it contained a semi-sedated cat unable for the moment to escape. I'd been reading the Bhagavad Gita, so I recognized my source—along, perhaps, with Dr. Seuss—but I thought this was a significant confirmation of something fundamental, so I hurried back to my notebook to write it down. . . though, as visions go, it was very small beer, and other than the understanding that I had a sack of my own to bear, nothing would come of it, not even a minor cult.

In the wake of Jill's departure, it had also occurred to me to wonder if she and the rest of our restless circle were running towards or away from something very much like the thing in a sack—though, after I'd written that down, it struck me as so banal that I instantly crossed it out. Besides, for several weeks after Jill left, the dragon repellent appeared to be working after all because neither Beryl nor anyone else in our crisis-prone circle of friends reported a serious mishap until, like a proverbial bad penny, Skinner turned up again, setting off psychic tremors by declaring to all who'd listen that Linda was merely a leech for whom he now cared nothing at all.

Though we did our best to tune him out, he rattled on incessantly about his fictitious conquests and, despite the stench of failure that clung to him so persistently or maybe because of it, he repeatedly claimed he'd soon be shipping out aboard a Norwegian freighter—the only shipping line, according to him, that required no union card. As what I, at least, took to be a total fabrication, he also held forth at length about a Polish girlfriend to whom he was sending money and was planning to meet in London, though always adding morosely that she'd momentarily run afoul of visa delays and couldn't get out of Warsaw.

For the past several months, it seemed, he'd been selling encyclopedias door to door for multiples of their actual price while loathing the venal distributorship that held weekly salesmanship meetings with banners and marching songs at which awards got handed out to its successful "bookmen," the ones whom they proclaimed to be "eagles" rather than "oysters." Though admittedly fallen from grace of late, he professed to have racked up earnings of five thousand bucks a week at first compared to a mere two hundred by a fellow novice bookman and his wife who, other than hawking their wares, aspired to nothing more than using their profits to skin-dive whereas he, with his Polish girlfriend in mind, had become as thrifty and sober as Silas Marner—from which I deduced that, whilst at Oxford, he must have read English too—and he'd vowed to keep it up until their rendezvous in England.

But all of that went by the board when Linda showed up again. He put her up in his apartment while she continued to sleep with anyone other than him and would have included either of us if we hadn't each demurred, though she'd probably told him otherwise because he didn't show up for a while until one day he met us for lunch at Sam Wo's to say it was over with Linda once and for all, insisting he'd only taken pity on her because without his financial support she couldn't have paid for food or rent despite her getting alimony—a comment that hung there unexplained as he added, "May she rot in hell," which prompted a further complaint that, while she was gone, he'd slept with a woman who'd clawed his back to ribbons and left him with a dose of the pox. He'd gone to the public health department and, among the assorted addicts and bums, been given a purported cure in exchange for filling out a form on which he reported the source of his clap, at whom and at which he continued to rail until we'd both heard enough.

All during his angst-filled monologue, Skinner was using ludicrous be-bop talk and, even after he'd ordered his meal from the cheaper Cantonese menu, he kept railing about "the wogs in Chinatown" in a way directed at me because I'd mentioned that I was working again at learning Japanese—and I realized with a shock that, recoiling from what he perceived as my bleeding-heart squeamishness, he was trying to put me down as even more of a loser than he. Not yet, I quickly assured myself, but something to think about.

"Women," he said, "they're nothing but two-bit whores."

After we'd eaten we made an excuse and told him we'd have to move on, but several hours later a message from Beryl arrived that Linda had swallowed a fistful of pills in an attempted suicide. It wasn't clear how Beryl had gotten involved or what was wanted of us, but we drove to Skinner's flat where we found that he and Linda were still at the ER. So, as if in some sort of waiting room, we sat with people we vaguely knew and several we didn't know at all, including a man with a Vincent Price moustache and a boy with a youthful clean-cut face who was probably there to socialize with Linda and told us in an eagerly genial way that his name was Lang—"l-a-n-g," he spelled it out if anybody asked, though he left in a flash when a landlord appeared and, after complaining about the darts randomly stuck on the ceiling, threatened to call the police as he must have done at some point after Beryl, Coren, and I decided to step outside for some air, a vantage from which we watched the cops go in, detaining some late arrivals including Linda herself who'd only just stumbled up to the door while the boy named Lang—who was waiting around the corner, birddogging her for as long as it took—looked on as

Skinner spoke with the cops, securing Linda's release... at which point Lang cut out.

It was clear by then that none of us was needed, but in a typical footnote to the evening, we were joined as we were walking away by the man with the dapper moustache who, in an inexplicably menacing way, refused to believe I was from South Carolina because he himself was from North Carolina and, though just recently back from Japan, he knew a southern accent when he heard one. When I assured him in Japanese that I was truly a South Carolinian, he grew more belligerent still and, as a subordinate threat, he was seconded by the squat quasi-British woman he had in tow who professed to be from North Borneo where, in what seemed at first a total non-sequitur, she said she'd become a lesbian by default, but had been so miserable either way that she thought about nothing but suicide, which was how she'd come to know Linda—though, with a sudden shifting of gears, she took up her escort's cause by accusing me of calling him a *funkorogashi,* a word I'd never heard before but which, according to her, meant "dung beetle," a term she'd learned in a women's internment camp in Sarawak during the war.

Attempting to make light of it after that, I assured her that I had nothing but the highest respect for people of every sexual inclination except sadism and necrophilia and not only had I not even mentioned *funkorogashi* but I'd been given to understand that dung beetles were actually highly useful creatures and, in some parts of the world, even considered edible—which infuriated her even further, and she kept her vituperation up until she slipped in the street while hurling additional insults and said she'd hurt her back, effectively ending our exchange.

"Clearly," I wrote that night, "we're all being turned into swine."

When Skinner was evicted following his landlord's visit, it was found that, before moving out, he'd dumped all of Linda's possessions into a pile on the kitchen floor and poured mustard and ketchup on top of them—like "a Compost Heap of the Vanities," as Coren wryly observed, though we never learned what had prompted such meanness other than Linda's usual betrayals and Skinner's apparent discovery that the woman from whom he'd gotten the pox had also attempted suicide, having had the health authorities visit her and swearing to them that whatever she had she must have gotten from Skinner. . . whereupon, in an odd bit of role reversal, Skinner had felt abjectly contrite and promptly moved in with her, setting up house together while both of them recovered.

Meanwhile, as if bereft of her vocation, Linda had disappeared, though for Skinner, in his new pox-ridden relationship, there were still more twists to follow when a heretofore unknown player—a man from Los Angeles who, because of a previous liaison with the unnamed woman in question, had been paying for her apartment in San Francisco— received word of what had happened and drove up in anger and haste to intervene. But providentially (for Skinner, at least), on the man's way to the hospital where he assumed his friend was still laid up, he had a nearly fatal wreck, suffering burns and broken limbs and, as far as anyone knew, had eventually flown back to L.A. without ever appearing center stage.

That's as far my knowledge of Skinner goes, and, for whatever reason, Coren, despite his assiduous notes, would never make use of that story or most of the others I've recounted. But I've got them still in summary form in my notebooks from that time, concluding with the terse remark that, after that episode, our contact with Skinner himself and his suicidal ménages had simply "Petered out." That's just as well, I think, records of even a crazy time seem too repetitive to retell at greater length. With only a few exceptions, including a later coda involving Linda and Skinner, my notebook entries broke off or dwindled into short paragraphs as other distractions arose, often improbable too but a good deal more upbeat.

For example, it was after we saw the last of Skinner that Coren got a call from Hollywood—from his black-sheep Uncle Sid who'd left England under a legal cloud and never been back in touch again. He'd reemerged, it seemed, as a furrier to the stars, and now, having gotten wind of his nephew's by-lines in *Punch*, he wanted to show him the town—in this case, San Francisco—along with one of his closest clients and friends, an actress named Kim Novak of whom we'd probably heard. Furthermore, as his obvious intention was to rehabilitate his reputation with his relatives back in England, he generously said his nephew's American friend from Oxford was welcome to tag along.

I was especially intrigued by Uncle Sid's invitation because the only fan letter I'd ever written to a movie star had been addressed to Kim Novak after I'd seen her in *Picnic* and heard her confide to William Holden in a shy but intimate way,

> You know, some boys. . . well, when they take a girl in their arms to dance. . . well, they make her feel sort of uncomfortable. But with you, I. . . I had the feeling you knew exactly what you were doing, and I could follow you every step of the way. . .

That, plus the deft one-two of her armor-plated breasts as, under the lanterns on a floating dock, she bedazzled her leading man, had struck me when I was in college as what I was looking for and, thinking I'd play the part of a younger if shorter partner of sorts, I'd invited her to a dance weekend at Sewanee. Unsurprisingly though, I'd never heard back—no doubt because her studio was as loath to tarnish her image as the handlers of Miss Universe had been. But implausible though it seemed, I might be getting a second crack, a prospect that struck me as brighter because of some recent changes I'd made for snapping out of my lethargy.

First among them was that, alarmed by Skinner's condescension when we'd met up with him at Sam Wo's, I'd adopted a fitness regimen and accepted a standing offer that, as soon as Uncle Sid had blown through town and I'd paid Coren back by helping him with another story for *Punch*, I'd move out of his digs and in with Janet and Rosemary—or, rather, in with Janet because Rosemary's plans had suddenly changed and she was returning to Ireland, having gotten so spooked by the Cuban missile crisis that was just then getting underway that she'd made up her mind she'd rather die in the arms of a man she'd known for most of her life—the graduate of an agricultural college, which probably meant he owned an Irish estate—than incinerate alone so far from home.

Though everyone thought her hysterical, it seemed that she was adamant, which would mean a free bedroom for me in the house that she and Janet had rented long-term on nearby Milvia Street. . . but with an implicit rider: Janet was feeling acutely depressed about having recently been dumped by an abusive biker boyfriend, Fred, who after much coming and going had definitively absconded, and I'd take on the task of trying to cheer her up, whatever that might involve. It would be my first go at becoming a gigolo of one sort or another, but it would also represent, I thought, a chance to concentrate on creating something myself.

In the weeks preceding that move, my personal great leap forward had involved a variety of positive steps including giving up smoking, buying a small zippered-up secondhand copy of the King James version of the Bible (reduced from $2.95 to a buck and a quarter) intending to read it from start to finish (or, as things turned out, from Genesis to Deuteronomy), and beginning to make extensive notes for the novel that I intended to write— about an addled old man who'd broken out of a rest home back in South Carolina and, in the company of a young Black Sancho Panza, would wander about the state in search of his boyhood home in the Kershaw County community of Jeffers which, when he was ten or eleven, had changed its name to Blaney to honor a New York banker who'd brought the railroad through, thus putting it on the map, but which, even as I wrote, was in the process of changing its name again to comply with the stipulation of a watch-making corporation from Illinois that would build an assembly plant there—thus assuring that my Quixote could never retrieve his past or his long-lost Dulcinea. . . or, in other words, the past is never dead, it merely gets misplaced or sold to the highest bidder.

At the same time, beginning to harbor doubts of my own about ever returning home, I was, in semi-Skinnerish mode, considering shipping out on a Norwegian freighter, a recourse for which I was getting into shape by jumping rope on the large flat roof of Coren's apartment building, a skill that I'd acquired in the course of my brief inglorious boxing career. Coren would later report that a woman who lived on the top floor had told the building's superintendent that she was going mad from hearing the pigeons stamp their feet, and, after he'd investigated and found there was nothing there, he'd agreed with her that she was losing her mind.

In any case, as the missile crisis worsened, Uncle Sid showed up with some disheartening news. Kim Novak had had a sudden emergency. When I told him that I'd been stood up before by the reigning Miss Universe, he clearly didn't believe me. But that was okay because, over a couple of spendthrift nights, he was as lavishly generous to us as a forty-niner who'd struck it rich, taking us to a succession of fancy expensive places—Ernie's, Finocchio's, Trader Vic's, Gold Street, and Bimbo's 365.

At Ernie's, Uncle Sid ordered a Nuits-Saints-Georges 1959, specifying that brilliant year which I'd guzzled as a *vin nouveau* in France a scant three years before. When the waiter grandly brought it forth, Sid took a slow appraising taste and, with a grand kabuki display that matched the waiter's artful con, insisted it wasn't a '59. He brushed the concealing napkin aside and saw it was 1958. The waiter developed rigor mortis.

"Let's get this right," said Uncle Sid, furrier to the stars.

The waiter conferred with someone else, either a sommelier or the ambassador from France, who was standing a few steps off. The waiter returned and said, "The maître d' is descending into the cellar, sir!" with all the majestic aplomb of, "The Bismarck is sinking, Admiral." Uncle Sid winked. He'd had his day—even if, as I suspected, it had been scripted in advance.

We were well into October by that point, and on the very next day Coren and I drove down to Big Sur to visit a survivalist group who'd set themselves up in an arroyo by the sea, a place which, because of prevailing winds, ought to be fairly safe in case of nuclear fallout. *Punch* was eager to get the story because of the ongoing crisis, now in its second week without any sign of being resolved, though as far as we were concerned there wasn't much reason to panic.

Arrangements had been made more than a week before to meet with the group, as they'd specified, in their arroyo at dawn—which seemed just the sort of melodramatic detail to illustrate their kooky West Coast excess. So we drove down most of the way the night before and grabbed some sleep in the car in order to be on time.

But when we got to their gate at daybreak, we were challenged and then turned back by sentries shouting from hidden positions that they had us squarely in their sights and would shoot to kill if we approached as much as another step. We didn't choose to argue and turned around. The back of my neck was prickling as we walked.

On our way back to Berkeley, in the vicinity of Castro Canyon—not far from where Henry Miller would spend the last four months of his longtime stay in Big Sur and fairly close to Carmel where Robinson Jeffers had died about nine months before—we stopped along the highway at a place called the Big Sur Inn which, as we learned in the parking lot from a tanned and supercilious bodybuilder, had been built in the 1930s by its German American owner using his own two hands. He was still on the premises, we were told, but the inn was currently being run by our strength-through-joy informant and the lookalikes he'd attracted. I'd only later discover that the founder and current proprietor was actually an immigrant from Norway by the name of Helmuth Deetjen, called "Grandpa" by the communards who, as I imagined at the time, must have kept him sequestered in one of the farthest cabins while they catered to their musclebound kingpin's whims

But the place had its attractions. When we entered to order coffee and soup, both of us unshaven in boots and turtlenecks— our notion of survivalist chic—a hi-fi Beethoven sonata was playing in an adjacent room and a girl named Susie or Sue who said she was from Seattle came gliding out to greet us. She was so purely angelic that I sat stunned on one of the stools while Coren, in search of an alternate story, was chatting with a couple of guys at the other end of the bar who'd parked a car and trailer outside, traveling and painting all over, they said, in inviting us to an opening in Monterey during the following week—each with his short and carefully tousled hair combed forward in an Augustus Caesar look and one with his teeth apparently filed in Borneo-headhunter style who'd tell me he thought I had a beautiful voice.

Actually, from watching the beautiful girl and having slept rough in the car, my throat was so constricted while dawdling over my soup that I'd uttered no more than monosyllabic croaks.

But at just that point—as Coren was paying his bill and telling the painters goodbye, another pair of Muscle-Beach types came sauntering in like cops on a neighborhood beat, smirking and greeting the girl. One of them was her brother it seemed and the other, in wire-rim glasses looking as vacuous as Clark Kent, was clearly there to fence her off or maybe to stake a prior claim and, in any case, to let me know—as I'd been advised in the first grade—that my ogling was out of line.

As if aware of my reaction, she held my gaze with a very long stare like the girl on the beach at the end of *La Dolce Vita* and finally uttered a nervous breathless sort of laugh that seemed to be questioning what I'd do. But, reviewing my options and finding none, I paid up in turn and left, sorry I'd never see the girl again.

As we were nearing San Francisco, we heard on the radio that the crisis in Cuba was growing dire with Soviet missiles spotted on ships that were then in the western Atlantic and that JFK had issued an ultimatum. As evening approached in the last long hour of the drive, we saw a strange dark cloud far out over the Pacific resembling a giant hand with its finger like a signpost pointing down at the city. Ten or fifteen minutes passed without it dissolving or changing shape until it was black-on-black and finally lost from view.

"Put that in the story," I said to Coren, thinking of Peter Koch's "it's coming soon" and of the snipers in the arroyo as harbingers of Armageddon.

He made a Bogart-like rasping sound and asked if I'd ever considered what I'd do if I knew the world was going to end five minutes from now. I said I'd need some time to think and by then it would all be over, though what was actually in my mind was Susie at the Big Sur Inn and rewriting that scenario. So I wasn't all that surprised when Coren said that he'd been pondering the matter and decided he'd "just sit on the beach with a woman he loved and watch the sun explode." No wonder we were friends.

I'd include that comment of his in one of my pile of notebooks that, in preparation for my move to Milvia Street, I put in a box along with a lot of my clothes to be shipped back home eventually at the cheapest possible cost. The rest of my things I packed in my massive Samsonite suitcase and lugged to Coren's car while he continued to fill me in about Janet who, to begin with, wasn't at Berkeley merely as a student but was teaching something too, though he wasn't sure what it was.

"As a graduate assistant then?"

"Probably," he said. "But it's also important to understand why she's taking you on as a roommate. You need to know about Fred."

I said we'd gone over that already—I knew she'd been dumped by Fred.

He'd treated her like dirt, Coren pressed on, asking me if I'd noticed her legs.

"Not really," I said.

"They're short and crooked," he told me. "From polio or something. You really hadn't noticed?"

I said I'd found her so intense that I hadn't paid much attention to her looks. I'd thought Rosemary very attractive, though—smart and unassuming in a quietly confident way and, if not exactly beautiful, easy to be around. . . whereas Janet was almost combative. "And resentfully needy," I added, confessing that, having to choose, I wouldn't have opted for her.

"Yeah, well, listen," Coren shrugged as we reached a busier street, "Rosemary has worried a lot about leaving Janet alone. It was her idea for you to move in after she'd left the scene. You need to pay her some attention."

"What sort of attention," I asked.

"Don't play so dumb. She needs to feel attractive."

I said I'd figured that one out, feeling a little queasy.

"You're getting free rent and lots more space. Just be nice to her, okay? She's really broken up."

"So this guy Fred. . . what'd he do to her?"

How Coren knew so much I'd never learn. But Fred had made her hide her legs in black net stockings, he said, whenever they had sex. Then he'd cut out on his Harley hog, sometimes for days at a time. . . and finally, just last week, he'd apparently left for good.

"You knew that, right?" Coren asked.

I said I knew he'd left, of course. The rest I didn't need to know.

"Look!" Coren burst out as we stopped for a light, sounding a little exasperated—which clued me in to the fact that our Damon and Pythias act was wearing a little thin. "We're not talking just mercy humps here. . ."

"But I need to be attentive. I get that, mate." I was ticked off too.

"Good," he nodded. "Good."

"Okay," was my reply.

Then he told me I should also know that, since Fred left, she'd persuaded Leslie Strickland to let her air some obscene and desperate poems over the radio in a bid to win Fred back. According to her account, he'd been a maverick genius, terrified of commitments, who'd showed up on her doorstep one day with nothing but what he was wearing and his bike, and now, impulsively as ever, he'd left to return to a wife and her kids with whom at bottom he couldn't relate. But Janet's friends had offered no help—not Cathy, whom I didn't know, but who'd reportedly married a sadist who'd kicked her in the stomach while she was pregnant, causing her to miscarry and nearly bleed to death; nor Decca Mitford, author of *Hons and Rebels*, who, for all her risky alliances, wanted no part in Janet's emotional life; nor an unnamed English woman who, as a previous roommate in what would become my bedroom in the house on Milvia Street, had at the age of twenty-two relinquished her maidenhead to the accompaniment of Bruckner's 7th and histrionics of her own, ecstatically crying out for days, "It's beautiful! Oh, God, it's beautiful!" That last had occurred when Fred was still around, and maybe her performance had been for him.

"But what Rosemary said about you," Coren concluded his briefing, "was that you're a really nice guy and you could make her feel better. Just keep sharp objects out of her hands if she gets really down."

"Hell is a city much like San Francisco," I said, paraphrasing his fellow Brit.

It was late when we got to Janet's house, so it was only a matter of chatting a bit before turning in for the night. She eyed me carefully as if to gauge my intentions.

Next morning, she'd left early for work, and I was alone in the house when I heard the telephone ring. It was somebody purportedly calling from Aer Lingus who wanted to know if Lady Rosemary was there. Taking it for a hoax, I told him that "Lady Rosemary" had recently flown the coop.

"I beg your pardon!" the voice reproached.

"You're wasting my time," I said as I hung up, ignoring repeated rings.

When Janet got back, I mentioned the call and got a blank look in return.

"Why did you do that?" she asked.

"Do what?" I asked by way of reply.

Rosemary, it seemed, had made previous reservations to fly to Ireland for Christmas, but she'd left early for the Second Coming. I remembered how we'd seen her off and how she'd briefly turned to me and, speaking of my country said, "It's much too young for me" as if she must have concluded it wouldn't be getting much older.

So okay, I said to Janet, Aer Lingus may have called for a reason, but what about the "Lady" bit? That was how I learned, after having known her for two or three years in England and then again in San Francisco, that Rosemary was in fact the daughter of the Marquess of Kildare which, though merely a courtesy title, had put him in line to become the 8th Duke of Leinster with one of the oldest peerages in the land. She'd borne her lineage lightly, but I wondered what else I didn't know, and Janet, with scathing irony, let on that the answer was "plenty," launching into a bitter tirade about the callous unfeeling triflers sightseeing their way through other peoples' lives, ostensibly meaning Fred but also implying Coren and me as if she hadn't been taken in by what I was doing there aside from cadging a place to stay and she wanted it understood from the start that she wasn't to be patronized.

I didn't know how she'd packed so much into a couple of innuendos but, as mating rituals go, it was not only full of anguish and pride but feral to the nth degree. For a guilty split-second or two, I entertained the thought that she must have been reading our notebooks or bugging Coren's car, but I knew it was just a measure of how much brighter and stricken she was than Coren or I had supposed.

I thought she'd leave it at that but, "Here's one for your files," she said, proceeding with an account of a guy I'd met once or twice who was, as I'd been told, the youngest photographer ever to have his work in the Museum of Modern Art's permanent collection. He was also a junkie, Janet said, something I already knew, while his wife was the errant daughter of wealthy socialites—which, of course, I didn't know—and whose baby's first word was cockroach because they were raising it in such squalor that its mother, the socialites' daughter, kept wailing "Cockroaches bad!" to stop it from putting them in its mouth which presumably it did anyhow, and those were the only words it knew before it was nearly two. After waiting a beat or two. "Cockroaches. . . baaaddd!" Janet repeated.

I shook my head with disgust while wondering to myself if things could have been much worse in the Cities of the Plain. I had to say something in reply but didn't feel up to thinking it through, so I simply shrugged and said somewhat nonsensically, "*Je suis le ténébreux, le veuf, l'inconsolé. . .*" at which Janet tossed off a nod as if I'd waved a flag of surrender.

A few days passed after that as Kennedy tried to negotiate with Khrushchev and the Soviets and the risk of a nuclear slip-up grew ever more alarming while I, in a ludicrous parallel, did my best to maintain a détente of my own with Janet, staying mostly in my room, reading whatever I found at hand and drawing up notes and diagrams for my non-existent novel.

I find in the last of my notebooks from that precarious time that my entries grew fewer and terser as if brooding on how shaky my tenancy had become. "Sex in itself is good," I wrote, "but devoid of love it's like Muzak, just rhythm without any meaning." On several occasions I simply copied out passages from books that I'd either bought secondhand or Rosemary had left behind, but they too were very short. One, from James Agee's letters to Father Flye, consisted of no more than, "At moments I wonder whether those who go, as I do, for a Full Life, don't get their exact reward, which is that The Full Life is full of crap." Another, briefer still, recorded a declaration from the poet Li Po that he wasn't, after all, the sort "to remain hidden amid the mugwort."

Neither was I, I thought, awarding that comment an asterisk even without the slightest idea that, among its other properties, mugwort is a mild hallucinogen used in some quarters to combat hysteria and might have been just the thing for my wretched landlady and me in our hellish *No-Exit*-style crisis. I'd reached a dead end again.

But things got steadily worse—both at sea with the Soviet missiles and on Milvia Street with Janet who, noting the toll her anecdotes took in the moments we spent together, found a seemingly grim satisfaction in describing the misery of people I'd met or might have heard about. I thought of how Skinner had goaded me by using racist epithets and, finally—when it was clear that, despite what I'd taken to be a standing invitation, I wasn't going to play the amorous consoler—we had a showdown of sorts that ironically coincided with unconfirmed reports that the Soviets might have blinked.

I'd just put the kettle on for a cup of instant coffee, when she cornered me in the kitchen and, as if she'd been reading my mind and knew I'd reached a point of deep pity for us both, launched into what I thought at first was a manic but pointless diatribe, concluding with a question out of nowhere about what I knew about Skinner and how he'd ruined Linda's life.

"By saving her from suicide?" I asked, puzzled by why she thought I'd care, but newly aware of how small their expat community was.

"By wrecking her marriage," Janet said, all but spitting the words at me. "You didn't know she was married, I guess?" returning to her theme of those who regarded themselves as tourists in the Inferno but also explaining the reference I'd heard about Linda receiving alimony.

What followed was a convoluted but seemingly pointless account of Skinner's maltreatment of Linda prior to my arrival, the sort of thing I'd have put in a notebook before—which may, in fact, have been her point, like tossing a dog a bone just to confirm what it was.

"They'd been renting a place in San Francisco with a man by the name of Glendenning. . . over on Van Ness Street," was how Janet started out while I obligingly listened. Linda's father, whom Janet described as a burly Italian immigrant with bulging eyes looking like Anthony Quinn in *La Strada*, had showed up one Sunday morning, pounding on the door and shouting out "bordello!" as Glendinning kept singing arias in the shower and the doomed dysfunctional couple lay chastely together in bed. An awful row had ensued and a "permanent rupture" of sorts that, by the following Christmas, had become even worse when Linda and Skinner, ruptured or not, had inexplicably stayed at the house of her parents who denounced them both as adulterers because Linda was legally wed to a man in the Navy named Larry whose only polysyllabic phrase was "intestinal fortitude," which he'd allegedly picked up from her and tended to repeat whenever he felt called upon as in, "My wife Linda has intestinal fortitude. . . which, in case you're not aware of it, means guts."

Though Larry was big and dumb, he wasn't abusive, but he often got drunk in bars, screaming out obscenities with "intestinal fortitude" mixed in until they hustled him onto the street or sometimes took him home where he'd gradually quiet down. It wasn't clear when Linda had taken to sleeping around, but Larry's binges grew longer until, on one occasion, he'd gone AWOL for a month during which Linda met up with Skinner and a relationship began that led to a confrontation in which Larry, three sheets to the wind, hit Skinner in the mouth—both Skinner and Willie Holst, in unrelated incidents, had been hit in the mouth, it seemed, with orthodontic consequences—after which Larry, all but comatose, was put on a train by Linda with the name of his ship on a tag about his neck and she, having moved in by then with the freakily celibate Skinner, got some sort of mail-order divorce, though not in the Church's eyes, which was all that mattered to her mother.

It was clear to me as Janet droned that she was wielding her monologue as a deliberate act of aggression, demanding that I hear it out and perhaps even write it down—as, of course, I did anyhow.

"That was when Charles showed up from Baffin Island," she said, scarcely pausing for breath as she cut to something I already knew while adding that, for Skinner at least, Charles had a special *éclat* because as a classmate at Oxford—at Univ, according to her—he'd been unabashedly gay and reportedly had a brilliant mind, though he'd never spoken a word in anybody's hearing.

There were other factors at play as well, such as Charles' mother's decision to marry a man Charles' age as Skinner's own father had done to a girl who was even younger plus the fact that, when Charles had appeared years later at Skinner's door, he'd just had his pocket picked by a Black girl he'd met en route who was pregnant by another Univ man who'd been a classmate of theirs, a Belgian-Persian harelip who went by the name of Basu, leaving Charles bereft of whatever he'd earned while icebound in the far north, a setback that he'd addressed by giving a televised interview that Skinner had somehow arranged, proving thereby that Charles was only mute as an exercise of will, and, in the aftermath, he'd bedded down promptly with Linda and just as quickly departed.

"Charles did," Janet emphasized. "Charles was the one who departed."

"You're sure the harelip wasn't a destitute Mexican homosexual named Napo?"

"Whatever gave you that idea?"

"These stories get very convoluted. . . but why bother recounting all this?" I asked, hoping to slow her down. "It's got nothing to do with either of us or what might soon turn out to be the end of the fucking world."

She smiled dismissively and explained that Fred had been on one of his walkabouts, and "I was chasing Basu too at the time but ended up with you."

And then it occurred to me that, so far from not being patronized, she'd expected nevertheless to be wanted and taken to bed or merely that I would try—but I'd reneged on playing the gigolo, and what she was laying on me in return was that I'd turned out to be no more than another deadbeat Skinner.

Then she doggedly continued as if she hadn't yet finished unloading on me. "There was also Melinda, remember her? The oversized folksinger nobody wanted to sleep with, who was keen on Jim Glendinning and wandered around North Beach singing in coffee houses."

I remembered Melinda, all right, who wasn't that oversized and had been in her way quite beautiful, I thought—though it had apparently been true that nobody wanted to sleep with her. She'd had the hots for Glendinning and was nearly as tall to boot in addition to having a nice contralto voice. To keep up with all the characters took a scorecard, but we'd gotten it down to two. She stopped and looked at me. The challenge was out in the open.

"Well?" she said.

"I think," I replied as if musing out loud, "I might ship out on a freighter."

She narrowed her eyes.

"Norwegian," I specified because it came back to mind that Skinner had declared they wouldn't require a union card.

"That would be good," she said. "Don't overstay your welcome here."

"Right," I said. "I won't."

And that was decided, though when I afterwards combed through the phonebook looking for Norwegian freighters, all I managed to turn up was the Seafarers Union in Oakland, where I thought I could get directions at least.

So, early the next morning, I set out like Herman Melville, but only to find the offices still closed—whereupon I went to the public library instead, intending to scan the *Chronicle* for any freighter ads as well as bits of nautical news I could use in an interview. That intention took me to the reference room where, on my way to the newspaper racks, I passed the *Oxford Dictionary of Quotations* and, recalling my tutor's parting advice about my Snark becoming a Boojum—which, despite being vaguely aware that it must be from Lewis Carroll, I'd never gotten around to looking up—I stopped to pluck it down and study it at a table. It sounds impossibly neat, I know, but that was how I discovered what Bam had actually meant. "For then," the quatrain ended,

> You will softly and suddenly vanish away
> And never be met with again!

It was, in effect, an oracular revelation, all the stronger because of its source. "Well, I'll be damned!" I said out loud as two Asian American girls seated across the table looked first at me and then at the librarian who'd just instructed them to stop their incessant giggling, prompting one of the girls to say to the other, "It's only because we're Orientals," referring to themselves in a way I'd thought taboo. The librarian also looked sternly at me but returned to what he'd been doing while I sat there wholly absorbed in my thoughts, trying to riddle out what I'd just read.

It occurred to me that, though most of those I'd met in my bargain-priced season in hell had probably also arrived with hopes of bagging their snarks, they'd been floundering on a precipice over which many had toppled or were dangling in mid-air while I myself had been at the very brink up until that very moment—and despite my wildly mixed metaphors, I belatedly understood that freedom lies less in having no boundaries at all than in earning the right to choose them for ourselves, which some would call growing up. Rosemary, like Jill, had pointed the way, and Janet had showed me the door.

I went to the newspaper rack and snagged the Oakland paper. In scanning the personal ads, I saw one seemingly put there for me: "Wanted," it began. "Someone to drive a late-model Volvo from Oakland to Jacksonville, Florida, November 1-3. All expenses paid plus other considerations." It was magically signed "J. Getty," and, once again—though that very day was the first— I could unmistakably hear the sound of destiny knocking.

I probably need to explain why the name J. Getty had leapt up so from the page. Now remembered mainly for his museum if not for his many marriages, J. Paul Getty was reputedly at the time the richest man in the world. He had lots of West Coast connections, though he'd once been a student at Oxford himself and was currently living in Britain. Furthermore, he was also notorious for his frugality, so it all seemed to fit together. I'd drive his car to Jacksonville, after which he'd probably say, "I like your face, kid—keep the car. . . and here's a million for your trouble."

Because it was still early morning, I hoped, if the ad hadn't been running for days, I might be the first to respond—as, in fact, I apparently was. The man who answered the phone gave me precise directions, saying in a peremptory way that he'd like to get his Volvo on the road as soon as he possibly could. I told him I'd need an hour or so, went back to Berkeley to pack things up, left a note on a table for Janet, and was out from under the mugwort for good.

As things turned out, it wasn't J. Paul or one of his errant sons but a hulking oafish man with tangled and matted hair atop a lopsided head. He told me he'd be a passenger on the ride, which I hadn't counted on—but, knowing all bridges behind me were burned, I agreed to his newly stated terms. He put a small bag in the trunk, and we were underway.

We weren't even out of Oakland before a clash of opinions arose, mainly about politics. I'd been making innocuous small talk intending to be amusing but found him slow and humorless in an ultra-Bircherite way, stubbornly disagreeing with any position I took. I'd initially replied with witty light-hearted retorts, though it was like debating an ox—and even when I conceded points to engage him at his own level, he merely repeated what he'd said in a sluggish emphatic way that verged on being belligerent.

He had a lot of rote phrases that he seemed to have memorized, telling me that the problem with "reactive" thinkers like me was that we always missed the larger point. What mattered was intuition of a mind-and-body sort along with an "auditing out" of what was obstructing its flow, something he'd learned, he told me, from Dianetics. I asked what Dianetics was and learned that he'd formerly been a disciple of A.E. van Vogt, the science fiction writer, who was teamed up with a man called L. Ron Hubbard about whom I knew nothing. He said they'd taught him how to liberate his mind in a way that made us know-it-all east coast elites completely irrelevant, but then he'd had an accident while working under his Chevy. The jack had slipped, and one end of the car had fallen on his head, after which doctors became alarmed because his brain was hemorrhaging, though van Vogt had declared no expert advice was needed because his problems were psychosomatic. When he went with the doctors' opinion, van Vogt had written him off—since when, J. Getty let on, he'd been feeling a little off.

"A *little*," he said again with a quick defensive look.

I decided to tone my cleverness down, and, after a few minutes more, he told me that we'd need to make our trip non-stop. I didn't argue then but, somewhere in New Mexico, I confessed I was getting exhausted and couldn't go any farther—

at which he reached into his pocket and produced a large blue
pill.

"What is it?" I asked.

"It'll help you drive."

"Why don't you take the wheel for a while?" I suggested. I
didn't really want him to, but hoped he'd agree to let me get some
rest.

"I'm not supposed to," was his answer, and I didn't argue
with that. Instead, I swallowed the pill, which was clearly a big
mistake.

I was instantly wide awake, though I wasn't inclined to talk
because such unsettling reactions were rocketing through my
head. So for hundreds of miles along the empty moonlit road with
me tuning in and out, J. Getty continued his ponderous
monologue, primarily talking about himself and musing on how
he'd lately become a very active patriot because our communist
foes enjoyed too great an advantage. When somebody in the
Kremlin made a costly mistake, he got quietly liquidated while
meanwhile here at home, in similar situations, traitors were being
promoted.

As dawn was breaking somewhere in the desert, he told me
that was the reason why, during the recent missile crisis—which
had ended only the day before—they'd had two of their best men
on JFK at virtually every turn "just in case it was necessary."

With that snapping me to attention, I told him it sounded
preposterous, so he elaborated. After giving up Dianetics at about
the time van Vogt gave up on it too, he'd decided to join what
sounded to me like an assassination cult that, on alternate Sunday
mornings, went up into the hills to practice their marksmanship,
popping the necks off bottles using telescopic sights. He was
screwy enough for me to suppose some parts of his story were
true, but I didn't believe him about the surveillance team
supposedly in D.C. and must have told him so because he
demanded that I pull over and stop right where we were.

I did, and we got out, and there in a Texas desert devoid of
noise or motion except for the sighing of oil rigs pumping like
giant dunking birds, I watched him lift a false bottom in the trunk
and peel back panels on the insides of the doors, revealing a

rolling arsenal of rifles and ammunition along with hand grenades.

I couldn't think straight at that point. The pills had wound my springs too tight, but I understood well enough that, whatever the truth of what he'd been telling me, I was definitely in that car with a possibly dangerous sociopath. In Louisiana, at roughly two o'clock, I started to hallucinate about gliding under giant trees that were letting in tiny specks of light, and I told J. Getty that I was afraid I might wreck the car. He agreed to stop at a motel, and I got a couple of hours of sleep before we started out again.

It was midway across the state of Georgia, after resuming our conversation and popping another pill, that I also understood, in a very confusing way, that I'd started to lose our debate. I'd conceded too much ground, it seemed, and his tortoise was passing my hare. But I didn't care—my mind was trashed.

We finally got to Jacksonville where I drove us to the Greyhound station, retrieved my bag from his car and watched J. Getty gliding away with drivers-ed aplomb. I had one more leg to go on a seemingly weapon-free bus during which I was able to doze until, in mid-afternoon, I was in Columbia again with my east-west odyssey done. In a couple of days I'd learn that, by sheer coincidence, I'd been in Jacksonville at the same time as my grandfather's closest friend, a physician named Heyward Gibbes who'd been a mentor to me and something of a maverick too as was evinced by the fact that his favorite book was *Tristram Shandy* and that in early middle age he'd owned the first known private movie camera anywhere in the state—with which he'd produced that cinematic trove including my mother and his daughter in their teens. He'd made his trip in less commodious style than I in J. Getty's Volvo, though it was all he required because, true to his free-thinking ways, he'd issued instructions for cremation when he died, a practice still so rare in the South that Jacksonville had the nearest legal pyre.

There were other things going on as I was now an uncle and there were people I wanted to see—one of them in particular, with whom I got wholly engrossed. So, caught up with such concerns, I failed to let Coren know how returning home had gone, but after about a month, I got a US Postal card, meticulously typed with images and ideas like buckshot from a gun.

Deducing from the postmark that he was in Berkeley still and from its explosive content that he was perfecting a style combining the Joyce of *Finnegan's Wake* with S.J. Perelman at his peak, I was amused to find his hundred-twenty-word paroxysm, addressing me as Kurt, was from a character named Werner invented for one of our dialogues, a maniacally learned Anglo-German polymath who, sun-stricken during the war with either Rommel's Afrika Korps or Monty's 8th Army in Egypt— he can't remember which—is as harmless and mad as a hatter.

"How now, Ole Mole?" the message begins, alluding to Hamlet addressing his father's ghost,

> Happy 1963, of course, but why do I not hear? I have fears of sandcaked lips grinning at the sun beside a burnt out Volvo. And did your clothes arrive? Are you vielleicht bei Uncle Sam, Kurt? Mit vollgepackt Achselgeträg und bb gun? Things are excellent here. I am finally winning at solitaire, and am busy embroidering the roof of my mouth, so es kommt few demands on lyf. Swich fyn harhar! I am writing a play in English. Candy sends her love; we are to be married next week & shall honeymoon in Oakland. Leslie has gone mad. Write. KPFA has been subpoenaed. Did you read about it? Bad thing. Write. In ranks of deth etc.

After that crazed mélange of banalities mixed with pseudo-Elizabethan spelling and allusions in various ancient and modern tongues that dart from my recent cross-country trip to the local news in Berkeley, Werner's signoff is stamped and sealed with a typed red-ribboned emoji.

The Stanford Daily's lead story for that day had, in fact, reported that Leslie Strickland had responded to a subpoena from the Senate Internal Security Committee by saying, "We are completely confounded by the investigation of our station. We can only speculate on the reasons for the hearings," although some suspected the charges had been prompted by a story lampooning J. Edgar Hoover, and *The New York Times* had opined not only that the station's "worst sin appears to have been the dissemination of offbeat ideas" but that the subcommittee's harassment seemed designed to enforce "a concept of speech that is pleasing rather than free." That hand we'd seen in the sky had been pointing in our direction after all.

There was an even more distressing footnote some twenty years after that when I met up with Coren in London and asked about the expatriate Brits we'd known in those rootless West Coast days. He reminded me that Rosemary had been right—we'd truly been on the edge of a nuclear holocaust. "Those silo doors were open," he said.

I agreed that we'd been blandly naïve. "But what about Janet Dawson?" I asked.

"Ah, Jan. . ." he answered. "That was sad."

"Janet, not Jan," I corrected him. "Jan Dawson writes for *Sight & Sound*. . . the best reviewer they've got."

"But they're the same," he told me. "When she came home, she shortened her name."

"Well, that's amazing! I'll look her up."

"She just committed suicide. Two years ago, I think—or the year before that. It's really sad."

"Awful," I said, remembering our time together in that weirdly hothouse *Inferno*. She'd deserved much better than that.

"Rosemary?" I asked.

"She married but got a divorce when the world didn't end."

"And what about Jill?"

He wasn't sure.

We were sitting at the big oval-shaped Punch Table with the famous initials carved all over its surface. Alan was then the magazine's editor, and, during the raucous staff lunch that followed, I once again, as I'd done with Alan Bennett a couple of decades before, held forth too much myself to savor the verbal fireworks on display.

When we were the last two in the room, we talked about other friends including Kristofferson who'd become so famous by then as a singer, songwriter, and movie star. Then I told him about a visit I'd had in October 1963, during my first year at Harvard.

An old friend of mine from Sewanee—who'd later become a novelist but was working for Bobby Kennedy for the nonce in the Attorney General's office—had come up for a visit from D.C., and we'd talked about the things we'd done since graduating from college. Eventually, I'd recounted the story of my encounter with J. Getty, and, in another month or so, an FBI agent had come to call, questioning me for an hour about J. Getty and his cult. JFK had been assassinated only a few weeks before but, though I'd never learn if there was any connection, it was further confirmation that the craziness wasn't over. Neither Coren nor I had ever supposed it would be.

11

Marriage and the Mob

Maybe it's true that, as a pattern-detecting species, we overrate coincidence, regarding it as a sign of destiny at work—though it's generally only in retrospect that we become aware of it, too late for all but irony. Had I known that Dr. Gibbes and I reached Jacksonville concurrently or that that I'd arrived in San Francisco just as Kerouac's *Big Sur* was coming into print, depicting his lurid nosedive in Ferlinghetti's cabin, would awareness of either have altered anything? That seems highly unlikely to me—and yet, if I'd known of the triple convergence of my returning home on the day that, halfway around the world, my cousin Hope was saying goodbye for good to Ginsberg and his crew on the Howrah Station platform in Calcutta, and that, at the exact same time, her astrological twin, the Athena-like Anne Boyd, had come home for a Christmas break from her job at a bank in Manhattan. . . I'd have said it *had* to mean something, if only by revealing what I'd really been hoping to find.

All it took was a sybil-like utterance from my mother telling me Anne was in town, and I was off to see her. I was still committed to my great-leap-forward workout regimen and, in an unusually warm December, wore what I hoped she'd recognize as English cricket attire consisting of white duck trousers and an open-collar white shirt with my Wadham summer sweater tied loosely about my neck—altogether, I thought, a dashing and casual look. But no sooner had I arrived than, having finished Harvard Law School and joined Anne's father's firm, my former Jamboree tentmate and fellow Sewanee alum, Kirk Finlay, showed up as well and, giving me a once-over, asked with his usual acerbic wit if I was now selling ice cream.

Stung but undeterred, I asked Anne to join me for dinner that evening and, though dining options in town were limited back then, I booked a table for two at the Forest Motel which, when I'd last bothered to ask during my undergraduate years, had been said to be the best of the sorry lot—but not anymore, we learned. The waitress licked her thumb after plunging it into my salad and, as for the filets mignons, we could have done with a chainsaw. . . though, because of my change of costume, much worse was still to come after I'd driven Anne home.

In addition to souvenirs like my Wadham scarf and sweater, I'd brought home with me from abroad the exact sartorial equivalent of the meal we'd just tried to consume—a pricey American knock-off of a baggy Harris tweed suit that I'd taken to Oxford but never worn because it looked like what it was, a pseudo-Englishman's attire that no native would ever wear. But doubling down on my cricketer pose and despite the unseasonable weather, I'd decided to wear the suit that night and, after we'd returned to Anne's house, assumed an urbanely nonchalant pose with my elbow on the mantelpiece in front of a festive fire. Anne's mother was a traditionalist, so the fire and air conditioning were probably going at once, though inside my baggy tweeds it was hot enough to bake bread.

Literally warming to the occasion, I was in the midst of a clever remark when I noticed the floor was rushing up towards my face. When I came to, I did indeed feel like a half-risen loaf of something yanked from an oven, though I quickly recovered all but my dignity and, making hasty apologies, drove just as speedily home and started to throw up—no doubt thanks in part to the waitress's thumb.

Next morning, my mother asked how the evening before had gone. She knew that, even amidst other girlfriends with Anne a full year older and attending a different school, I'd carried a torch for her and even told her so during a house party at the beach in the spring before leaving for college when we'd climbed up into the moss-draped limbs of a spectacular old live-oak and, surprised by my own impulsiveness, I'd suddenly blurted out, "You know I've always loved you!" to which she'd calmly replied with the faintest hint of a shrug, "Well, what can I say?" I'd said it was simply a fact, that's all, and that would have to be that. But now, as I told my mother, I feared I'd blown it again. . . though, just as I was saying so, the telephone rang downstairs, and, less than a minute later, I heard my mother thanking Anne for being so concerned, adding I must have picked up a bug but was feeling much better already.

Taking Anne's call as a signal, I asked her out on another date, which went far better than our first. We kissed and meant it at last, and I was thinking I'd like to pursue things further when she looked me in the eyes and asked if I was really serious—"because," she said in a no-nonsense way, "I've got a rent-controlled apartment in New York, and I'm not risking it on a whim."

I realized that I'd caught my heart's desire and didn't know what to do with it. "Is this a proposal?" I jokingly asked, but Anne's expression didn't change.

"Okay," I said, "give me twenty-four hours to work things out."

In twenty-four hours, I'd applied to Harvard, the Peace Corps, and the medical school down in Charleston while also arranging with the local University of South Carolina to teach a night school class during the spring semester while taking a couple of graduate courses in English and Russian literature. Then, before Anne had returned to her Park Avenue job at First National City, I asked her to marry me and afterwards, in courtly fashion, asked permission from her father who was a man of utter probity and very little chitchat, like Beowulf in a business suit. He assured me that his daughter was a good girl with a more than adequate mind but added as a word to the wise, "If you cross her, though, she's mean as a snake."

As a fellow Southerner, I understood what he meant. If I ever did her dirty, it would be war to the third or fourth generation like the Hatfields and McCoys. I nodded and told him I loved her, which I did and always had—for, as I said and subsequently jotted down in a journal, love's not what you feel for a moment but what you do over many years. I meant it, of course. . . though, like so many things we think we know at the time, it's often long after we've made such grandiose declarations that we learn what they really involve.

So it was that, suddenly on the brink of that commitment but without any second thoughts, I reminisced about others I'd loved or thought I'd loved for weeks or months or, in one case, years and all the entrancing might-have-beens that blinked for a dazzling moment and vanished like shooting stars—including the girl on Nantucket at summer's end on a rainy cool night in the harbor when we stripped down to our skivvies and swam out to a little boat bobbing about in the dark, laughing and swigging brandy snitched from a shelf in the cockpit and shivering with an awareness of what might happen next but didn't for reasons neither of us would regret; or the bright-eyed girl in Manhattan with whom I sat in friendship deeper than desire, holding each other in our arms in a grassy hideaway just north of the U.N., watching the barges' red and green lights drift past a Nabisco sign that was throbbing across the river; or the girl with whom I'd shared a consanguineous kiss as we paused from running through orchard trees on an island not far from Dubrovnik and stood locked in an embrace while the towering freighter we'd raced to see slipped by in a deep narrow channel no more than ten meters away. . . Circe, Calypso, Nausicaa, all preludes to my coming home!

I heard first from the medical school that I must have been out of my mind to apply without any MCAT scores or the courses required for admission. "Your loss," I sniffed a day or two later with two other letters in hand, one of them from the Peace Corps, then barely one year old, offering a slot in Nigeria but only if I was single, and the other from Harvard's graduate school, awarding a full scholarship commencing in the fall with marriage not an issue—so the choice was simple, and I took it.

With that whirlwind of details worked out, Anne returned to New York for a month prior to coming home again for our matrimonial marathon. We were married on the 8th of June with hundreds of invited guests, most of them friends of our parents, and trunkloads of wedding gifts which my highly practical father-in-law, knowing we'd have little use for them over the next few years, packed up in shipping barrels where many would remain for three or four decades to come. They ranged from wastebaskets, ashtrays, and bowls to what might have ransomed an Inca king—though once the nuptial dust had settled, what we had as cash on hand was a hundred twenty-five bucks plus my former Nantucket summer job and a 1951 Mercury, which had stood like a sentinel in our driveway since my grandfather's death in January. Like everything he'd possessed but his heart, it was still in stellar condition, and I felt his presence under the hood like a familial Saint Christopher.

So, despite our paucity of liquid assets, the stars seemed well enough aligned as we blithely "saw" Rock City after detouring through Sewanee on our way up to Cape Cod, where I was once again to be billed as a Green Line "native driver" for bus tours and taxi rides while Anne, whose job at First National City job had mostly consisted of greeting a handful of the bank's wealthiest depositors on a floor off-limits to others ("Why, good morning, Mister Onassis, how lovely to see you again!"), soon got herself hired as a bar maid at a new and supposedly posh hotel inauspiciously called The White Elephant.

Things started out well for her because few cocktails could be ordered that she wasn't familiar with, but a Lothario on the permanent staff made a pass at her one night and, outraged bridegroom that I was, I staged a melodramatic scene complete with a butcher knife and dire Italian curses, severing that connection.

Actually, though brandished merely as a prop, the knife in question had been so ready to hand because, for a virtual pittance, we'd rented an empty restaurant formerly known as The Lighthouse which, with a ten-foot red-and-white replica of the Sankaty Head original looming beside its door, took on a risibly Dadaist air compounded by its interior where a single enormous dining room had been emptied of everything but a solitary table along with eight tubular padded chairs and an incongruous double bed shoved up against a partition behind which lay a largely non-functional industrial-scale kitchen with dimensions like a Pullman car. Among the few operative means of preparing meals other than the aforementioned butcher knife were plastic glasses and plates along with a midget refrigerator, a double-eyed hotplate lying atop a decommissioned blast-furnace stove and, in lieu of a tub or shower, two capacious metal sinks for acrobatic splash baths.

On the more positive side, each of us had a clearly designated toilet and, because the restaurant's address was 73 Pleasant Street on what was then the edge of town, we had only to slip out of our front door and cross the little-traveled road to find ourselves in a spacious butterfly-haunted field—though, unhappily, around mid-summer, a noisy traveling fair was permitted to set up there, and, for what seemed a very long time, we had to endure the death-defying routine of "Thamar the Impossible" or something of the sort who, despite the origin of the name, turned out to be a man whose act consisted of climbing a sky-high flexible pole each night and, to the repeated recorded strains of Nat King Cole's "Fascination," swaying back and forth in an arc that seemingly took him over our roof while a spotlight followed his metronomic stunts and Portuguese fishermen sat on our stoop drinking and applauding as if Thamar was a relative of theirs—which wasn't wholly out of the question—creating a sonic illusion for us as we lay together in bed that they'd somehow entered the premises and were, with equal enthusiasm, commending our conjugality. So it went for one largely sleepless night after another during Thamar's seemingly endless two-week run, like a *son-et-lumière* of the London blitz with a slamming and banging of carnival rides in the background and searchlights raking the clouds while, over the low-pitched muttering of those camped out on our steps, an emcee's urgent bulletins kept intruding on our embraces.

When the fair had moved on at last, vast numbers of monarch butterflies, presumably headed towards Mexico, once more took over the field. So with Nabokov in mind on a rare free afternoon, I decided to capture a specimen and, as a memento for my wife, mount it on velvet and frame it. My first steps were buying some cheesecloth and taping it to a coat hanger refashioned into a hoop, then attaching that to a broomstick. Next I went to buy some chloroform, but, wearing my Green Line uniform, got questioned by the druggist concerning my intentions (as in "Heiress Kidnapped by Non-Native Driver") and, after I'd explained, was obliged to settle for something less lethal that smelled like Listerine.

In any event, because the butterfly swarms were so dense, I netted a large black-and-yellow specimen in a second and conveyed it back to The Lighthouse and my waiting if dubious wife. But it was like trying to kill Rasputin—when the pseudo-chloroform failed to work, I tried depriving it of oxygen by putting lit matches beside it under a glass bowl, though just when I thought I'd succeeded, I'd lift the bowl to check and it would feebly start thrashing its wings again. Finally, in desperation, I stabbed it with a hatpin, hating myself for doing so, and in a bitter finale, disposing of its mutilated corpse, feeling as if I'd strangled one of the muses while my wife discreetly kept her thoughts to herself.

But that wasn't my worst debacle of the summer as, accompanied by my endlessly patient wife, I went to the Hospital Thrift Shop—again in my Green Line uniform—hoping to find some interesting cast-off books. But shortly after entering, my eyes fell on a glass-topped case in which, amid some floridly engraved flat silver, I spotted a pair of serving spoons. Then, squinting to read them, I indignantly howled, "These were stolen from my family!" A pair of Nantucket ladies raced at once to the ruckus, but nothing they did or said could allay my righteous rage.

"F-T-W?" I theatrically told my wife. "Those initials stand for what? For Francis Thornton West! And he was my great-great-grandfather!"

The ladies looked truly distressed, though my wife kept pulling my sleeve.

"Ah, no, my dear!" I shook her off. "It's a matter of ill-gotten plunder. Yankee vandals stole these spoons from our old place in Virginia. All we had left was a punch ladle."

I held the two ladies transfixed as a third arrived to hear me out.

"How much more of this loot have you got?" I ranted. "I'll buy every piece in the store!"

The ladies scurried about, turning up one more piece and apologizing to me for not finding any more. I bought the spoons at a bargain price and, only after we'd gotten outside, did Anne irately hiss in my ear, "Why wouldn't you listen?" She grabbed a spoon. "You read this monogram upside down. What it says is MLJ!"

"It does?" I asked, but she was right. I could never go back there again, I thought, though our unborn children would someday inherit the spoons.

I settled down after that for the better part of a blunder-free month, at the end of which I returned to the thrift shop after all— slightly disguised by a long overdue haircut while decked out in yacht-club mufti and affecting a Long Island accent. I was browsing about for things we could take to Cambridge for the unfurnished apartment there that Reeve Parker had helped us find, having himself gone straight to Harvard after Nike and encouraged me to follow.

There were all sorts of items in the shop that caught my eye—like a handsomely framed engraving of a painting by Thomas Cole from his series *The Voyage of Life* in which an adventurous youth, oblivious of the choppy waters ahead, sets forth alone in a skiff towards a visionary goal. Except for adding a passenger in my boat, it seemed ironically to the point, so I tossed it in with more mundane stuff that at once won Anne's approval because all that we'd managed to transport from home and leave for safekeeping with Reeve was some bookcases and a bed.

Thus it happened that several days later, as naïvely as the voyager in the painting, I crossed with Anne on the ferry to Woods Hole with a sideboard and a dining room table strapped to the roof of our car along with other movables including a captain's chair plus a trio of silver spoons, looking very much like a vandal myself or a Frenchmen retreating from Moscow lugging a plundered armoire. It all would serve us well in our four small second-floor rooms on picturesque tree-shaded Gray Street, luxurious digs on the whole marred only by a guitarist who practiced and sang overhead, unfailingly off-key.

Anne got a teaching job at a private school in Brookline, and I signed up for courses by Douglas Bush, Harry Levin, Jerome H. Buckley, and Walter Jackson Bate—names that, in those now-distant days, rolled like thunder across the Charles. On a fairly regular basis, I also attended lectures by Perry Miller, bumped into John Kenneth Galbraith at a newsstand near Harvard Square, and rubbed elbows with Robert Lowell who'd eye me with a quizzical look before sliding away at an angle. I developed a special kinship with Alan Heimert who, though less than a decade older, had been Perry Miller's protégé and, as a still youthful professor, oversaw my study of Southern history & lit, a subject I'd afterwards teach there as well while, in a different pursuit, I myself became a protégé of Alan's colleague Jack Bate in whose seminar on Keats I managed to enroll just as his magnum opus on Keats' life and work was coming into print.

Bate, who always entered the seminar room like a boxer from his corner in a crouch, had a critical acumen both razor-sharp and deeply humane. He was an inveterate bachelor, but, when I introduced him to my aunt—a Wellesley alum who, in her lovely solicitous way, had represented for me as I've noted before, the most widely read person I knew—Bate saw that she was appointed to the Radcliffe Board of Visitors and during its annual meetings, held dinners for her in Eliot House, maintaining what I somewhat romantically took to be *une amitié amoreuse* about which neither I nor my uncle need feel the least discomfort.

Most importantly for me, Bate, Heimert, and Perry Miller shared a conviction with the other great teachers of literature with whom I'd studied that, despite the decree of a still ascendant New Criticism that the exercise of their trade "must become more scientific, precise, and systematic," they'd been called to be much more than analytical technicians. To paraphrase something Bate once said, reading a poem well isn't like taking a shower, just a matter of turning the knobs and letting it issue forth. It should be a collaborative act, "like performing a Mozart sonata, using whatever we know and feel to bring it fully to life." That seemed agreeably romantic to me, demanding of us as students that we be both mirror and lamp.

When I repeated all that to my wife, she said, "So it's like a recipe, then."

"In a way," I politely replied—though, when I repeated what she'd said to Alan and Arlene Heimert over my first encounter with both moo shu pork and hot and sour soup at Joyce Chen's restaurant, Alan gallantly observed that all his best ideas had come from his wife as well.

With such Olympian mentors at hand, I was as fortunate at Harvard as I'd been at Oxford—and at Sewanee too at that earlier stage of finding a path to follow. As far as critical doctrine went, we were in a trough between waves of change which sometimes seemed to result in a sort of persnickety zeal among non-tenured professors. I encountered one such instructor whose insistence on an absurdly pedantic *explication de texte* prompted me to respond with an equally preposterous *reductio ad absurdum*—a twenty-eight-page dissection of a single three-line sentence by Sir Thomas Browne which, though worthy of *The Harvard Lampoon*, earned me a gullible commendation for my apparent conversion coupled with a gratuitous dismissal of my former Oxford tutor, Lord David Cecil, as "rather too fruity for me."

Ironically enough, given how competitive admission to any of the more prestigious seminars could be, Harry Levin would welcome me into his because of Cecil's imprimatur. As the Irving Babbitt Professor of Comparative Literature, he himself was like a last surviving column of the New Humanistic temple, fastidiously aloof from the fray of critical fashion and, in the classroom at least, more impressive for breadth than depth. Though we'd actually met more than five years before I enrolled in his course on Utopia and the Golden Age, I didn't suppose he'd remembered that other than looking at times as if he almost had.

That encounter had occurred during the summer of 1958 when I stayed with two of my Camden cousins in Cambridge— to which they'd been removed for a number of reasons, including death threats by the Klan that I've reported before. One afternoon while there, I accompanied my cousin Sam, the future novelist, to look up a girl he'd met in school whose resonant name was Marina—derived, as I assumed, from Shakespeare's *Pericles* or T.S. Eliot's poem or maybe from both or neither by her famously erudite father who was, as I already knew, the author of nearly a dozen books, including one I'd read at Sewanee about Hawthorne, Melville, and Poe. At some point during our visit, I casually said to Marina that, as an English major, I greatly admired her father's work.

"Would you like to meet him?" she asked.

I said I definitely would, and she led us through a series of rooms and into an unlit corridor, tapping lightly on a closed door at its end. Without a word being spoken, the pocket-door panel slid open to reveal a mandarin-like figure resembling a Madame

Tussaud's display of which I can recall only his dapper moustache below a serenely incurious gaze and a silken red *robe de chambre* over his trousers, shirt, and tie. If any courtesies were exchanged other than my name, I have no recollection of them and after a brief silence, the door slid shut again and the audience was over.

When I found myself in his very wide-ranging seminar, I produced a long and, to my mind, very Levinian study of similar motifs in Southern history and letters and, because it was based on such a large number of works with all my references noted in the text, my bibliography at its end simply listed the books along with the pages in my essay where citations had occurred. It was a last-minute shortcut at a time before computers had made such compilations easy, though I still expected unstinting praise instead of what I got when my essay was returned with no comments of any kind except on the bibliography, which Levin declared inadequate as if the whole assignment had merely been a style-sheet exercise. . . or more likely, as I thought in a snit, it was all he'd bothered to read.

He had a point, of course, but it struck me as picayunish and ended all thought of pursuing comp lit if he was the guardian at its gate. I'd be better off, I concluded, with the guys who hailed from Chicago like Heimert and Perry Miller who ruled the Warren House roost in the company of Jack Bate of Makato, Minnesota, where Sinclair Lewis had written *Main Street*. It would never have crossed my mind that Harry Levin himself was also from Minnesota.

Meanwhile, across the Charles, the so-called Boston Strangler was still at his grisly work, and the body count was growing. It was in that alarming context that late one Saturday night, after hearing shrill screams outside from somewhere below in the street, I once again, as if by conditioned reflex, grabbed a long-bladed butcher knife and rushed to the victim's rescue. As best I could later discover, a young woman had been going towards or returning from an adulterous tryst on foot when she'd been caught in the headlights of somebody else's car as it turned into a driveway. She'd been taking a shortcut of her own and, finding herself lit up between the car and its garage, had frozen and started to scream before she recovered her wits and ran back the way she'd come.

Unluckily for me, by the time I reached the street, she was nowhere to be seen while, from windows and porches nearby, a half dozen bright-beamed flashlights were probing the shadowy scene. . . and I was what they revealed, clutching a knife in my hand.

"I thought there was someone in trouble," I sheepishly called out.

My neighbors were unimpressed and tended to look away whenever I nodded in passing, even long after the Strangler was caught and put away.

A few weeks later, in late November, I was working at home on a borrowed desk that belonged to my cousin Virginia when, in the midst of a broadcast of *Fidelio* on public radio, a voice broke in with the news that President Kennedy had been shot while on a visit to Houston. Boston and Cambridge went into shock and, the following day when the outcome had been confirmed, Perry Miller, whom JFK had praised as his favorite professor at Harvard, broke down at the start of his class and sat there blubbering like a child while everyone quietly left the amphitheater.

Stunned like everyone else, Anne and I went to a drug store nearby on Mass Ave where we could watch the coverage on TV as a pall fell over everything and people were kinder to each other. Less than three weeks later, Perry Miller died as well. He was only 58, just 12 years older than JFK.

Five additional months dragged by. We still had no TV—and no time to watch one if we had—but, as classes were ending late in the spring, we decided we'd saved enough to buy a KLH, a portable hi-fi record player made just a few blocks away, and we had enough left over to buy a couple of record sets—one of them a Julius Baker compilation of Bach's flute-and-harpsichord sonatas. I opened the windows and listened ecstatically, and later that afternoon, with the music still ringing in my ears, we drove in our Merc with Reeve and his new wife Pat and a couple of other friends to swim in the Waltham reservoir. That was a mild transgression, but the friendship and the weather and the Bach sonatas waiting at home made swimming illegally under the moon seem worth whatever it cost.

As things turned out, the cost would include having the whole left side of our car rolled up like the lid of a sardine can as a hit-and-run driver sped away. Astoundingly, no one was hurt, but our apartment had been sublet beginning at noon the following day when, according to best-laid plans, we'd be heading for a freebie summer back in our native state—but not, it seemed, without major repairs. We managed to rattle our way to A&J Body Repair on Beacon Street in Somerville but couldn't have driven much farther.

When we got an estimate in the morning, it was four hundred fifty bucks just for putting the Merc on the road with inoperative windows and doors on the driver's side. That was more than its blue book value but less than the cheapest used car that could get us safely home and was, unhappily, a huge amount for us. Our insurance company offered us two-fifty max with no immediate pay-out date, and, though the police in North Billerica, where the accident had occurred, confirmed that they'd apprehended a drunk and reckless driver the night before, they insisted that, because the case was still under investigation, they couldn't release particulars, including even the driver's name or any insurance details. That left us in utter limbo with no place to stay and no way to leave.

So Reeve, who'd organized our ill-fated moonlit swimming party, arranged with one of Pat's friends for us to use her housemate Peggy Means' bed—but only during the daylight hours when Peggy wouldn't be in it and, in order to make that schedule work, we'd have to spend our nights at A&J Body Repair seated on empty cartridge boxes kibitzing with its night watchman, a guy our age called "Benny the Waif" because he'd spent his childhood years at a Catholic foundling home connected somehow, according to him, with "Honey Fitz" Fitzgerald, grandfather of JFK.

Benny was a friendly guy—heavy-set, shy, and, like everyone else, instantly sweet on Anne. He tried to tell us the score concerning the hit-and-run driver and North Billerica police but, with his nickname and manner of speaking straight out of Damon Runyon, I thought at first he was having fun putting us Harvard-types on. It was simple, he insisted as I nodded as if in assent—the cops had gotten a pay-off, see? and, unless I could offer them something too, they wouldn't divulge the driver's name no matter how long we waited.

"Listen," he told us on our second nightlong vigil, "there're two kinds of justice in Massachusetts—one for fat cats handled in court that's managed by lawyers and politicians and another one for the rest of us. The second one'll cost you too, but it's a lot cheaper. . . and it works." He waited a beat, then added while looking sidelong at Anne, "You know what I'm saying? It's run by the mob."

"Aw, come on, Benny," I countered. "You're pulling our legs."

He looked only slightly offended. "So . . . I'll give you a personal example," he said, leaning earnestly towards us from his box and chopping the air for emphasis. "My brother-in-law hires a carpenter to do some work on his house but pays up before he's finished the trim. That's always a mistake you know, but he gets a promise from the guy that he'll wind things up as soon as he can. Still, months go by, and every time he gets asked, all the guy has got to say for himself is, 'Naw, I'm really sorry, but I'm finishing up another job. I'll get there when I can. . . just like I said.' Finally, my brother-in-law says, 'This is the last time I'm asking, you know—can you finish up with my trim in the next two days?' When the guy refuses again, my brother-in-law then comes to me and says, 'Okay, Benny, get your friend—I'll pay whatever he charges.'"

Benny looked at me hard to make sure I was following his story. I was skeptical, but I listened.

"So the friend he was talking about was in the foundling home with me, a guy who's known in the trade as 'The Rotisserie,' which pretty much says it all. He works with this assistant of his. They wait for their mark behind a hedge, and when they get him on the ground, his assistant spins the chump so my friend can stomp on his knee . . . like this, like this you see?" Benny showed us the technique, rotating his finger and hitting it with his fist. "He breaks the leg in four places, okay? The advantage of which is scientific—the way they set the pins, the jerk'll be in traction for maybe six months or so. It's a pretty sweet deal all round and worth it to my brother-in-law."

"You're kidding me, right?"

"Why would I kid you?" He looked offended again, glancing at Anne for support. "He gets four hundred for a job, gives fifty to his assistant and pockets the rest for himself. Besides, he likes his work." He let his story sink in. "Just think about it is all I'm saying."

The following night he had good news. He said he'd talked about us to his friend The Rotisserie—how down-to-earth we were despite the Harvard connection and what had befallen us while living in Massachusetts—and his friend had said it was a shame for visitors like us to be treated that way. . . and, as Benny reported, he'd offered to do a charity job, saying he'd use some contacts of his to get the hit-and-run driver's name. He wouldn't disclose it to us so we couldn't be implicated, but the mystery-man in question would be getting a lot of bed rest.

I told Benny—and I meant it—that, with tears of gratitude in my eyes, I wanted to thank both him and his friend. But, pleased as I'd be by the thought of having our unknown assailant in traction for a spell, we'd still be stuck in Cambridge if we couldn't raise the dough.

"Just tit for tat, you know?" Benny said, nodding his head to drive the point home, and, for just the slightest split-second, I wondered how my insurance rep would react to being in traction too.

But, no, I shook my head

Anne smiled at him and said, "It's really nice of you, Benny"—and that was as close as we got to the mob—the non-academic one, at least—but it was a moment of truth of sorts.

Though I'd hoped to manage our own affairs, I realized that the time had come to call in some help from home. In a couple of hours, my father-in-law had arranged for a young lawyer from Columbia, whom both of us knew and liked, to straighten things out in a hurry. Joe Gibbs was working at Choate, Hall & Stewart, a big-time Boston firm, and it cost him a single piece of stationery to let the folks in North Billerica know that some heavy artillery was moving into place. The name we needed was instantly released (I remember it to this day), his insurance company said they'd pay our bills, and we got the bodywork done in a day and a half. Then we drove home for the summer.

By my second year at Harvard, I'd begun to learn the ropes, including some basic skills that I either hadn't been taught or had failed to learn on my own at either Sewanee or Oxford. I had most of my language requirements down—one ancient, two modern, plus Anglo-Saxon (or Old English as it was increasingly called)—though, towards the end of the spring, in addition to a grad assistant's load tutoring juniors and seniors in American History & Lit, I still had to pass a Latin exam before beginning my dissertation. I'd sailed through French and German in the fall but had only found time to brush up a bit on Caesar, Catullus, and Ovid and hoped the texts would be easy.

But they weren't, and midway through a knotty passage from Virgil, I experienced something totally new to me. Ever since the second grade, I'd thought of taking tests as my only highly developed skill, but suddenly, inexplicably, as I stared down at the page, it came across like cuneiform. I blinked and tried to refocus but could make no sense of it. I'd never panicked like that before and couldn't expunge the awful thought that all our plans for the coming year were about to fall apart. That only worsened my brain-cramp, of course, as for the first and only time in my life on any sort of written exam, I froze and, putting my pen down, looked helplessly at my watch as more and more minutes flew by while the chill in my stomach spread outwards to every limb.

Then, with less than ten minutes left, as rapidly as the panic had set in, a calm resolve took over, and all my confusion was gone. I examined the text again, and it was as if the complex Latin syntax had been magically rearranged into lucid English sentences that I proceeded to transcribe as fast as my fingers could move, finishing just as time ran out and getting an almost perfect score—along with a near-certainty that our plans were still intact. I'd never known that fail-safe button was there, but then, I'd never needed it and hoped I wouldn't again.

After that near-disaster, it was altogether golden. My teaching became a constant joy, and no sooner had I started research for a dissertation on Keats than I was offered a full-time position in the English Department—one of only two, I was told, out of a very large number. "But," Alan Heimert advised me as if we were back at Joyce Chen's, "no tickee, no washee, understand?"

Those were his actual words, hardly thinkable today, but regarding my dissertation the message was crystal clear: don't dawdle addressing posterity, just wind it up and join the club. I'd never considered staying on, but learning at the same time that Anne was several months pregnant caused us to agree that having that on my résumé would open more doors in the future.

So I agreed to their terms and buckled down, changing my topic from Keats to William Morris under Buckley's direction, primarily to assure that I finished on time, which I did in May and got my degree—and six weeks later, as Doctor Lamaze might have said, our baby arrived *comme une bombe*.

We were standing with a loaded shopping cart in the middle of a Star Market aisle, having just encountered Julia Child and her husband in the fructuous produce section, when Anne assumed an odd expression evincing both excitement and alarm.

"It's happening," she said with great composure. "And fast," she added more urgently.

Her water had broken, and what had seemed as theoretical as *Being and Nothingness* was suddenly inescapably real. We abandoned the cart and drove straight home, hurriedly packed what we thought we'd need, and sped across the river towards Boston Lying-In.

Despite the challenge before us, I was brimming over with confidence—partly because our obstetrician was none other than Clement Yahia who'd studied under Pierre Vellay, the protégé of Fernand Lamaze himself, the guru of pain-free natural childbirth. I felt secure in our hospital too, which, among obstetrical institutions, was considered one of the best in the world, and I was confident in my wife and me—we'd attended classes, we'd practiced faithfully, and I was equipped with all I'd need to coach and support her at every turn. I was, after all, a nascent Harvard professor.

It was eight in the evening when we checked in. Yahia briefly examined Anne and said to our great relief that her labor was slowly progressing and promised to be routine. When he left at nine-thirty or so—to catch a little sleep, he explained—he told the nurse to let him know right away if any significant change occurred.

It must have been a slow night in obstetrics because, over the next several hours, the nurse on call, having checked in once or twice and finding nothing amiss, showed no further special concern and virtually disappeared. But I was still there, of course, ready with stopwatch and notebook, recording each contraction and coaching Anne's huffing and puffing, supposing the role I played was like a helmsman's in a storm.

At one o'clock, Anne's pains got worse. She said the breathing didn't help, so I tried to persuade her it would. After a while she started to curse. I told her I'd get the nurse but, once outside our closet-like room, I looked in vain for directional signs and, in the darkened hallways, couldn't locate the nurses' station. A janitor stopped to help me out and led me to a secluded nook I'd apparently overlooked where our nurse was immersed in a telephone call to somebody she was joking with. She was clearly annoyed at my intrusion and impatiently let me know that nervous first-time fathers should go sit in a waiting room, though nevertheless she said she'd go have a look at Anne. Then, telling the person she'd call him back, she stalked her way to the labor room with me following on her heels.

After briefly checking on Anne, she informed us in a peremptory way that delivery was still a long way off. She left and we tried to settle down, but Anne's pangs began to grow sharper with every passing minute, and soon it was inescapably clear that, though her pain threshold was much higher than mine, she was fast approaching agony. Beads of sweat had broken out on her brow, her teeth were clenched, and the pain that was wracking her never stopped.

She fixed me with a furious stare. "Something's wrong," she managed to gasp.

I nodded and raced back down the hall. The nurse was again on the telephone. As I strode in, she swiveled her chair, turning her face away from me.

"Something's *really* wrong!" I said.

She covered the receiver with her hand.

"I've told you it's fine," she instructed me. "Go back to your wife."

I started to object, but she repeated what she'd just said with an additional, "Now!"

I felt enraged and desperate. It was like the end of *A Farewell to Arms* except that I wouldn't just walk away. I looked around, surveying the room, and saw a portable sterilizer—at least, that's what I thought it was. I grabbed it, lifting it over my head.

"I'm going to start demolishing things," I told the livid nurse.

She saw that I meant it and coldly replied, "I'm going to deal with you."

She said goodbye to whoever was on the phone and brushed out past me into the hall. When I got back to the labor room, it was barely in time to catch her frantic expression. She pushed a button, and lights went on with people converging from every direction. Code Red was clearly underway, and we'd later be given to understand that, during the last forty minutes or so, the baby had turned a somersault to enter the world feet first, compressing its umbilical cord and cutting off any oxygen. A couple of minutes more would be the absolute limit, and, as I was ushered out of the room, I caught a glimpse of Yahia rushing rapidly past while fumbling to tie a mask behind his head. He must have been sleeping nearby, but because it had entered the birth canal, our baby's only chance was if all of it could slip through.

I reflexively pushed the fail-safe button that I'd discovered inside my mind and, foolishly or not, felt an absolute calm descend and with it an assurance that luck would trump negligence in the end. . . and I had after all played a role that was more or less essential in getting us through the storm, if more like manning the pumps than taking control of the wheel. My thinking had gotten no further when Yahia stepped out of the opened door to tell me we'd had a baby girl—something we hadn't known before—and to say she'd arrived with all her fingers and toes, good Apgar scores, and a beautifully shaped if completely unmolded head. He wouldn't look round at the nurse as he apologized to me for all the undue distress before directing me up some stairs to a place where I could see our new daughter for myself through the neonatal ward's glass window. When I entered the empty corridor, her wide-eyed face was turned towards me as she fixed me with a lemur-like gaze, and I felt a surge of unbelievable joy. She knows me, I thought, and I know her—we've been waiting to meet each other.

Of course, every young couple's birthing tale gets recounted in great detail as if it had been miraculous while all aftermaths just as quickly become a humdrum blur of sleepless nights and groggy days with frantic learn-as-you-go concerns. We were the same as everyone else except for calling our daughter "Boykin," which wasn't on standard baby-names lists. We'd named her for my mother-in-law, who'd been baptized Frances Boykin, but we chose to use the surname instead because, as I persuasively pointed out, John Cleland's long-banned and cheerfully salacious *Fanny Hill* had been published only months before and dealing with that might be a built-in embarrassment. It was on our daughter's behalf as well that, having been told that doctors got diaper-service discounts, I put my new prestige to work over the telephone.

After identifying myself as "Doctor Dunlap," I was asked by a voice with a streetwise Boston accent where I was practicing.

"Practicing?" I stupidly repeated.

"Yes, at what hospital?" said the voice at the other end of the line.

"Well, I'm not actually a physician," I confessed. "I have a PhD and. . ."

"Then you're not a real doctor and don't qualify for a discount."

Clearly, I wasn't the first credentialed imposter to be put in his place by Tidy Didy. But in the wake of that humiliating rejection, I began to wonder if I was a real anything, especially after I'd been given my first full-time teaching assignments and found that, in addition to adding a lecture course while tutoring still in History & Lit, I'd be teaching an introductory fiction-writing course during the following spring. . . and that was what gave me pause.

It wasn't that Harvard meant to abet my innermost aspirations. It was, rather, that teaching creative writing was so little regarded there that it was taken for granted that anyone could do it, and as if to test that assumption when the end of January arrived, for my class's initial session, made up mostly of freshmen, I shared some excerpts from Chekhov and Welty, led brief discussions of each, and told the students to go away and write short stories of their own employing whatever they'd praised in class. When we convened again on Thursday, I collected the results and read them over the weekend. Most were predictably derivative—accounts of sex and drug busts—but one was startlingly good about fighting in the Negev.

No one in the class had struck me as mature enough to know such things firsthand, so the obvious conclusion was plagiarism. On the other hand, I was myself a newly minted professor and didn't want to begin my ascendancy with such a strident accusation. The safer course would be to award its author a B+ with a comment like, "This is very promising, but you can make it better—please revise." I struggled with myself and finally decided to say what I really thought. "This is brilliant," I wrote. "I think it's publishable."

The student spoke to me after class. "I'm glad you think so," he said. "It's been accepted by *The New Yorker*."

That was Harvard for you, and he was Mark Helprin, who would shortly become not only one of his generation's most celebrated writers, but also, in time, a Fellow of the American Academy in Rome and a Member of the Council on Foreign Relations. I never asked if that first story was true, though I afterwards learned that, because of some vagaries during his teenage years, conceivably during the Six-Day War, he wasn't a first-year student as I'd supposed and certainly not a conventional one.

Whatever the case, nearly everything he submitted in the course of that semester would reappear in *The New Yorker* and afterwards become part of his first collection of stories, *A Dove of the East*—which hardly seems surprising now because, even at that early stage of his career, Mark had a mind that, like Keats' comparison of the imagination to Adam's dream—"he awoke and found it true"—seemed to convince itself that whatever he conjured up on the page had actually taken place whether fighting a war in the desert or gazing out at a bitter cold sea through the eyes of a lonely sea captain's wife with torrents of words piling up in her head like shells on an unpeopled beach. To my credit—and, from my present vantage, relief—I told him early on that I had nothing to teach him about the writing of fiction but that I'd give him an honest opinion while doing my best not to obstruct his communing with the muse.

So my better instincts had won, and my sails were set as a teacher—which worked well until later in the semester when I read in the morning paper that a young alumna of my wife's former college in Virginia, someone we'd recently met, had been murdered in her Cambridge apartment a block or so off Mass Ave. According to the report, her body had been found in a locked room without the apparent murder weapon, suspected to be a butcher knife. The mystery was being investigated.

We were living then at 40 Mount Vernon Street, just off the other side of Mass Ave, and it crossed my mind that some of my former neighbors a few blocks away might remember my night-time derring-do. But, while I was mulling that over, I got a call from Mark Helprin who said he'd just completed the best story he'd ever written and he'd really like me to read it. I reminded him that we'd be seeing each other later that afternoon, but we could meet up, if he wanted, just shortly before that. He said he'd really prefer that I read it right away. He was weirdly persistent, but I figured he was still in the throes of inspiration and reluctantly agreed to meet him at a café near our classroom in Holyoke Center as soon as I could get dressed and down to the Square.

Though feeling a bit like Raskolnikov when I thought of my neighbors on Gray Street, I detoured past the house where the murder had taken place. There was no indication of a crime scene but, knowing the address, I peered up at the second floor where the victim had rented her rooms, then examined adjacent houses, the yard, and a sycamore tree, all of them mute witnesses to whatever had taken place. From there I continued on to the café where Mark, with his usual wild-eyed look and sporting a confident grin, had staked out a table off to itself.

"Read it," he said as he handed his story over.

I read it, and my blood ran cold—a condition that frequently seemed to afflict me during my Cambridge and Boston days, what with word of my parents' sudden divorce, the death of a friend in
Vietnam, a Mafia shooting down the street when we lived for two years in Somerville, and the fate of a student I'd taught the year

before who, after a postcard from the Galapagos about tracking Herman Melville, had vanished into thin air (or into the briny deep) pursuing what was to have been his senior-thesis topic. Mark's story was of a piece with all such battle, murder, and sudden death—a vivid first-person account of stabbing a young woman near Harvard Square merely for the thrill of doing it. It went into telling detail, describing how he'd cased the scene, entered the girl's apartment by crawling along the limb of a sycamore tree and in through an upstairs window. Then when the deed was done, he'd exited via the tree limb again leaving his weapon behind—imbedded high and unseen in the crotch of the sycamore. . . the perfect murder, he boasted.

I could feel Mark watching me closely as I read. I got to the end and, casually glancing back at an earlier page, I looked up at him and said, "This is fascinating, Mark—a sort of *Crime and No Punishment*. We've still got more than an hour before we meet with the class. Let me take it back to Adams House and give it the time it deserves." As he nodded with that strange smile, his eyes were still on my face.

I went to my office in Adams House and phoned my friend Roger Rosenblatt, who'd taught Mark during the fall and been at the same party where we'd met the murder victim. I told him we needed to talk, and he joined me in my office a few minutes later.

Wordlessly, I handed him the story. He read it and muttered, "Great Scott!" or something of the sort, no less appalled than I. "No way to check it out, I guess?"

I told him I'd cased the house on my way down to the Square, and the tree and the window were there, all right—which didn't necessarily mean. . .

"I know, I know," Roger said.

"Raskolnikov," I shrugged.

He was thinking *The Tell-Tale Heart* instead. "So he's giving himself away, you think?"

"Deliberately? Yeah, that's possible."

We worked out a strategy. I'd ask Mark to wait until after class when we could go over his story again. Then I'd confront him with my suspicion. Mark was short but heavy set and, if he made a run for it—as good as a confession—it would probably take the two of us to keep him from getting away. . . unless, of course, he'd armed himself and had actually fought in the Negev. We'd have to run that risk, Roger said, but Roger's own presence would be a surprise, and, because of the seminar room's glass wall along the corridor, he'd be able to keep an eye on what was going on and, after the other students had left, he'd casually block the door as if waiting to speak to me. We reminded ourselves that Mark could be innocent but, though we regretted not having time to make sure the knife was there in the sycamore tree, we also agreed that Mark was behaving erratically and his story was deeply disturbing.

My class assembled, and I seated myself where I could keep an eye on the corridor—though, when Mark took a seat next to me with a slyly amused expression, I worried he might have sniffed out that something unusual was up. But despite that troubling distraction, I got halfway through the class before I saw a figure appear wearing a belted trench coat with its collar turned up in back like a B-grade private eye. It was Roger, of course, who started making furtive signs, drawing attention to himself in a way that threatened to give us both away until it finally got so out of hand that I asked the students to please stay put while I addressed a personal matter.

Carefully closing the door and keeping my back to the class, I gestured for Roger to tone it down.

"They've caught him," he said.

"Caught who?" I asked.

"The murderer. It isn't Mark."

I glanced into the room and back at Roger. "That was close," I said. "It would have been a debacle. But why the hell. . .?" I added, nodding at his attire.

"It seemed appropriate," he shrugged.

I understood. He's a fellow fox at heart, I think, with a quick and mordant wit which, in retrospect, was appropriate too. We'd nearly deprived American letters of one of its future luminaries— or maybe ourselves of our jobs. But then, not unlike Oxford, I mused, Harvard was, in effect, an international stage where far-fetched farces occurred as often as great ideas. In my first or second year, I'd been to a lively bash hosted by Jim Watson, the molecular biologist who, whatever he might have cribbed *en route* to a Nobel Prize, had a weakness for blondes with ponytails and laughed like a fraternity boy during a big party weekend, and only a few days before our near fiasco with Mark, I'd had lunch in Adams House with Jorge Luis Borges, who might have invented Roger and me as a pair of sleuthing buffoons tracking our wily suspect through Harvard Yard's forking paths. . . except that Borges at that point was almost totally blind and wholly caught up in Anglo-Saxon verse, which was all we'd talked about—*Beowulf* and C.L. Wrenn and a couple of lines in the text in which Grendel is described as prowling the misty fens "though nobody knows where demons of that sort roam," which seemed true enough as well of the world that we were in.

In other words, in that uneasy calamitous time at that stage of my career, it truly seemed the unthinkable might occur, which was certainly proved to be the case only a week or two later when, as I was giving Boykin a bath in a tub in the kitchen sink and Anne was hacking a leg of lamb to rend the last of its meat from the bone, Boykin—who, because of her traumatic birth according to Berry Hazelton, was in a hypertonic phase—shrieked and stiffened her limbs when I lowered her into the water.

Anne looked up at the shriek, and her greasy hand slid down the serrated blade. "Oh, God!" she said with a gasp.

I looked and saw to my horror that the little finger of her right hand was dangling by shreds of tendon and skin, almost completely severed. While she struggled to wrap the bloody mess in a towel, I dashed to the apartment overhead clutching our naked baby and found that my cousin Virginia—who was Boykin's godmother as well and was living there at the time—just happened to be at home. "Anne has cut off her finger!" I cried, shoving our baby into her arms, and rushed Anne to the emergency room at Cambridge's Mount Auburn Hospital.

With great good luck again, there was a surgeon there on call who'd recently been in the news for reattaching the severed arm of a boy who'd fallen in front of a train, but he declared Anne's finger a much trickier proposition since all the tendons had retracted. It would be far simpler, he added, to complete the amputation. But Anne, who'd been given narcotics to ease the appalling pain, stirred at overhearing his opinion and trilled as if we were on that special floor at First National City Bank, "But I couldn't possibly go to a ball with only four fingers on my hand! We wear long white gloves, you see."

That swayed the decision since we were obviously of the Brahmin class and could afford whatever it cost. So the finger was reattached, though the awful pain persisted for months—for which the only solution was letting Anne's mother take both her daughter and still nursing granddaughter home with her to Columbia while I soldiered on in Cambridge looking to find a way to cope with the medical bills, which to my relief and surprise were fully settled by Harvard because, as a full-time faculty member, I qualified for its special rate which, except for pocket-change from me, would amount to whatever Blue Cross-Blue Shield agreed to pay for the service.

Three ghastly months went by with Anne completely spaced out on the phone, like a princess in a far-off tower that happened to be an opium den. My daughter was growing up, I thought, while I was nine hundred miles away merely helping to refine the already hyper-refined. That had to change, I felt—and at just that moment, as if preordained, a delegation showed up from the USC I knew best, the one in South Carolina, to make me a tempting offer. The salary would be much better, my family reunited, and my vocation more ennobled in a less prestigious place, though I was somewhat perturbed by the implicit condescension of thinking that I'd go home in order to save my people or the folly of supposing they'd acknowledge needing it. As a further incentive to stay, I'd just learned that I'd receive an elevation in rank and concomitant raise in pay, extending my three-year contract for another five years at least—and, according to legend among us junior profs, no one had ever turned a Harvard promotion down.

And yet, though troubled by a suspicion that somebody meddling at home—like a mother-in-law determined to end her daughter's protracted exile—had somehow been behind my sudden unsought recruitment, I was bothered as well by the thought that I could join any mob at Harvard without examining my conscience. Growing up in South Carolina, I'd largely defined myself by swimming against the current, and as much as I dreaded self-contempt for merely skimming the surface, smug pedantry would be worse. After all, I tried to persuade myself, some people drill down deeply in life while others explore more widely in search of broader connections—like none other than William Morris, of course, who wasn't just a jack of all trades but the ultimate master of many despite the fact that, in the end, poetry hadn't been one of them. . . and wouldn't be for me either as I increasingly knew in my heart.

Morris was truly a case in point. What had drawn me to his work from the start was the number of interests and skills he'd managed to weave together and how they'd unerringly led to matters of social justice. It was the spring of 1968 following the Tet Offensive in Vietnam, and as I've mentioned in passing, a good friend who'd stood beside me as a newly selected Rhodes Scholar had been killed in that dubious war while racial conflict at home was growing steadily worse despite and because of the Civil Rights Act. Dr. King had just been murdered in Memphis and demagogues like George Wallace were running for president which made taking a stand in the north seem a piddling sort of commitment compared to doing so in the south. Even while at Sewanee, isolated as it was, I'd gotten somewhat involved with the Highlander Folk School nearby when James Bevel and Septima Clark were there, she being from South Carolina too and, however self-serving the question might seem, wasn't that where I ought to be?

I went to see the Arts & Sciences dean and told him about my dilemma. He repeated their offer of a promotion with a raise at least as high as the one I'd be getting at home and, as if in a tale by Grimm or Perrault, he tendered three bits of advice. The first was that, if I chose to leave, I'd be stepping off the escalator—"and once you're off," he warned, "there's no getting back on again."

I told him I could handle that.

He said I was a thoroughbred, but the choice that I was considering meant "going back to haul cartloads of slag."

I said okay, but maybe that wouldn't be the case.

Then he cocked his head and squinted at me. "I believe you misspoke," he said. "You must have meant North Carolina. So far as I'm aware. . ." he paused to let his words sink in, "there is no University of South Carolina."

He knew better, of course. We both knew that. He was saying that what I was contemplating would be academic suicide. So be it, I thought. I was out of there.

12

Vital Signs

To the best of my knowledge, I've only saved one other person's life and, ironically enough in view of having been drowned myself not long before the event, I did it underwater. That may have been even more commendable because, as destiny or my gene pool would have it, I'm one of those people who, owing to body density or something of the sort, won't under any conditions bob back up like a cork—except in the Dead Sea as I discovered a decade or so ago, though rescuing somebody there wouldn't amount to much.

Nevertheless, my persistence in sinking used to irritate my highly aquatic wife who believed it to be an affectation and, despite my numerous demonstrations, continued to maintain that, for whatever aggravating reason, I was deliberately failing to float. She was right about this much at least: my notion of swimming has always been to jump into the water, thrash about for a minute or two, and then move on to something else—whereas she liked nothing better than bobbing for hours like a seal with her snout just out of the water.

And yet I too was semi-amphibious as a boy. My family visited Pawley's Island each summer as my mother and her family had done from even before there'd been a causeway over the creek—or so my mother had told me. One attraction there was that its wide and gently sloping littoral made swimming especially safe, and, once I'd learned the rudiments, it was fun to body-surf a long ride back to shore. There were other beaches along the coast with steep and treacherous drop-offs amidst a single short line of breakers, dangerous for even good swimmers whenever the surf was rough, but in general we avoided them.

Garden City was the worst—which was one of the reasons I didn't want to go when a friend named Eddie Roberts invited me to join both him and his family there in a house they'd rented for a week. Eddie and I shared an interest in books, though I was an athlete too and he definitely wasn't. I was also, so far as I knew, more interested in girls and in chance encounters at the beach, but I was unnerved by a sense of doom that had settled over his home since an older brother's death of a malignant brain tumor. His mother especially bore what I'd have later described as a *mater dolorosa* sort of grief that not even her Catholic piety could dispel, a loss so ghastly and profound that my instinct was to hide from it. . . though, nevertheless, I went.

Eddie took his 45-rpm record player with him to the beach, and I remember listening over and over to my own extended-play version of Robert Schumann's *Carnaval* while we were there— music which, amid its ostensible gaiety, struck me as morbid too and weirdly insinuating, adding to my unease. What provided a little relief was that Mary Alice Cloyd, whom both of us knew from school, was vacationing with her parents in the cottage next door to ours. Her father had a withered left arm, as I noticed when I saw him on the beach looking paunchy and middle-aged in a tan-colored bathing suit, though Mary Alice herself was—as a caption in *Pageant* magazine might have observed—enticingly curvaceous. She looked good enough, in fact, for me to hang out doggedly after lunch on the lookout of our house high up over the beach, reading a sci-fi novel about traveling to the moon while waiting for her to appear.

One cloudy and blustery afternoon with a storm far out at sea, I was alone on my voyeuristic vigil when Mr. Cloyd showed up, strolling down towards the water and wading cautiously in. Almost at once, it seemed, an aggressively big wave rose up and loomed above him like a predator's paw, yanking him out and under. I could barely hear his feeble calls for help over the buffeting wind and surf, but, as recklessly as I'd one day rush towards a voice I heard screaming in the street, I raced from the porch and into the surf, was hit myself by a furious wave, and tumbled and swam as best I could towards where I'd last seen Mr. Cloyd.

Submerged by a second thundering wave, I was blindly flung up against him, grabbing at his waist, and struggling to get a gulp of air before the undertow sucked me under again. I couldn't get traction with my feet and was suddenly being attacked by Mr. Cloyd who, in frantic self-preservation, was trying to clamber atop me, hammering on my head with his useless walrus-like flipper. It was precisely the situation for which the *Boy Scout Handbook* had instructed us without a lot of detail to sock a recalcitrant rescuee on the jaw, but that wasn't remotely possible—and I realized at that moment that I was going to drown a second time. My lungs felt as if they were bursting, the turbulence was relentless and Mr. Cloyd as hyper-energized as panic and fear could make him. I was desperate to regain control, but both of us kept being tumbled about and pressed back down to the bottom like ants in a washing machine.

For only the briefest of respites, I felt the water recede before gathering itself to pound us down again but, in a maneuver surprising even me, I managed to somersault and solidly plant both feet in the steeply sloping sand. As the next swell loomed behind us, I steadied myself as best I could and shoved with all my might, propelling Mr. Cloyd like a riderless surfboard towards the beach. Then, verging on blacking out, inhaling salt water as I gasped, I got another half-breath of air before going under again.

The wave threw Mr. Cloyd up onto the shore but drew me out like flotsam again before flattening like sheet metal and swiftly sliding sideways towards the beach, thrusting me as I tried to swim on a seething and thinning diagonal some twenty yards farther along. As I crawled out sputtering onto the sand, I caught a glimpse of Eddie—who at some point must have seen what was going on down below and descended from the porch—as he took Mr. Cloyd's good arm and gave it a vigorous tug. That was when Mary Alice emerged, saw Eddie with her father, and rushed to embrace them both, saying Eddie was heaven-sent.

It baffles me to this day that no one took any notice of me as I dragged myself half-drowned from the sea like Odysseus on Scheria and that Eddie himself, though modestly saying when praised that he'd only done what anyone else would do, would never refer to me either—an omission that Mary Alice, the

Nausicaa of Garden City in a highly becoming one-piece suit with a sort of ruffled skirt and a mole like a beauty spot next to her mouth, would never find cause to correct. Eddie was the hero of the beach, and, seeing that it was useless trying to claim any credit, I took consolation in the thought that I was lucky to be alive.

That was my second close brush with the Reaper. My third would occur some fifteen or sixteen years later, in the spring of 1970 when, on a year-long grant from a Rockefeller Foundation-funded Cooperative Program in the Humanities, I'd been awarded faculty status at both Duke and UNC-Chapel Hill in order to do research for a book on William Morris. The only catch was a housing shortage in both locations, and, by the time we were able to look for a place to stay towards the end of the previous summer, there was literally nothing to rent in Durham or Chapel Hill.

Finally, through a nonacademic friend, we'd managed to find a partly furnished two-room retreat in the woods about twenty-five miles from Chapel Hill. It was built atop an empty garage and storage space on a bluff above the Deep River some four or five miles from Moncure—which was at the time, before the dam that would later create a lake flooding some fifty thousand acres, little more than a rural crossroads next to the Seaboard railway line for which it had been a watering station in the days of steam locomotives.

The community, such as it was, consisted of a smattering of modest one-story houses, a plywood factory a mile or two down the road, a cement-block hair salon painted pistachio green, and a fly-blown general store that looked like a movie set for Faulkner's "Barn Burning" tale except for an adjacent P.O. for which the store's semi-retired proprietor also served as postmaster along with overseeing the volunteer fire department of which the only evidence was a truck in knee-high weeds next to an antique gas pump with a couple of road-worn tires propped up on either side.

In the three or four miles between the general store and where we lived, there wasn't much else to see other than tin-roofed shacks surrounded by flat dirt yards and chinaberry trees strung out along the highway near the turn-off to our house, and, except for the Aussie editor of a farmers' magazine with ultra-rightwing views who, shortly after our arrival, had started to renovate a two-story clapboard house a few hundred yards past us for himself and his put-upon pregnant wife, we three were alone on a dead-end seldom-scraped road and the only whites within miles—a fact prompting such paranoid racist fears in the mind of our Aussie neighbor that he set out each night on armed patrols along his "safety" perimeter with all-clear rifle shots at different coordinates.

At the opposite extreme and naively inspired by Thoreau and *The Whole Earth Catalog*—as well as by Arthur Godfrey's son who, much closer to Chapel Hill, had combined some old tobacco barns to create a place of rustic charm—I planned to live deliberately too, adding some touches of my own to enhance our year of bucolic bliss, especially for Anne and Boykin, who'd just recently turned two and for whose sake I'd need a space to work apart from our one big living room.

The cement and concrete-block downstairs was much too large to heat and would soon be too cold as well, so I took a page from the Godfreys and had the skeleton of a former nineteen-by-twenty-foot mule shed hauled up next to our rented retreat and mounted on concrete blocks than I scrounged up from inside the garage. Next, with some rudimentary carpentry, I converted the slatted walls of the shed to fairly tight board-and-batten, added some two-by-twelves to support a plywood floor, and, as my trickiest addition, installed three double-hung window units measuring two-by-three-feet each—which would have been much easier if it hadn't slipped my mind that parallelograms too can measure two-by-three. But in the end, with only a hammer and handsaw, I'd created the sort of writing hut envisioned by Yeats at Innisfree where I could pursue my study of Morris as well as whatever else the muses might inspire, which turned out to be precious little other than one long poem in *The Sewanee Review*.

That somewhat limited productivity was largely due to the fact that, as many before me had found, living the simple life can be very time-consuming, though by early October it seemed I'd gotten things under control—commuting to Chapel Hill once every week or so, picking up groceries and mail at the local country store, and devotedly watching the debut season of *Sesame Street* with Boykin, especially after learning that a state commission in Mississippi had voted to ban the series because of its integrated cast. For the next three months, our sojourn felt Edenesque—"almost," I crowed in my journal, "as if the Aquarian Age has dawned on us here in the sticks."

That supposition ended abruptly late one night in mid-January when my brother called with the news that, on their coldest night of the year, my father had either been mugged at his house in Myrtle Court or had a bad fall when the lights went out or maybe had suffered a stroke before or after his furnace quit— and may have frozen to death, which also remained unclear because, although he was breathing still and in an ICU, he wasn't fully conscious and seemed to be sinking fast.

I got there in the early morning hours and was permitted to go to his bedside where I found him not only awake but calling me by the name we shared and then repeatedly "son," complaining about how cold he was and how badly he needed to pee—whereupon the nurse came in and told me I'd have to leave until seven or eight in the morning while assuring me he'd recover.

He didn't, though, and following his death just short of his sixtieth birthday, the three of us drove to Rock Hill for a desolate funeral service and afterwards back to Moncure where, when picking up our mail, I learned that a pack of wild dogs was marauding across our area threatening people and livestock— including a number of horses with several reportedly bolting through a fence.

Next morning the pack showed up at our house, drifting in eerie silence across the driveway in a disciplined single file some forty or fifty feet away as I, having been alerted by our secondhand collie-shepherd, stood with a loaded shotgun in front of the ground floor metal door while Smokey, as our adoptee was called, sensibly stayed by my side, trembling from nose-to-tail with what I took to be a city-dog's well-placed dread—that despite the fact that within the pack were breeds that looked like former household pets, some of them rather puny. . . like middle-class recruits for a Manson Family raid, the subject of much lurid recent news.

With their second pass the ravagers drew closer, emerging out of the woods and into the driveway's gap as if to test my nerve. At their third appearance I fired—only the second time in my life that I'd actually used a shotgun—and though, given the buckshot's widespread field, I must have hit one or two, they kept going without a sound and simply disappeared.

I was still coming to terms with both of those events—one an irreparable loss, the other a surreal threat—when a day or two later outside my hut I heard Smokey's frenzied barking a few feet from the sandbox I'd built in the woods for Boykin adjacent to our driveway. As I cautiously approached to learn the cause of the uproar, I watched Smokey charge down into a shallow pit largely concealed by underbrush and suddenly reemerge with frantic yelps. I yanked a large pine tree limb aside and saw, to my disbelief, some twenty or thirty copperheads slithering about.

I'd never learn how many times she was bitten, but Smokey's head was soon swollen to jack-o-lantern size. We rushed her to the nearest vet a dozen miles off in Sanford, and after a shot of cortisone and grateful coddling from us, she was back to herself within a day or two while a man in overalls whom I'd contacted through our Moncure store turned the pit and its environs into a DMZ, including my arts-and-crafts sandbox.

We wondered what else could go wrong, but then, one morning in March, I tripped over a bit of stone jutting up from the hard-packed dirt a couple of yards from my hut and, with a little digging, quickly uncovered a millstone—dragged there, I surmised, from a mill that must have stood on the river far below, perhaps as long ago as the Revolutionary War, or possibly, as my Aussie neighbor opined, it might have been a treadle-driven wheel for grinding and polishing that must weigh, he guessed, as much as two hundred pounds. My plan, in any case, was to dig it completely up and, in lieu of the now-toxic sandbox, mount it on wooden blocks as a play table for our daughter where I could keep an eye on things.

Here I should note that, partly in response to my father's death, I'd launched myself again on an all-out fitness program—sprinting back and forth along the empty dirt road and tossing off fifty or sixty push-ups at a time—so, given my strength-through-joy routine, it never crossed my mind that, once it was full excavated, I wouldn't be able to lift the stone which was nearly as wide as manhole cover and six to eight inches in depth.

Somehow or other, I did in fact manage to get the lower rim braced on my knees while holding the upper rim like a steering wheel, after which I tried to take one or two crab-like steps towards the blocks I'd just set in place. But at the second step, I felt an odd sensation in my gut, painless but disquieting, like a weather-degraded garden hose being yanked and ripped apart. Momentarily concerned, I dropped the stone and waited—but nothing further occurred, and, with a sense of relief, I postponed my plans for a table.

In the middle of the night, however, I awoke in agony and was rushed by my wife to the UNC Medical Center where, as I lay supine on a gurney with what felt like a stake through my chest, an EKG was administered.

"Not a heart attack," an E.R. doctor said as the pain subsided a bit, after which I was given a couple of pills which I swallowed and went home.

But no sooner had we gotten there than the stake through my chest recurred and, with Boykin bouncing about in the car, we raced back to the medical center. This time the ER was full, and my records had been misplaced with the apparent consequence that, until my previous treatment was known, nothing could be administered except another EKG, which was done with the same results. Then, with me laid out on a gurney again encircled by pale green curtains, Anne and our daughter were led away to a nearby waiting room.

I remained in undisturbed agony until shortly after dawn when a section of the curtain was pulled aside to admit a frowning physician trailed by a handful of young interns who clustered about as if to study me. It was, I'd been told, a teaching facility.

"Thirty-three years old," the doctor read from my chart, missing it by eight months or so. "Severe chest pain, no heart attack, awaiting diagnosis." Then, reaching to pry my eyelid up, he turned to address the group. "How many units of pain in our measurement scale?"

"Ten," one of the interns replied.

"That's the limit," snapped the doctor, "but where would you place this patient?"

Silence and then a tentative, "Eight?"

"Eight and a half?" ventured another.

"Close," the doctor nodded with approval. "You can see from his eyes that he's almost wholly unresponsive. I doubt if he's even aware of those tears." He traced their path on my cheek, surveying his students with what I took to be a look of satisfaction. "This patient's at nine and a half," he said. "The pain that he's experiencing is the most intense a conscious patient can feel."

The interns examined me closely until they were led away. Then the curtains were abruptly drawn, and I lay there alone again, feeling a curious sort of pride and the reassuring thought that, no matter how bad it was, the pain could get no worse—and from that point on, it was as if I were surfing a dark malevolent wave rolling on hour after hour towards some distant unknown beach. I was still in that state of mind, focused solely on maintaining my virtuosic balance, when a brashly confident young surgeon appeared and announced to his entourage that, though my gallbladder had exploded or was in the process of doing so, he, through surgical intervention, intended to save my life. Presumably, my records had been found.

I had no say in the matter, but, as far as I could tell, his bravado was more than a bid for acclaim because, in what used to be called a trice—as soon as I'd undergone some ablutions and anesthesia—he by all reports went in with scalpels flashing and removed the organ in question, though I was through with my surfing by then.

The operation was considered a great success with the unforeseen downside that what remained of my body fell into a drastic form of post-operative shock, shutting some basic functions down and leaving me on life-support that continued for several days—for so long, in fact, that my wife and mother were summoned and told that, most regrettably, the odds would be very much against me unless I began to respond in the next twelve hours of so.

As if that ultimatum had been conveyed to my innards, I began to recuperate from that moment on and, in scarcely more than a day and a half, had improved from critical status to a prognosis of full recovery. But, to me, the duration of my time in

ICU—tube-ridden and semi-comatose, sustained by intravenous drips and mechanical devices—seemed absolutely timeless. It could have been five minutes or an eternity.

All things are relative, of course, though even as I began to recover, there was one specific aspect of the long drawn-out ordeal that seemed supremely obnoxious—the tube that ran through my nostril into my newly gall-bladderless depths, complemented by a suction apparatus that steadily drained saliva from my mouth—and as I became increasingly aware of it, the thirst that I started to feel seemed unendurable. My tongue was as dry as a camel's hoof in the Great Sahara Desert—or so I told myself, paraphrasing the dauntless wit of *archy and mehitabel*, which I quoted to myself at considerable length along with Coleridge's mariner, begging with him in unison for a merciful drop to drink. I grew so obsessed with the thought that, as my recovery progressed, I dwelt on it night and day.

And then one blessed mid-morning, with his phalanx of nurses and interns, my life-saving surgeon appeared to declare that, thanks to his ministrations, I'd rebounded sufficiently well to have the tubes removed from my nose and mouth and be given a sip of ginger ale.

Never have I felt such gratitude as I did for him at that moment—Dr. Stanley R. Mandel, my healer and extractor, my sommelier extraordinaire, a prodigy who just months before had completed his residency and promptly carried out the hospital's first-ever kidney transplant, though he'd never so much as witnessed one before.

I awaited his benefaction as, with imperious self-command, he gave one of the nurses instructions while, as I watched from my bed as if with telescopic vision, I saw her approach the nurses' station, noted how deftly she popped the cap of a red-and-green ginger ale can and unhurriedly poured its contents into a glass containing four frozen cubes that, thanks to a preternatural sharpening of either perception or fancy, I could hear as they started to grind and crack like icebergs in the polar night and could see the sublime effervescence kick in, bubbling and bursting around them.

I observed how gracefully she turned, lifting the tray with both hands, and then, in extreme slow motion, came gliding towards my cubicle bearing the benediction of Canada Dry, placing a plastic straw to my lips, and, with the beatific smile of an angel in the presence of divine forgiveness, urged me to taste and swallow.

Words can't describe the ecstasy I felt at my first sip. I was suffused with a radiance so extreme that tears of happiness began to course down my cheeks. I turned my head and looked out a nearby window and saw that, while I'd been lying there in suspended animation, spring had come to North Carolina, and a breeze was blowing the new green leaves, and all the world was lit up with the same transcendent beauty and joy that arose in the pit of my stomach and was spreading throughout my body.

I took another sip of the cosmic ginger ale and cried, "It's beautiful! Oh, God, it's beautiful!"

"Oh, oh," muttered my wife with patient exasperation. "Here we go again."

As she knew all too well, I was prone to such ecstatic moments, and, admittedly, my euphoria might have come across as an over-the-top reaction to a little ginger ale. But it was truly a moment of quasi-mystical elation, partially produced perhaps by sensory deprivation, though not by sedatives or drugs but by entirely natural means. It lasted for maybe a quarter hour, gradually diminishing and leaving behind as its residue a haunting recognition that, at least theoretically, such ecstatic awareness might be accessible every second of our lives if we're sufficiently attentive—though admittedly, I suppose, it's a good thing for the efficient operation of chainsaws and high-speed trains that, on that variety of endeavor, we forego such extreme elation.

Still, two things occur to me now. One is that I'd totally forgotten having mocked a young English woman in San Francisco for having a similar if somewhat more plausible reaction to sex as opposed to ginger ale, and the other is an ironically related thought that Emily Dickenson—who, except for the fizz released in her verse, seems to have kept it bottled up—would instantly recognize what I've attempted to describe, for as she once dryly confided,

Did life's penurious length
Italicize its sweetness,
The men who daily live
Would stand so deep in joy
That it would clog the cogs
Of that revolving reason
Whose esoteric belt
Protects our sanity.

Before I left the hospital with most of my cogs unclogged, I was visited by a former Sewanee roommate, Warren Holland, who was at the time a cardiologist at Duke. He remarked first that I was an unlikely candidate for gallstones, not being fat, female, fertile or forty. So I showed him the souvenir gallstones from my operation with which I'd been presented.

He poked at them and shook his head. "But this is a random collection," he said, explaining that there are two types of stones, calcium and cholesterol—though, depending on the progress of an infection, no one produces both at once. So the buckeye-like objects I'd showed him weren't exclusively mine—if any, in fact, had come from me at all—and, as if to confirm what he'd told me, I'd find myself repeatedly over the next several years in various emergency rooms, having the very same stake-through-the-chest attacks that had put me in Dr. Mandel's hands.

After innumerable EKGs, it was finally recognized that I'd ruptured my diaphragm in playing about with the millstone and given myself a hiatal hernia, which I've managed to control ever since by sit-ups and strenuous exercise—though, without a shirt on the beach, I look like a fortunate survivor of battlefield surgery with a ten-inch keloid scar running from gizzard to gullet. Still, the relevant bottom line was that, despite a foolish blunder by me compounded, it would seem, by a virtuoso's mistake that left me literally teetering on the brink, I'd managed to cheat the Reaper again.

I should have taken that as a warning to forego further recklessness, but as soon as I'd returned to USC, I got myself a motorcycle—partly because I'd so much enjoyed my free-wheeling scooter in England but mainly to defy the Fiat-to-Buick transition that signaled success for the senior profs who were still waiting in vain for me to become "productive," though as a nod to that intention I'd recently joined The William Morris Society and was in regular, if desultory correspondence with its office back in London. For the Society's part, its missives dispatched sporadically to distant members like me were mostly confined to necrology notes in black-rimmed envelopes containing the doleful news that another aging printer, designer, or agitator had recently taken the ferry.

Those notifications became a running joke between my wife and me as returning home each day, after parking my bike behind the house, I'd stride inside and ask, "Any interesting mail today?" And on very special occasions, she'd gravely shake her head and report, "Only another necrology note from the William Morris Society."

Then one afternoon in July when, as a junior professor, I was working the sign-up tables for summer school registration, a thunderstorm blew up, and on my way home in the rain, I got into a nightmarish situation where, under a railroad trestle, guardrails funneled the traffic into two very narrow lanes with no room to spare on either side. When a pickup zoomed out from a power company lot, the car ahead of me jammed on its brakes compelling me to do the same—but under those circumstances safe distances don't exist, and I went into a skid, sliding into the opposite lane in which I saw a large white van that was barreling towards me dead ahead.

I tried to focus my mind, and once again, as I had with my cosmic ginger ale, switched to a hyper-slow-motion mode in which, seeming to have forever, I calmly asked myself if somehow I could get off to the left.

"Noooo!" was my regretful reply.

"Or possibly back to the right?"

"Noooo!" the answer came again.

Then maybe if I could lay the bike down, slide under the van, and, ". . . uhhh. . ." a cry went off in my head. "That's it! Too late! I'm dead!"

That was my final conscious thought before colliding with the van. I'd later learn that the cars and the van had all sped off— the cars, perhaps, unaware of the wreck, the van for the opposite reason—leaving me in the roadway, a bundle of broken bones and rain-soaked rags amid the debris of my bike, in danger of being hit again by whatever happened along.

As things turned out, what happened along was my old friend Eddie Roberts, who'd by then become a lawyer and been divinely appointed to work his bad karma off for usurping my life-saver status at Garden City. He stopped, got out, and inspected the bundle. Then, waving the next passing driver down to send for an ambulance, he stayed with me in the rain until it finally arrived.

I came to in an emergency room with my shoulder crushed and head broken in, surrounded by a weeping wife and three or four somber-faced doctor friends. The one who addressed me first was Julian Adams, who'd become a neurologist.

"Listen to me, Bernie," he asked. "What year are we in? How old are you now? How long have you been married?"

None of that seemed relevant, but I did my best to answer—though, unbeknownst to me, my traumatized brain had, for the moment it seems, completely erased the past two years, causing an incorrect answer to every question. I saw him look up at Anne and gravely shake his head—by which he meant, of course, that I'd suffered some memory loss and maybe brain damage as well. But I, still absorbed by my last thought just before the wreck, assumed he meant the worst.

So, summoning all the strength I could manage, I reached up with my only functioning arm to pluck my weeping wife's sleeve. She bent over to hear me better as I uttered the one immortal line of my life—"*Notify. . . the William Morris Society!*"—and then with a drawn-out groan lapsed back into unconsciousness.

I ruined it, of course, by returning for an encore—at which point I found my nose was on the other side of my face and my right arm totally out of commission. But, other than that and a few other cracked and misplaced parts, I was reasonably intact. The nose would be cranked back into place, though without the Augustus Caesar look I'd asked for—possibly because another old doctor friend, who'd promised me a pleasantly pain-free nose job, had failed to requisition the anesthesia of choice which happened to be cocaine—and, given my pain-wracked ordeal and the fact that the procedure itself was a good deal more like changing a tire than tucking a sagging eyelid, I apparently got a rush job, leaving me with the nondescript result that's on my passport now.

As for my shoulder, I switched temporarily to my left hand for everything, including writing, and doing it with such ease that it seemed to corroborate my insistence that, despite my mother's denials, I was a natural-born lefty. My biggest problem lay in the fact that, after six months had passed, I'd failed to regain even half the use of my injured arm. So, having taught a number of Gamecock football players, I went to an Athletic Department trainer who told me in a folksy way that, in order to recover, I'd have to learn that pain was my friend—on the basis of which he prescribed a gymnastic regimen that had me doing vertical push-ups and walking up flights of stairs on my hands before the year was out. That could have left me crippled, but it didn't.

The most memorable consequence came three weeks after the wreck, when my arm was still in a sling. My motorcycle had been totaled, and, by way of Freudian compensation, I'd quickly grown a moustache. But I wasn't yet able to drive, and that was a definite problem because my wife was at that point more than eight months pregnant. We'd made arrangements for the baby to be delivered across the river in Lexington County—a decision that caused even greater dismay among our childhood friends than that our firstborn had made her world debut as a Yankee up in Boston.

Columbia was still a very conservative place. When Anne had informed her obstetrician that she wanted to try Lamaze again with her husband in the delivery room, he'd told her that wouldn't be possible. Actually, what he'd said was to tell me to get a girlie mag and a six-pack of beer and forget it, which so incensed my wife that she asked around and, having found a monitrice across the river whose name was Marie Campbell, announced that she'd have our baby there. That prompted her friends to protest that having "Lexington County" on our offspring's birth certificate would be an unbearable stigma. But my wife was undeterred, and she found a new obstetrician named Dr. Bodie who'd happily work with our monitrice.

Not long after that and sooner than we expected—just twenty days after my wreck—our second daughter, Susannah, decided to make an even more precipitous arrival than her older sister's had been, letting us know as darkness descended that she was in a considerable hurry. We urgently called my mother, who rushed to pick us up in her Volkswagen Beetle and drive us to the hospital where I dutifully donned a doctor's mask and scrubs and, despite my orthopedic handicap, had the stunning experience of helping with the delivery, making a one-handed catch with four hands backing me up.

Wildly euphoric, I made my way to the waiting room to share the good news with my mother, then started back to rejoin my wife and newborn daughter—though in the course of our precipitous arrival I'd failed to notice that, located next to ours, was another delivery room that was exactly the same in every respect but one. In order to talk with my mother, I'd pulled my mask below my mouth and, while doing my best to tug it back into place, I walked up to the bed and looked down at my wife—only to see it wasn't my wife.

For whatever reason, no one else was in attendance for the moment, and when the woman, who was clearly well along in labor, turned to me with a pleading look and groaned aloud, "Ohhhh, doctor!", I felt a sudden compelling urge to shoot for a daily double. I was sure I could pull it off—or out. There was really nothing to it.

But reason prevailed. I patted her on the shoulder and said as reassuringly as I could, "Don't worry about a thing. . . it's going to be okay." Then I exited and found my proper location.

My imposture was never mentioned, though I've often wondered since then if, somewhere in Lexington County or beyond, there's a woman who recalls her surreal hallucination of a mustachioed one-armed obstetrician appearing out of nowhere during her labor.

Our brief sojourn across the river had been so positive that we were back in a year and a half for the birth of our son Ben who was launched like a ball from a bat—but, off the injury list by then and fielding with two hands again, I easily made the catch.

13

A Close Call for Topeka

As every reader to this point will have noted, I was neither born famous nor had I achieved any fame by the time I had tenure thrust upon me. I'd earned multiple degrees, fathered a trio of offspring, and won plaudits for my teaching. But becoming a full professor would require a couple of books that, in the aftermath of my wreck and other life-threatening events, I was no longer inclined to write. I needed a *deus ex machina* and, out of nowhere it seemed, the machinery lay at hand.

So it would come about that, at the age of 38 and while still an associate professor, I was allotted a brief but glamorous sort of fame that, if it was prompted by anything, was the result of having a student who'd told her father how much she'd enjoyed a film history course taught by a guy who'd made some movies in England. In point of fact, I'd never laid claim to anything more than the truth—that, during my years at Oxford, I'd been a mere factotum for an undergraduate film purportedly underwritten by J. Arthur Rank. Nevertheless, my student's father, Gene Upright, was the programming head of our local ETV network, and it may have been that bit about the famous producer that snagged his full attention because, though it was at that early stage little more than a personal pipedream, he had a big project in mind involving the national schedule and the Exxon Corporation.

I was called in for an interview on the topic of classic films, and, having been proclaimed a prospective "on-camera talent," I'd undergone a screen test during which what had seemed so natural in the classroom became an unnerving ordeal featuring terse demands rasped like a taxi dispatcher's from a box on the studio wall.

"Okay, relax," it urged as if to a slow-witted cabbie. "Just think about who you're talking to."

"Whom," I silently said to myself, ever the English professor.

"Invite them into your living room."

Why would they be in my living room? Weren't we going to screen a movie?

"All those housewives in Topeka," it added, which somehow came across as luring them into the casbah. What came next was an admonition. "But keep what you say to them simple! You're sounding like a professor."

I *was* a professor, of course, and wasn't at the moment anywhere remotely resembling a living room. I was rooted under blinding lights in front of three hulking cameras that, responding to orders I couldn't hear, were gliding about like mastodons on wheels, peering with their unblinking eyes at my piteous *rigor mortis*.

"Why Topeka?" I weakly croaked, but the box had no reply as the director whose voice had been goading me came striding into the studio.

Actually, once transmuted from his disembodied state, he—the director Larry Lancit, which sounds a lot like a stage name but wasn't—was highly congenial to work with, a decade younger than I but already balding up front with a circle of hair like a laurel wreath and a slightly anxious look that, as soon as we started to talk, would instantly change to a smile. He had a wry sense of humor that I both shared and enjoyed as well as what I feared might be a highly implausible hope that, on the strength of what we'd create, he'd move up a rung or two to Boston, New York, or L.A., the system's premier production centers—just as I harbored thoughts of not only teaching films but eventually writing them too.

Both of us were still young, and it was, after all, a time that encouraged such overwrought dreams when, for most of the country as at home, there were only four basic networks and, though PBS was less than a decade old, we had at least a farfetched shot at making its national schedule as my student's father had envisaged. I had lots of ideas to share, but what I'd failed to reckon with was how difficult it might be to deliver the goods on tape.

"Just *talk* to them, Bern," urged Larry in his encouraging way. "Coax them into your home."

I knew he must mean susceptible viewers in Kansas because I could guess without being told the reaction of housewives closer to home whose preferences didn't run to Eisenstein or Cocteau. I could see them in my mind in kitchens all over the state, a half million Norma Raes with sweaty wisps of hair and avidly needy eyes locked in seamy rapport with genial afternoon hosts like Bob Barker or Chuck Barris while I stood leering in Studio D, game but catatonic in an artsy-fartsy turtleneck, inviting them instead aboard the Battleship Potemkin.

But stuck on viewers in Kansas, Larry conjured them up again from back inside his control room.

"I don't know any housewives in Topeka," I objected.

"You will, Bern. You will," he boomed from the black box on the wall, "soon as we go nationwide. LET'S HAVE SOME LIGHT ON THE FLOOR!"

With a blinding glare and searing heat, the furnace doors opened overhead as I noticed my upper lip was immovably paralyzed.

"That's it, Bern! Give 'em a smile. Can you see the prompter okay?"

I peered out from the Saharan blast. "I can see it, but the writing's too small. I can't come close to *reading* it."

"Well, it's got to stay where it is—just glance at it every now and then. But keep looking at the camera. . . and try to relax, Bern, just *relax!*"

"Larry. . ." I couldn't seem to pronounce my words. My tongue had become a wooden clapper.

"Somebody do something with his hair. He looks like Dennis the Menace. That's it. Okay, tape's rolling now. Give him a countdown there, Eileen, and QUIET IN THE STUDIO!"

I was alone once more at ground zero as the voice from the box became a beguilingly unctuous purr. "Remember those housewives, Bern."

A sudden silence ensued as if a fuse had been lit. I licked my lip as my heart began to thud like an overloaded washing machine. One of the crew stepped into the light with a Star-Wars headset over his ears, pointing in my direction. That was my signal to begin. I turned my rigid features towards Topeka and spoke into the camera. "I'm Benjamin Dunlap," I bleated, "and this is *Cinematic Eye. . .*"

"CUT!" the abrasive voice ripped through my casbah hideaway. "What's the matter with that front-screen?"

The hot lights started to fade, prompting a half-dozen crewmen to leap to life around me—but what did they have to worry about? Life was still sweet for them. Their tongues still \worked, their lips could move.

"Look, Bern. . ." The voice was patient, like Walter Cronkite on Quaaludes.

"Huh?"

"You don't have to shout! You've got a mike on. Listen. . . when you gesture, I want your hand between your shoulder and your lapel. Three inches either way and it's out of the shot. And try to relax, okay? Welcome them into your living room. Believe me, they're gonna love what you got."

"Larry?"

"HOLD THE TAPE! What's the matter, Bern?"

"None of this feels natural."

A pause, followed by an indistinct conversation in the control room. Then the voice was back, coaxing me again.

"Trust me, Bern. You look great. I mean it. . . really *sexy*. Just don't move your hand past your shoulder, okay?"

"Okay."

"Give him another countdown, Eileen."

The lights went down, and the spots rose overhead again like a half-dozen midday suns. A girl in aviator glasses stepped in front of me with a slate indicating that this was for real.

"Cinematic 'A,'" she said, winking with a conspiratorial leer.

I felt a wave of gratitude as if a nurse had let me out of the chair while the dentist was on the telephone.

"Quit screwing around, Eileen!" said the ruthless dispatcher's voice. "Let's focus, okay? And get it *right*!"

The girl in the tinted glasses made an obscene but eloquent gesture towards the box, and something about her sheepish defiance put me in mind of Diane Keaton in Woody Allen's *Annie Hall*, the same goofy but fetching Madonna-on-stilts sort of style.

Then I had a further thought, a shock of self-recognition. If she was Diane Keaton, who was I but the Alvy Singer of professorial movie critics setting my chessboard up on a sun-bleached studio beach for my match with Ingmar Bergman— since it was his script for *Torment*, the first of Bergman's career, that I was about to discuss and Woody was on the current cover of *Time*. . . witty, neurotic, relaxed. For a moment of calm resolve, I forgot about hard-to-please viewers in Kansas or anyplace else and the lights, the heat, the illegible teleprompter. I had a sure sense of who I was and what I was doing there. It was Woody whom I was addressing.

"Ready, Bern?" asked Larry over the box.

"Ready, Larry," I firmly replied, propping my foot on a stool with relaxed urbanity. It was there for me to sit on during the course of the shot.

"Roll tape!" Larry told the technicians.

I leaned forward with my elbow on my knee, my other hand wagging expertly between my shoulder and my lapel. The man in the headset pointed. But as I began my spiel, the sole of my slick-soled shoe slipped from the rung of the stool, propelling it like a bazooka shell towards a slide-projector stand from which movie stills would be beamed to a screen on the set behind me. As I watched in mortified disbelief, the stand collapsed in the wake of the stool as it caromed in the direction of Annie Hall. But she deftly stepped aside, and it clattered over the floor with one of its legs dangling loose. For a moment nobody moved.

"Sorry, Larry," I said, as if welcoming him to my living room.

There was a silence of the sort that, in a movie cliché, often precedes an explosion—then, in a strangely diminished voice, "No sweat, Bern," before the box went dead, though I could still hear the muffled reverb of Larry's despondent reaction. Things were wordlessly repaired, and after a while we resumed.

That was how it had all begun, the year and a half of my life that my wife would later see fit to deride as "A Close Call for Topeka"—though I suppose, in a symbolic way, it had actually started long before when Kenneth Clark and Jacob Bronowski emerged from their august research to cavort with the sirens of television. I can well remember the excitement in even the farthest outposts of our academic world. If there had been two, we told ourselves, any one of us with a polished shtick might someday be the third—third among the PBS sons of light!

Of course, Andy Warhol had by then promised virtually everyone a short happy snatch of celebrity, but as I've suggested already, we were greedy. We wanted much more than fifteen minutes of airtime, a season-long series at least, which in my improbable case would never have come about but for my friendship with the novelist George Garrett who, before he'd become a colleague at USC, had scratched out a pair of screenplays as a lark, one for a Hollywood film entitled *The Young Lovers* that got mercilessly panned and the other a low-budget spoof called *Frankenstein Meets the Space Monster* that was, as he himself found fitting, universally ignored. What George and I had in common, in addition to a love of film and highly revved-up metabolisms, was an underlying conviction that Balzac had gotten it right in calling his most serious work *La Comédie humaine*—and it was entirely in that spirit that, while in our cups one night, we'd decided to launch a movies-are-worthy-of-study scheme before a rival department could beat us to it.

That was in the early days of film study as part of a collegiate education, but within a couple of years we were teaching nearly forty per cent of the students in upper-level English courses—which, because our departmental budgets were based entirely on enrollment, led to big emoluments for our three or four dozen colleagues and an oversized load for me when George, to my great dismay, decided to move on.

That was when, as sheer chance would have it, the Exxon Corporation chose to underwrite a package of classic foreign films for broadcast on Public Television, and somebody at the local network began to worry that even such arty subtitled flicks might jeopardize state and federal funding—which is why, when my student told her dad about the class she was in, I was called upon to allay such qualms by popping up for just long enough before each movie began to tell any skeptical watchdog, "You might think these movies are nothing but fun, but I'm a film professor, and, as I intend to demonstrate, they're painfully edifying."

I knew what the network wanted, and that, as far as they were concerned, it was strictly for local consumption. But abetted by Larry from the start, I also knew, as few outsiders did, that SCETV was actually number four among the system's top producers—an anomaly mainly due to the fact that, when southern legislators were threatening to shut down public schools rather than integrate, a shrewdly far-sighted network head had persuaded the politicians that, in our recalcitrant state at least, educational TV might somehow serve that strategy. So, for the worst of reasons, one of the best of public networks was born and, with it, a rare opportunity for aspirants like me—especially by way of contrast with Boston, New York, or L.A. where the queue of famous scholars competing for such a shot was long and impossibly daunting.

But even with that advantage, I still faced major challenges like adjusting my presentation from the classroom to the tube and a problem much harder to address derived from the simple fact that, in graduate schools like Harvard, they don't teach you how to write for housewives in Topeka. I'd have to learn to express myself in a wholly different way with the added concern of knowing that, so far from being stuck in their seats, my viewers could cut me off with a testy flick of the wrist.

I tried to persuade myself that great numbers of them were starved for what public TV supporters liked to call "intelligent fare," embracing the hopeful notion that it was only the crassness of commercial sponsors that kept the medium's focus on blind maws while we instead were addressing people's minds. Hence, I decided to let a thousand flowers bloom—I would make of that guttural wasteland a polysyllabic garden.

Inevitably, of course, among those who'd seen my screen test, there were a few misgivings—though not about my vocabulary or even my odd southern accent. It was my artless haircut and the style-averse cut of my jib that made the front office nervous. So they brought in a very mod hairdresser from an Atlanta salon as well as a local haberdasher who specialized in revamps for rural legislators. But the outcomes were mixed at best. My new hairdo was disturbingly reminiscent of Derek Jacobi's in the recent *I Claudius* series while, according to a receptionist, the bill for my cream-colored trousers, which made me resemble something between a pimp and a fugitive from *The Love Boat*, had caused a minor uproar because of such extravagance for a virtual unknown's wardrobe. Eighty bucks was a lot of money back then, but that was how public TV worked if bigwigs thought it worth the while, and Larry had persuaded them it was.

"We're gonna make it, Bern!" he kept assuring me, though what he chose to gloss over was that, as we both were aware, we'd only been asked to produce five minutes per weekly show—five measly minutes, I thought, in which to tell posterity what I was burning to say about any given film, to rummage through my cinematic soul and divulge what smoldered within it.

I took our case to the highest-ranking network official I knew, the son-in-law of my mother's next-door neighbor who was an aunt of the CEO, and said to him that, though I understood the immediate need, fifteen minutes would have to be the absolute minimum and, if we hoped to go nationwide, thirty at the least. In order to humor me, it was eventually agreed that, as long as I wrote and delivered a dozen five-minute stand-ups, we'd tape a medium-length pilot of maybe ten minutes to be broadcast only locally as the last of the introductions. Production costs would be minimal and, as the head of the department pointed out, tape as opposed to celluloid could always be erased and used for something else.

So I was back to the matter of adjusting my delivery, about which the girl in aviator glasses would observe after my awkward first attempt that I'd come out of the chute on air as if riding a Brahma bull in eighty-dollar britches. "Note the vertiginous complexity of Piranesi's doleful fantasies," I said about a shot in that Bergman-scripted film—and even my wife confessed she didn't know what I was talking about. One day in the Piggly Wiggly, a total stranger came up to me as if to do me a favor. "Why don't you cut the crap," he fumed, "so we can just watch the movie!"

Even my friend Jim Dickey, whose opinion along with my wife's I tended to value most, said that listening to my rapid-fire spiel was like trying to read a boxcar when you're stopped at a railroad crossing as a train goes hurtling by. "You know it must say something," he grinned, swiveling his head to demonstrate, "but it's gonna cost you whiplash guessin' what!"

That was a poet's way of talking, but I knew he had a point because, in addition to being a brilliantly gifted poet critic, he'd written the script and played an on-screen role in adapting his novel *Deliverance* while George and I had been launching our courses on film.

As a matter of fact, George had also been publishing some of his finest work while we were working together, and, a few years later while Jim was knee-deep in other commitments, he and I would collaborate too on a number of video projects, the first of which involved an on-camera introduction for an hour-long documentary based on Depression-era photographs from the Farm Security Administration along with several newsreel clips and a number of field recordings recorded by the father-son team of John and Alan Lomax, the latter of whom I'd afterwards consult for a series on dance ethnography in the south.

For most of the scribbling tribe, of course, fame is a sometime thing, and Warhol's notion of its brevity applies to nearly all of us in the end. George and Jim were both immensely talented and at the top of their games, but, as they used to say in Hollywood westerns, the town just wasn't big enough for them both. Jim had gotten there first, and George felt obliged to move on to what were literally greener pastures, but I'd remain close to George for the rest of his life whereas friendship with Jim was a lot more complicated, a factor that came into play when we collaborated.

For that documentary project, I'd signed on as the writer only but, inspired by Humphrey Jennings' wartime film entitled *Listen to Britain*, I proposed dispensing with narration and bringing the photos to life by slowly zooming and panning using a close-up lens while appending natural sounds or solo instrumentals. This was well before Ken Burns had adapted the same technique while retaining voice-over commentary, and my producer thought it too radical. So, to make it appear more conventional, I suggested doing what we'd done at first for *Cinematic Eye*, using a brief introduction and even briefer conclusion—and to sweeten that compromise, I said I'd try to get Jim Dickey who was then in great demand for everything from late-night talk shows to presidential inaugurations. The producer declared we had a deal if Dickey agreed to do it for a fee that would be quite modest but not miniscule.

The further complication turned out to be his other more lucrative gigs, but Jim did agree on the sole condition that I'd compose his commentary, so he'd simply have to deliver it, assuming there'd be a teleprompter or cue cards of some sort. It was only at that point, after plotting out everything else, that I started to realize how awkward for our relationship that might potentially be—mainly because, despite the great disparities of age, achievement, and fame, our friendship was based on a sort of détente that literally putting words in his mouth was likely to put to a test.

It's easy enough to maintain, as many have done, that Jim was an egomaniac, but wary though I am of facile psychologizing, I think the truth of the matter is that going from football at Clemson to war in the Pacific had changed his view of the world from a Kiplingesque sort of game to a conflict of hunter and hunted or predator and prey which, however much he tried to define himself by affecting a feral swagger, was at odds with that other bookish self that aspired to be a poet. A lot of his best work derived from that contradiction and much of his worst from its absence. He openly identified with wolverines and sharks as well as those who killed with compound bows and planes, but what he kept concealed was that he wasn't in fact or at heart a former fighter pilot but instead a navigator, a man with a sextant and guitar who wrote about courage and fear as if he'd frequented both. Like Hemingway and many more who'd come of age in a war, he was also an alcoholic, and that gnawed away at his talent until, as he neared its end, that in itself was his subject—but his acuteness as a critic would never wane.

With friends he didn't play the alpha male, though with strangers his opening moves were often overbearing, and the closest we'd ever come to going head-to-head was during our first encounter at USC. His being older by fifteen years was somewhat offset by the fact that we'd both just joined the English Department for reasons that weren't that dissimilar—because, as he liked to say in interviews, it was "where the action ain't," meaning that he was pretty much free to do whatever he wanted. Supposing that to a lesser degree the same might apply to me, my wife and I, when the fall semester began in 1968, decided to give a drop-in for colleagues we already knew, one of whom was Cal Winton whose wife, Elizabeth, had grown up in a Sewanee-campus house where my weekend dates had sometimes stayed. Our party was a casual affair and, because the Wintons had known Jim and his wife Maxine from long before, they brought them along as well. That caught us by surprise because, by some previous arrangement, Jim was spending the fall at Georgia Tech while Maxine and their children were settling down in Columbia.

He was already a celebrated poet at that point, and, though I still bore a very faint sheen as an Oxford and Harvard hot-shot, I kept my distance while he prowled about our compact living room examining titles on the shelves of a tall Globe-Wernicke bookcase that had once held my father's law books. As I approached, he turned towards me pugnaciously and asked, "Who've you got here that you really like?"

I knew what books were on the upper shelf and named the most improbable. "Trumbull Stickney," I said in a similar tone of voice.

He plucked down my copy of Stickney's verse and, without opening it, began to quote, "Be still. The Hanging Gardens were a dream. . ." It was the obvious choice, one of only a couple that I could quote as well.

"That over Persian roses flew to kiss. . ." I tossed the next line back at him, and we finished the sentence together,

The curlèd lashes of Semiramis. . .

which, whatever the case for Jim, was as far as I could go.

He weighed the book in his hand, prompting me to think he'd probably reached his limit too, but then he muttered another phrase, "Apollo springing naked to the light." I knew it was from Stickney but couldn't recall any more. He saw that I couldn't and nodded as if he'd edged back into the lead. Then he scowled and asked, "How old are you?" as if we were squaring off again.

"Thirty," I told him, like the smaller of two billy goats.

"My God!" he said. "If I were thirty, what I would do!"

"How old are *you*?" I asked him.

He looked me up and down. "Forty-five," he said.

"My God!" was my retort. "If I were forty-five, what I'd have already done!"

It wasn't great repartee, but that's how it went verbatim—I wrote it down that night as if I'd just seen Shelley plain—and, to Jim's great credit rather than mine, we were friends from that point on. Knowing him was a privilege, but, as I've implied already, there were eventual complications with all the *grand guignol* and alcohol-soaked fiascos that made too close a friendship border on all-consuming. And yet, it was more than worth it in its intensity and excess for most of the next twenty years until both our lives had changed in ways that took us each in totally different directions.

When Jim's celebrity was truly stratospheric, just after *Deliverance* had hit the screen, there was a constant heady circus at his lakeside house on Lelias Court, hobnobbing with authors of every stripe but especially with writers from the south like Styron, Warren, and Tate. We spent evenings with Lowell again and with Wilbur, MacLeish, and Eberhart as well as with Spender and Yevtushenko—whom I'd meet up with again in thirty-five years on the campus of Wofford College, where he'd be as passionate in performance as he'd been on his visit to USC. . . so much so, in fact, that he and my friend Pat Conroy were the only two authors so over-the-top at their readings that I feared they'd collapse at the podium.

Jim, who knew no Russian, hadn't let that hinder his "translations" of Yevtushenko's poems, and, on the occasion of the Russian poet's visit, things were at such a fever pitch that, before the evening was over, Yevtushenko had taken to drinking from my wife's shoe while crooning "*malen'kaya mama*" into her ear, literally "little mother," and comparing her to Natasha at the end of *War and Peace*.

But much would change in the years after Maxine died in 1976 and Jim had married again, though we still were schmoozing at length whenever we happened to meet—and that was probably why, when I sat down to write the script that he was supposed to deliver, I managed to channel his voice and style so much better than I'd anticipated that we both were relieved and surprised. When we went over the lines together, he paused at a point where I'd written about the haunting sense that Walker Evans' photos evoke of sharecroppers in their cabins, how the austere lucidity of their stares is echoed amid the bare swept wooden floors by the white enameled basins hanging like shields on otherwise unadorned walls. Inspired as much by *Let Us Now Praise Famous Men* as I was by Jim himself, I'd tried to conjure, as Agee had, the futility of their dreams during sweltering hard-bitten nights and the straitened illusion-less dignity of their gaze.

"This is good," Jim said. "This is really good." Then he added deferentially, "Would you mind if I inserted a couple of words?"

"Of course not," I said. I knew the script was good enough.

He wrote two lines in with a pencil and handed them to me.

"In these photographs," he'd written, "they're trying to tell us something. They're trying to say they do not want to die."

With their simplicity and directness, they were worth more than anything else in the script. He himself was simply that good, like a painter who adds with a single flick of his brush the equivalent of a Mona Lisa's smile. All I could do was nod—and, though the program went on to win a couple of big awards, the only on-screen credit I got implied that I'd done nothing more than edit Jim Dickey's remarks as opposed to having specified every image, sound, and camera move in the course of its hour-long running-time for which, when the kudos began, the producer snapped up the praise as if it was her due. . . which according to Jim—who'd learned it the hard way, he said—was how it was always done.

"You've heard the one about the starlet. . .?" he asked.

"So dumb she slept with the writer? Yeah," I told him, "I know."

I guess he knew far better than I, but our friendship was intact and, though the housewives of Topeka were undoubtedly safer with me than they would have been with him, he was godfather to my son—and a couple of years before my series on film had aired, I'd gone with him to the hospital and was holding Maxine's hand just minutes before she died. It was out of deep feeling for both of them that, barely two months later, I declined to serve as best man for his marriage to a young student of his, and, though we saw less of each other after that, the bond between us remained. I was touched when, shortly before the pilot was taped for *Cinematic Eye*, he presented me with copy #1 of his poem *The Strength of Fields* that he'd read at President Carter's inauguration, repeating for me in a handwritten note that "we know simplicity is close to the source that sleeping men search for in their home-deep beds"—both admonitory advice and the source of some of the words I'd later put in his mouth.

I've already quoted what Jim would have to say after seeing that pilot aired. So when he joined my wife in suggesting that, in that initial attempt, I'd "overloaded every rift with sesquipedalian ore," I took his whiplash comment to heart and got Larry to let me revise the script and tape the pilot again—for which I deleted "doleful fantasies," merely urging my viewers to note "Piranesi's vertiginous complexity." Jim was silent after that, but my wife continued to shake her head with obvious consternation while, somewhere in the midwestern night, the unsuspecting housewives of Topeka slumbered fitfully in their beds.

But I was beginning to learn, and after thirty short introductions, the front office pronounced our pilot ready to take to New York which, in terms of editing rights for the films I'd be talking about, would be a crucial moment—our show-down with the cinematic muse. . . or, at least, with the big-time distributor who had her under contract. His name was Saul Turell.

At our Production head's suggestion, I'd be wearing the state-owned togs throughout the up-and-back trip, but at the very last minute I learned there'd been a change of plans. Because of some other business there scheduled the day before, I'd have to fly up by myself and meet our network's team at the office of Janus Films. That involved a still further complication because VHS was still such a new technology that the distributor lacked a playback unit—which caused some front-office type to conclude that, rather than rent one in New York, I'd have to carry it up myself along with a color monitor, ten newly-printed press books, and two copies of the tape, totaling fifty pounds or more.

Nothing was compact in those days, and my debonair silhouette was quashed by the things I carried as I staggered across La Guardia and into a cab for Manhattan. By the time I reached the Janus Films conference room high over Fifth Avenue, sweat had ringed my shirt cuffs with grime and tangled my blow-dried hair that had just begun to grow out and look less like a toupee. My wardrobe had lost its housewife-appeal, and I myself, in the eyes of Saul Turell and his fellow magnate Bill Becker, was taken for a delivery boy until our network's vice president affably hailed me by name.

They'd clearly been waiting for quite a while, so small talk was kept to a minimum while someone assembled the playback unit and a jittery picture leapt to the screen, paused, and then proceeded as a white-faced robot in natty attire leered at the camera and said as if from the heart of the casbah, "Hi! I'm Benjamin Dunlap, and this is *Cinematic Eye. . .*"

In fifteen minutes it came to an end, leaving us tensely huddled by the light of a color-bar haze. As I wondered if anyone noticed I was wearing the robot's clothes, it occurred to me that once upon a time Bob Barker had sat like us in suspense and even Merv Griffin perhaps—but surely not Jacob Bronowski or Kenneth Clark, whose ex-cathedra authority would have needed no such approval, nor would Andrew Sarris or Pauline Kael.

The lights came on overhead, and the bigger big-time distributor looked at me more closely. I could tell he recognized the wardrobe as, with a sudden change of expression, his face flashed a wide venal grin that reminded me of the ads for *Jaws*.

"At last!" he chortled expansively. "Something to sell to the BBC!"

Everybody relaxed and began to congratulate each other. With his backing assured, the rights would be cleared, and we'd be going nationwide with a thirteen-program series.

"Listen," the mogul said, brushing a speck of dust from my state-owned cream-colored trousers, "how'd you like to have lunch with François Truffaut?" His *Jules and Jim* would be the final film in my series.

I managed to gasp I'd like that fine, and, only a few minutes later, we strolled along Fifth Avenue together, past the spot where horse-drawn carriages picked up tourists and would-be lovers for movie-like rides in the park, the place where I'd always felt on the edge of somebody else's dream. Then, while we were crossing a side street, a spotlight of sun reached down and plucked us from obscurity—the tycoon and the delivery boy. . . and for that single cinematic moment, I was Scott Fitzgerald in my lost city. Forget Topeka, I thought, Manhattan was mine!

Truffaut and I had lunch with Saul Turell at the Sherry-Netherland. It was a peak experience for me, though I got off to a shaky start by addressing him as "Cher maître!" at which he seemed taken aback. He was only in his mid-forties then, just five years older than I, but, if indisputably a master, who was I to say so? For, despite such bracing encounters, I was still—in that high-stakes world—an utter amateur with nothing to my credit yet but a clever quarter-hour pilot and, on the deficit side, thirteen unwritten scripts that I'd have to come up with by September, not to mention my novice attempts at acting, producing, and editing tape.

On the other hand, as Jim Dickey generously said, I seemed to be getting the hang of it and hadn't so far been tossed off the set—an allusion to what had happened to him resulting from dueling egos while *Deliverance* was being shot. But Larry and I were a team, and with a national slot locked in, our network was suddenly thinking big, offering to underwrite such remote location sites as Monhegan Island off the coast of Maine for a program on Robert Flaherty's *Man of Aran*. My scripts were nearly intelligible, my delivery less spasmodic, and I was almost cocky by the time we took our crew on the road for that particular shoot—though I should have known better, of course.

The island, onto which no motorized vehicles are permitted, was the privileged haunt of those with refined but simple tastes, like the painter Andrew Wyeth and Jamie, his gifted son, whom we glimpsed as we disembarked from a lobster fisherman's boat. We'd been told that the island's rocky cliffs on its eastern side were among the highest on the east coast, so an almost plausible lookalike for Flaherty's wild Irish landscape. But the downside was that once again, as on my trip to Manhattan, there'd be a long portage to reach our scouted location and, wanting to help our undermanned crew, I carried a 12-volt battery—a portable power source that leaked a little acid onto my shoulder, burning a couple of holes through my state-owned turtleneck in a way that Larry applauded. It looked authentic, he said.

As we passed a modest-sized graveyard hemmed in by a picket fence, I glanced at the picturesque scene and was starting to turn away when I heard a woman call out, "Come on now, Zero! Get up already! We've got to get a move on!"

To the best of my knowledge, there was only one person in the world who went by the name of Zero—the actor Zero Mostel, best known in theatrical circles for *Fiddler on the Roof* and by movie buffs like me for *A Funny Thing Happened on the Way to the Forum.* So I scanned the burial ground until I spotted him lying supine on a mound with a tombstone as his headboard, eyes closed and fingers clasped across his famous stomach.

"Come on, Zero!" the woman repeated.

He didn't move, as if in some sort of rehearsal for what would, in fact, occur within a couple of weeks when he'd die of a sudden heart attack—though, whatever his premonitions, it struck me at the time as merely macabre clowning about of a sort that was tempting the gods.

That mood was still fogging my brain along with the acid burns on my shoulder when we reached our steep location where, with the same daredevil bravado I'd succumbed to so often before, I let Larry persuade me to inch my way out to a sliver-like perch high over the rocks below. According to his instructions, I'd turn and gesture out to sea, then back to the camera again while delivering a 90-second spiel—which, though that may sound like no time at all, was actually an eternity during which to talk and gesture and turn without a safety line or any net below.

For the initial two or three takes, I felt like a Wallenda. But technical glitches got in the way and suddenly, without warning, something enthralling entered my brain that I'd never felt before—what the French so vividly call *l'appel du vide*, the seductive siren-call of the abyss. On the thirteenth or fourteenth take, I began to feel an urge to soar like a bird from the cliff. After two or three more delays, the impulse to give it a try was all but overwhelming.

"Sorry, Bern!" I heard Larry shout from his safe and snug position. "We'll get it right. Just try to *relax* and. . ."

"I know! I know!" I howled into the wind. "Those horny housewives in Topeka!"

Whatever was in my head was certain that I could fly, and it took my full concentration to stop myself from demonstrating.

"Where's my body double?" I groused from the ledge amidst yet another pause for some sort of camera adjustment during which some cantankerous gulls discovered that I'd encroached on their domain. I tried to wave them off and nearly lost my balance.

"Pass him the gin, Eileen," Larry directed the girl in aviator glasses, who promptly swung a bottle on a string down to me from above, driving the gulls into a frenzy.

Though it wasn't an ideal way to steady my equilibrium, I took a purifying swig, like iodine on a cut, and the housewives' call—if that's what it was—at once began to fade.

"Show biz, Bern!" Larry shouted again. "You're in your living room, right? But quit fooling around with those gulls or you'll get bird-doo on those britches. . . state property, you know."

So, apparently, was the body inside them that managed somehow to survive the twenty-one takes of that perilous shot for a show that we'd later have to re-tape less ambitiously in a studio while working against a merciless series of deadlines that would have me frantically doing research and toiling over the rest of the scripts from breakfast to lunch each day while taping during the afternoon and editing throughout most of the night—using a new and highly innovative time-code-based technology that enabled me not only to juxtapose the famous Odessa Steps sequence from Eisenstein's *Battleship Potemkin* with Goya's *The Third of May 1808* and do it with relative ease but to demonstrate the manipulative power of Eisenstein's use of montage by re-cutting the sequence's shots to make heroes of the Cossacks instead and villains of the mutinous sailors. The catch-22 of that new technology was that I was tempted to take full advantage of it, and, like the complexity of the preceding sentence, each of our half-hour shows had literally hundreds of edits strung together—which, if we'd been cutting and pasting on an antiquated Steenbeck, would have been like building the Eiffel Tower out of Legos.

Ideally, of course, I would have completed all the scripts, then taped the shows and edited them for broadcast. But just as we were rolling into full-tilt production, Larry had gotten an offer he couldn't refuse and left overnight for New York. The network briefly hired a director from outside whose higgledy-piggledy rock-show style was based on *A Hard Day's Night* but, after a costly fiasco on location in Atlanta amid the faded opulence of the very same Fox Theater where I'd gone to see my first movie some thirty-odd years before, I feared our series would be scuttled.

Actually, when the results were in from our more than twenty straight hours of taping in Atlanta, it seemed that I myself had been scuttled as, in the roughly-edited course of a twenty-eight-minute program, I appeared to have gone from youthful middle-age to haggard decrepitude. It was at that desperate point that I beseeched the network's senior director—a man I hardly knew, named Sidney Palmer—to take the project on, and he reluctantly agreed with several important provisos: that we'd tape exclusively in the Studio D where our pilot had been produced and that we'd redesign the set.

To my great good fortune, Sidney was one of the princes of this earth. From a distance, he resembled a quizzical be-spectacled third brother for Tweedledum and Tweedledee, but up close he had the sternly appraising gaze of Johann Sebastian Bach with just a hint of amusement at the corners of his mouth while, on the production floor, he was totally in command. In a matter of days, we had three giant plywood reels stacked atop each other with a fourth one upright on its edge spilling out classic movie stills as, without any prompting needed from him, I welcomed the housewives once again, this time to German expressionism.

It was a spare but elegant set of an understated but functional sort that, as I'd come to understand was typical of Sidney himself—a former musical prodigy who'd spent his childhood concertizing with some of the world's great orchestras in addition to teaching at Juilliard, conducting and composing on the side while studying with Olivier Messiaen. In his early twenties, he'd been commissioned—in what he modestly claimed was a case of mistaken identity—to compose a coronation march for Queen Elizabeth II, but then, while still quite young, he'd experienced the sort of neuromuscular disorder that had afflicted Robert

Schumann, and, knowing he'd never perform again at his best, he'd walked away from the piano and taken up television, directing opera, film, and ballet instead—though, every now and again, he'd do a little composing, as he would as a gift for me more than twenty years after we met for a college inauguration.

Naturally enough, as a performing artist himself, he was comfortable switching live from an editing board offstage which was relevant for my on-camera work for which he tutored me expertly, and his preparation was done with such erudition and finesse that even Leonard Bernstein had asked to work with him. But despite his often-underappreciated brilliance among many who knew far less, Sidney was self-effacing and generous to a fault along with being a wonderfully loyal friend as well as a masterful teacher—though like some of his favorite composers, he tended to favor established styles as opposed to unorthodox novelty so, inevitably and forthrightly, we had occasional disputes. When the playfully off-beat script I'd written for *La Strada* struck him as too Fellini-esque, he declined to direct it himself but turned it over without rancor to "Ditsie" Weynand, a talented young assistant who, later in her career, would understandably revert to her given name of Diana and become a leading expert on CMX editing, with regard to which we were literally on the cutting edge.

But we were frantically under the gun. By the time we'd gotten back underway after Larry's abrupt departure and the debacle in Atlanta, our first air date was approaching fast and, with panic beginning to bubble up, the three of us had realized—Sidney, Ditsie, and I—that even our best projections would have us at work on show number five when show number one was airing. The squeeze soon left us half-demented, which came across as verisimilitude when I stumbled into a blue-screen shot and started holding forth on the lunacy by design in Caligari's world—and our all-night editing sessions in a dimly lit cocoon were becoming hallucinatory with Ditsie at the keyboard and me calling out time-coded numbers like sleepless U-2 pilots headed for reasons we couldn't explain on a mission over Topeka.

Not so coincidentally perhaps in terms of that far-fetched metaphor was that that one of our technicians during those nightlong sessions had served as a chopper pilot in Vietnam and had a tendency, when things got too intense, to lapse into manic flashbacks, screaming that we were going to crash and doubling our anxiety. But after a while, as the schedule got even tighter, Ditsie herself grew so adept that the two of us could pretty much manage on our own—notwithstanding the panic we ought to have felt when, with ten days before our first air date, we only had three shows in the can. . . or the fact that as Peter Anderson said (he being our droll production head), I'd started to look like Marley's ghost dragging my celluloid chains behind some fancy state-owned britches while Ditsie resembled Bob Cratchit.

Our lead time narrowed week by week. In the midst of a shot for show number six, a mirror fell off its camera mount and smashed onto the studio floor, but we managed to edit around it. In show number nine, without marring the shot, Eileen, my sometime Annie Hall, deftly managed to swat a fly that, after circling my head for several takes, had lit on my cream-colored trousers—which were cleaned and back on the set in hardly more than an hour. Whatever occurred, we kept rolling tape, hoping to edit the rough spots out while maintaining continuity. We finished the final show a half-day before it aired, dispatching it via satellite. Then we simply collapsed.

A few months later when each of us had moved on to various new undertakings, an odd report from Master Control just happened to get to Peter Anderson's desk while all three of us were there. During the night, it seemed, some drunken prankster kept teeing them off by trying to place a call to anyone there in charge.

"How'd you know he was drunk?" asked Peter over the inter-office phone.

"Oh, he was drunk, all right," insisted the tape technician. "He kept rambling on about *Cinematic Eye* and how it might be getting an Emmy at Lincoln Center. We finally took the receiver off the hook."

But they called again that afternoon, and the unbelievable news was true. In all its inscrutable winnowing of video wheat from chaff, the National Academy of Television Arts and Sciences had indeed seen fit to nominate our series for an Emmy—for "Outstanding Program Achievement"—and, as the nighttime caller had said, our team of three was invited to attend the ceremony which would, of course, be televised nationwide.

I wore my on-camera duds again. As we approached Lincoln Center on foot, I spotted the paparazzi and autograph hounds clustered about the entrance, mobbing each celebrity as he or she tried to enter.

"Brace yourselves," I cautioned Sidney and Ditsie. "I'm afraid my britches will give us away."

"Which as you know," added Sidney on cue, "belong to the people of South Carolina . . ."

". . . and could end up in a museum someday," Ditsie loyally pointed out.

". . . like Judy Garland's slippers," I said.

We'd become a close-knit team.

"These bricks aren't yellow," Sidney complained.

At thirty feet, the mob began to take note of us. At twenty feet, they appeared to hesitate. At less than ten, they parted like the Red Sea, and we passed through unmolested. Despite my signature look, I seemed to be incognito.

At the banquet before the ceremony, we sat with our main competition, the producer of CBS's long-running *Camera Three*, along with three members of the Academy who, to my guileless eye, looked more like shopping-bag ladies—three crones decked out in red, black, and platinum wigs as luridly as the Fates in a Bob Fosse musical, confiding as we talked that they always knew in advance who was going to win.

I chatted with them uneasily, half expecting to be hailed as the upcoming Thane of Cawdor.

"I think they'll win," I said to the crone in the platinum wig. "I used to watch *Camera Three* when I was a kid."

"Here in New York?" asked the shopping-bag lady.

"No, no. In South Carolina."

"From so far away!" she shrieked. "Agnes! Did you hear that? He's here from North Carolina!"

"From even farther than that," I said.

"Listen, honey," Agnes advised from her cloud of scarlet nylon. "Don't feel badly if you lose." She gestured at the producer from *Camera Three*. "He just got cancelled after twenty-six years on air."

"I knew you weren't from New York," observed the brunette Fury, bending over to give her Supp-hose a tug. "You talk like Andy Griffith."

"It's time to go to the theater," grumbled Agnes.

The platinum blond tossed me a ghastly smile. "Well. . . break a leg, dearie," she said, then caught herself up and put her hand on my arm as if giving a tourist directions. "That's what we say in show business when we wish somebody luck."

I didn't want to disappoint her. "Ah've already broke it twict," I replied, the leading movie critic of Mayberry, R.F.D.

She rolled her eyes and reached for her shopping bag to head for their seats inside. The encounter with them had been ominous, but Manhattan was a long way from Topeka.

The ceremony itself was like a re-run of *Hollywood Squares*. All the high rollers of daytime TV were there, the hot shots of the game shows and the soaps. We were there along with them because, though our shows were mostly broadcast at night, our national feeds had gone out on Saturday mornings—like *Camera Three* on Sundays, most recently over PBS like us.

Bob Barker was the host, smarting because, by filling that role, he'd disqualified himself from the first nomination he'd received in twenty-three years and counting. I thought about guys like Barker who'd been slogging their way for so long through swampy afternoon schlock and realized how at odds with them our category was—not feeling so much superior but as if I'd arrived expecting *As You Like It* and found myself instead in a seat for *The Price is Right*.

The show was resolutely garish. Some hyped-up kids performed a rambunctious song-and-dance that brought the whole house down when they urged their beleaguered parents to take away all their books and baby brothers but not their afternoon TV. I squirmed in my seat and looked around at Marlo Thomas squeezing Phil Donahue's arm and Burt Reynolds sprawled across the aisle sitting with Dinah Shore—at least, I thought it was Burt Reynolds, though he seemed to be in disguise because something about his hair resembled the shopping-bag ladies.

Our category was listed fifth in the program with the biggest awards to follow. But I knew my wife would be watching at home and conceivably some of those numberless hordes that Larry had foreseen invading my living room—insatiable housewives spinning their dials, searching through tasteless alternatives for a man in a garnet turtleneck and the hint of a southern drawl. I mused on the whitened bones of other star-struck professors amid the video shoals of eastern Kansas, and I thought of Clark and Bronowski, strapped to the masts of their series, hearing that plaintive cry as it rose from the prairie night not only for them alone but, puzzling though it must seem, for Benjamin Dunlap too!

I calmly reviewed what I'd say if we somehow managed to win. "First of all," I thought I'd begin, "I want to thank D.W. Griffith. . ." Bob Barker would shake his head and laugh. "What a guy!" he'd probably say on mike and, if you could read his lips, "Amazingly cool for his first time out." If I lost, I'd keep my composure in case the cameras were zeroed in. Even Dinah would wonder who I was, though maybe Burt would confide that we both were friends of Jim Dickey.

As things turned out—though I don't know how they determined this so early in the program—the event was running long, and our category was announced during a Gaines dog-burger commercial. We lost to *Camera Three*, just as the Furies had forewarned. I caught its producer's eye and saluted congratulations. He looked at me and shrugged. After all, he was out of a job—I was still a professor of sorts, if something of a has-been as a so-called on-camera talent.

I got home much later that night, but when I checked at the network next day, there was a stack of long-delayed fan mail waiting for me to answer along with an urgent message that Don Simpson had called from Hollywood. I tried to return the call at once but could only get to his secretary who reported that, while relaxing in his hotel suite before a production meeting, Mr. Simpson had caught an episode of my series for PBS and wanted to discuss it. I asked if I should call him back, but she said he'd call me again when he could find the time. She added that I should know "he's a *very* important man"—though needless to say, I'd not only never hear from him again but, when he died in 1996, I'd learn he'd been so erratic throughout his movie career because of cocaine addiction. He'd probably done a lot of impulsive things while idling here and there.

It would be the only occasion when, albeit very faintly, I'd hear the Hollywood mermaids singing each to each, but that was okay, I told myself—not only because I knew in my heart that such a life wasn't for me but because, at the bottom of that pile of accumulated mail, was the letter that I'd been waiting for. . . from Milwaukee instead of Topeka, but unmistakably *the* letter.

"Dear Benjamin Dunlap," it began, proceeding to quote a line of mine about the movie experience. "*'Like those long Etruscan banquets smiling in the dark'*"—she'd underlined my words before going on to declare, "Oh, yes! I murmured to myself on hearing you speak that phrase at the end of our thirteen weeks and deciding that I'm in love with you. My only question now is whether you'll come to Milwaukee, or I must go to wherever you are in the wilds of South Carolina." It was signed, "Impetuously, Lois Hindenburg."

I examined the letter closely. Was it a hoax? I asked myself. The last name sounded suspect, but lots of German Americans were supposedly in Milwaukee and, though the handwriting looked a bit juvenile, the wording seemed wholly sincere. . . and, since beggars couldn't be choosers, maybe Larry had gotten it right about those housewives tuning in.

I composed my answer carefully, striving for a light touch. "Dear Lois," I wrote in longhand. "I've hoped for quite a while that someone would detect in me what you suppose you've seen, and your extremely flattering letter is the closest reassurance that I've received. But, even on PBS, television can be a deceptive medium. I fear I'm much too old at forty-three, too short at five feet seven, and in other respects, most regrettably, unsuitable for you."

I paused to consider the past few months and my brief celebrity before adding facetiously, "However, if you choose to persist in your folly, please send me a photograph, a lock of hair, or some other such memento by which I may determine if I am, as I suppose, too old, too short, or otherwise unsuitable for you." I signed it, "Prudently, Benjamin Dunlap."

I studied what I'd written. It was wry enough, I thought—I trusted she'd see that and understand as well that I had nothing untoward in mind. But something still was missing, and I was curious. So I tacked on a P.S., "Have you ever been to Topeka?"

The reply arrived by return mail. "My dear Benjamin Dunlap," it began. "Words too are often deceptive. I am not a schoolgirl, as you seem to have supposed, but a spinsterish schoolteacher who writes such letters once every year or so, usually to Paul Newman or Willian J. Brennan. Yours is the first truly personal reply I've ever received and certainly the only request for a photo or lock of hair as opposed to sending me an autographed 8x10. But I am fifty-seven years old, just under five feet ten, and unable to fit inside a photograph—for, as you might have guessed, my name is but a descriptive *nom de plume*. So you see, my charming, naïve professor, it is I, alas, who am much too old, too tall, and in other respects unsuitable for you." It was signed, "Realistically, Lois."

In an instant they'd been expunged, all those restless red-cheeked housewives lying awake amid the alien corn aching for what they'd glimpsed so elusively on the screen including, on moon-soaked prairie nights, even Benjamin Dunlap. All that romantic yearning gone, dispelled by an epistolary blimp writing to me from Milwaukee, and not even those luminous britches— a gift from the treasurer's office now hanging in my closet— could ever lure it back again, though I'd keep them in reserve there just in case.

More than forty years have passed since then, in the course of which I'd go on to write—and, as often as not, produce—some fifty additional programs and series, mostly of a similar sort with several, including dramas, winning desirable prizes. Except for seminars now and then, my professorial days have recently come to an end, and, though their books are still on my shelf, both Clark and Bronowski are gone along with François Truffaut and my friends and sometime collaborators George Garrett, Jim Dickey, and Sidney Palmer. Though largely forgotten now, Carl Sagan was third among the PBS sons of light in a wardrobe very much like the one so anxiously chosen for me, and a program entitled *Sneak Previews* that debuted shortly before my own turned out to be the one that would stick around for another twenty years just as Larry Lancit—who'd escorted me from obscurity, as it were— would find a more reliable superstar in the person of LeVar

Burton and, for twenty-three stellar seasons, direct a program called *Reading Rainbow*.

In my own long post-celebrity glide, life seems as fleeting now as a thirteen-program series and innocence as remote as *Camera Three* or *The Andy Griffith Show*. But what's most salient from the past is often what seems in retrospect most comically absurd—such as Larry's image of me rampaging through bedrooms in Kansas or my letters from Lois Hindenburg, whoever she might have been.

I used to think of her late at night when, as if from a box on the wall, our neighbor's barking dog was keeping me half-awake. "Ah, Lois! Lois!" I'd sigh to myself, having long since shared her putdown with my wife, who'd laughed and said it had served me right—though, with my vanity battered but still intact, I'd continue my silent monologue, assuring the flighty Ms. Hindenburg that, "I'd have welcomed you into my living room, relaxed, and acted so natural that I feel sure we could have been friends, discussing favorite movies of ours. . . or the effigies of Etruscans, if you preferred." But she'd never seen fit to write again—which may have been in the end, as Jim Dickey might have put it, a deliverance of sorts for us both. She was probably better off with Newman and Justice Brennan.

Then the box on the wall would go blessedly dead. The dog's fifteen allotted minutes were up. My wife slept on serenely by my side.

14

A Votary of Terpsichore

What are the pathways to wisdom? Confucius reportedly declared that "A man who hasn't studied music needn't be taken seriously," while at roughly the same archaic time—though half a world away— Pythagoras would presumably have agreed since harmony and proportion were just as important to him. More than two millennia later, Albert Einstein was equally explicit. "The theory of relativity occurred to me by intuition," he said, "and music was the driving force behind that intuition."

So, without purporting to be wise, where exactly does that leave me? Not only do I lack any formal instruction in music but, for all their twisting and turning, neither my model Odysseus nor my totem the fox is noted for euphony—though Homer certainly was, and who can say whether his hero too, once reinstalled on Ithaca, didn't beat his spear into lyre? He was an inveterate bard of sorts, and as for foxes, they also, when I hear them yapping in my woods at night, are starting to sound a bit closer to song than I myself can manage and, in any case, are quick and nimble-footed—which leads me to my essential point that Terpsichore is the muse of dance as well as of lyric verse and that, despite his admonitions about playing the wrong sorts of music, even Plato considered the study of dance to be crucial for future leaders.

All that's by way of dignifying a decision I made when, in the wake of my PBS success and prior to any subsequent series, I set off in a direction that, to many who otherwise wished me well, seemed absolute lunacy or, at best, a hopeless mid-life crisis.

To begin with, it's not as if I was obeying some sort of genetic imperative for, aside from my grandfather's baritone rendering of
his Rotary Club repertoire, I can find no indication among my recent forebears of even the slightest musical aptitude. My mother loved painting and literature but was completely indifferent to music and warbled "Jingle Bells" as if it had been arranged by Arnold Schoenberg. My father had been a highly gifted athlete but took no interest at all in art of any kind. And yet, though they wouldn't have seemed a propitious pair for turning out future musicians, if their positive traits were added together and given the right sort of soundtrack, they might plausibly have produced a reasonably talented dancer—and my wife's great gift to me in midcareer, when that option had seemingly come and gone, would lie in urging me to pursue it.

But where'd that proclivity come from? I can only guess it derived from an all-pervading rhythm antecedent to music or words or even awareness of myself, something akin to what I'd later suppose I'd remembered from the womb impelling me to be born and take up the dance of life—an impulse I'd obeyed, of course, and though I'd sing off-key like my mother, even at three or four I could beat out intricate time and used to rock to cadences heard only in my head like a conch shell held to my ear.

Then, while still in my early teens, I had a curious dream set in a greenish-blue grotto that, as I realized at the time, was based on a picture seen long before in a version of "Puss in Boots" with the monarch being a lobster king seated upright on his throne surrounded by animal-courtiers decked out in human garb. I can't say if I was dreaming in technicolor or merely recalling the illustration, but the crux of the matter was straight out of Charles Perrault because, as in his fairytale, I'd just performed some heroic deed for which I was being awarded three wondrous gifts from the king.

I can still recall what ensued in the dream as if I were watching a movie, beginning with a drumroll of sorts and a lizard-like herald who then announced that, as the first of my great rewards, I would have bestowed on me an immense amount of wealth, at which everyone started to mew and crow like an afternoon quiz-show crowd, though I myself was distinctly underwhelmed. Still, there were two more prizes to come, and I hoped they might get better.

The second announcement was that I'd live to a very old age, enjoying blissful pleasures of every sort. Again, the ooohs and ahhhs broke out, but I felt bitterly disappointed as if the gifts were going nowhere. Then, after clearing his throat and scrolling a bit further down, the herald proclaimed in a slightly puzzled voice, "And, lastly, his majesty has decreed that, from this this moment on, whenever you choose to speak, the sound of a lute will accompany whatever you say."

The crowd expressed its bewilderment but, despite the fact that in all probability I'd never even heard a lute, I was so ecstatic that I woke up suffused with joy and rushed to write it all down, noting as I did so that the way the dream had ended had almost certainly come from another tale by Perrault in which a young girl was rewarded for her kindness by having jewels and flowers scatter from her lips whenever she started to speak as opposed to her rude older sister who had toads and vipers spew forth. But, regardless of its source, I was vaguely aware at the time that my dream was really about the gift of gab—of "eloquence" I'd have later said—which was something I truly craved as, like one of the young adventurers in so many such stories I'd read, I wanted to make the most of life.

At about the same time, just as I was setting out on my early prize-winning career, I ran across a copy of *Walden* and Thoreau's ferocious resolve "to put to rout all that was not life, to cut a broad swath and shave close, to drive life into a corner," and I understood something more about my dream—that prizes were only a means, not in any sense the end. . . and experience and expressiveness were the key.

It's odd that so childish a dream should have borne such symbolic freight, but I see quite clearly now that the lute, as a key detail, bespoke a much deeper desire, and the fact that it was so distinctly musical makes it all the more inexplicable that, even today in my eighty-fifth year, I still haven't actually studied what has mattered so much to me so much for so excruciatingly long. I can only read music laboriously and noodle about on the piano, but no one would mistake me for an accomplished musician despite the fact that I'd always promised myself that when I retired, as I more or less did after turning seventy-five, I'd take on that task at last. But here I am merely dabbling again which may require some further explanation if, in the Elysian Fields not all that long from now, I should find myself face-to-face with Confucius or Pythagoras —though I'm about to rehearse what I'll probably say for myself while trusting that, should I encounter him, Einstein might cut me a little slack.

I'd begin by telling him a story that goes back to my childhood in the '40s when I was still in grammar school. My parents, especially my father, wanted a "regular" boy, and, in that far-off time and very provincial place, though I did all the things a regular boy should do, I had a small radio in my bedroom, and on Monday evenings I'd crouch down next to it with my ear pressed up to its speaker—so closely, in fact, that I toppled a couple of lamps while keeping time to the music played on *The Voice of Firestone* and *The Bell Telephone Hour* and, as I'd start nodding off and was crawling into bed, to stirring Sousa-like strains from *The Band of America*.

I can't remember on which of those programs I first heard Borodin's gorgeous and frenzied "Dance of the Polovtsian Maidens," but it rattled around in my head for months, and I became so avid for more that I begged my parents to let me study piano. We weren't well off—but no one I knew was well off, and yet most of the girls and some of the boys took lessons and had recitals.

My father refused. "You want to be a sissy?" he asked. "You want to be like Alan Taylor?"

I didn't know who Alan Taylor was, but eventually I'd learn that he was my parents' age, unmarried, and played the cello. It was clear I shouldn't set out to be like him, so when, in the fourth or fifth grade, my school was visited by an itinerant music teacher named Mr. Krueger who had a foreign accent as well as wire-rim glasses, a carefully trimmed moustache, and an imperious old-world manner, I signed up for an interview without my parents' permission.

When I met with Mr. Krueger, he asked what instrument I wanted to play.

"The trumpet," I told him.

That sounded manly, I thought, so my father might approve. But Mr. Krueger demanded to see my teeth. "Nein! Nein!" he bristled when he saw them. "The teeth are wrong. Show me your hands."

I held them out.

"So!" he said. "You play the cello. A beautiful instrument. You will be happy with the cello."

But I knew I wouldn't and couldn't, even if we could afford it. Becoming like Mr. Krueger was almost certainly as bad as being like Alan Taylor.

I later learned that Mr. Krueger himself was a cellist. He was also a Holocaust survivor who'd ended up somehow in South Carolina where he wangled a living by teaching kids in schools that didn't have music programs. He had a young daughter I never met or saw, but she died when she was eleven, and someone long afterwards told me that at her funeral Mr. Krueger had played the cello in the rain next to her open grave. "The Dying Swan," they said.

I've carried that scene in my mind for many years, conjured up like an image from Perrault but as indelibly imbedded there as if I'd witnessed it myself with Mr. Krueger savagely sawing away, rain mingling with his tears and trickling down through his moustache, his daughter inert in her coffin, his students and their parents bewildered and distraught by such histrionic grief. Each time I hear the Saint-Saëns piece, that tragedy comes to mind as if, however remotely, I'd been complicit—like the flapping of a butterfly's wing or the swatting of a fly.

With several of my friends, I joined the junior choir at Trinity Episcopal where my grandfather, who'd formerly been its senior warden, always sat in what we regarded as our family's pew just a few feet from the pulpit so he could hear the sermon, cupping his hand behind his ear as if deeply immersed in what was being said. After decades of hunting ducks from blinds in the lowcountry marshes, he could barely hear on his shooting side, but our minister, Louis Melcher, had a stentorian style that, though I could hear him well enough, I couldn't begin to decipher even when he'd drawn his text from "Hickory, dickory, dock, the mouse ran up the clock"—which, on one wholly baffling occasion, he'd declaimed with all the gravity of tablets bought down from Sinai.

But directed by Robert Van Doren, a Juilliard alum and highly accomplished organist, the senior choir was spectacular and featured a home-grown tenor named Ed Betsill who later befriended me and, as I'd then discover, had become good friends as well with some of the world's great singers.

As an aspiring vocalist, I sat with others my age on the opposite side of the chancel—and of the musical spectrum—in stalls that were closest to Mr. Van Doren's sternly perfectionist gaze as we waited in cassocks and surplices for his signal to begin. I wanted to sing well, but, hampered as I was by faulty ear-training at home, my notes, though clear and strong, almost always went awry. On one occasion as we rehearsed, he abruptly rose from the organ bench and, waving his arms to continue, moved in a querulous crouch from one of us to the next, listening as if for something I couldn't hear.

When he got to me, he cried, "Aha!" Then, instructing everyone else to stop, he repeated the last few notes we'd sung and gestured for me to repeat them. I mumbled, and he frowned, "Again!" My second attempt was flatter than my first, eliciting snickers from my friends. Nervously, I started to smile, compounding my erring and straying ways. Mr. Van Doren folded his arms. From now on, he said, I should simply mouth the words without any joyful noise. For several weeks I did as I'd been told, but the verdict was painfully clear—my singing career was over.

That was a definite setback, but it left me less dismayed than I might have otherwise been. I continued playing various sports, drawing up comic-book dogfights between Zeros and P-40s, and writing heroic adventure tales, merely biding my time because I knew when I got to the seventh grade I'd have a music class at last. It wouldn't be too late, I thought, and though I'd heard that Miss Swearingen, the teacher, could be a holy terror, that wouldn't matter to me. At least, I didn't think it would until the long-awaited first day of class when she asked for a show of hands by all who were studying music. Most of the girls predictably waved their arms along with a few of the boys, the ones who were generally chosen last when teams were picking up sides.

Miss Swearingen rearranged our chairs. Those already studying music were clustered about her piano while the rest of us were told to move our desks to the other side of the room and silently work on something else. I couldn't believe my misfortune. All the mysteries and treasures of music were going to be discussed and enjoyed but just beyond my hearing. Surreptitiously on the second day, I edged my chair-desk closer. But Miss Swearingen caught me in the act, and perceiving it as a deportment problem, kept me in from recess, letting me know in no uncertain terms that, if I disrupted her class again, I'd be suspended from school.

I was old enough by then to make a little money from an afternoon paper route with my old friend Harry Scrivener, and I knew from the radio what recordings I wanted to buy. So, as I accumulated what was needed, I made my way down Saluda Hill to the Five Points music shop owned by a Hungarian violinist who, with his pianist wife, was part of a struggling local orchestra made up largely of amateurs. Mr. Racz was testy with me at first for rifling through the record bins but began to relent when, after lengthy deliberation, I decided to buy a single disc at a time—of Rubenstein, for example, performing a Chopin Polonaise (the one in A-flat major) or the First Piano Quartet playing three of his Études. All the records I bought were breakable 78s which, not wanting to explain, I smuggled into our house wrapped in an old windbreaker. We didn't have a record player but, after hiding my collection in the closet that I and my younger brother shared, I'd take the recordings out when I was alone in our bedroom, running my finger over the grooves and trying to replay the music in my head.

Needless to say, as my cousin Hope Savage would learn, that was the sort of irrational act that could mean big trouble if you got caught, so I was desperately concerned when I came home from school one day to be confronted by my mother. She'd found the records and, looking very perturbed, demanded to know where they'd come from. I told her, and, to my utter disbelief, my father bought us a 45-rpm record player and, not long after that, an upright piano as well. He told me I could teach myself to play, and, along with a few additional recordings that he bought from a shop uptown (one of which was "Bongo Bongo Bongo, I Don't Want to Leave the Congo"), he reckoned that would do it. . . and maybe it would have if I'd worked at it hard enough, though I evidently didn't. I painstakingly worked a few pieces out, even some simplified Chopin preludes, but after that I bogged down and didn't progress much further.

On the other hand, there was my second cousin twice removed, Samuel Latimer, who was also my godfather and, in a way, my great uncle because, when orphaned in or around the turn of the century, he'd been raised by the family of my father's mother, Mary Jo Witherspoon Dunlap. He'd become the editor of *The State* newspaper, which meant, among other things, that he got complimentary tickets to whatever Sol Hurok chose to present at our city's Township Auditorium.

Although Sam was a lifelong bachelor with a nervous tic of sniffing and jerking his head to one side, he was full of family loyalty and tediously insistent on the subject. But he'd had a moment of stage-struck glory once. . . as a doughboy in France towards the end of World War I.

Probably because there was no one else to do it and because in his civilian days, as a copyboy first and then as a reporter, he'd already formed the habit of attending every theatrical event that paused on its way to Atlanta, he served as a sort of unofficial morale officer and, following the Armistice, was officially put in charge of entertaining his idle brigade. More or less single-handedly, it seems, he'd created a sort of vaudeville review that General Pershing himself just happened to attend, and, after the general commanded that every soldier still stationed in Europe should have a chance to see it, it was taken on the road and Sam got a giddy taste of an impresario's life from which he'd never recover.

Through the years in Columbia as I was growing up, he took me to see every classical musician from Rubenstein to Ormandy and back, always with the best seats in the house and often with trips backstage to meet the great performers. I saw Rubenstein more than once, and on the first occasion, he played the Chopin Polonaise that I'd come to know so well along with other works I recognized like de Falla's "Ritual Fire Dance"—and I can vividly remember seeing and hearing the latter as an encore at a concert to which I'd gone with a very high fever, watching his jack-hammer hands pounding out cadenzas while I reeled in my front-row seat, absorbing the notes like bullets from a gun while returning fire with the flu.

Sam took me to operas too, including Boris Goldovsky's troupe performing *Il Trovatore* for which I got to super onstage as a spirited Gypsy boy which, to my great relief, didn't involve any singing—though, disappointingly, I wasn't entrusted with a hammer during the Anvil Chorus. I can also recall a D'Oyly Carte *Mikado* which, to my delight at the time, seemed as much about beheading and seppuku as about its ostensible subject of love. If it rained on Saturdays and there was nothing else going on, I listened to broadcasts from the Met which lasted all afternoon, replete with mystifying thumps and the sound of clattering chains amid blood-curdling shrieks and, every now and then, a mirthless drawn-out howl that choked on its own laughter.

But the greatest revelations of all were the ballet companies—the Ballet Russe de Monte Carlo and American Ballet Theatre that arrived on a regular basis and, until it failed to reappear one year, Colonel De Basil's Original Ballet Russe. Despite their travel-worn costumes and sets, the uncertainty of recorded scores and often lackluster performances, there was always at least a glimpse onstage of intensified states of being that were as stunning to me as any Parisian might have found Diaghilev's truly original troupe when it first appeared like the Golden Horde galloping out of the steppe. But though I couldn't have expressed what I felt, I sensed it was more than mere spectacle or embellishment of the music with acrobatics and mime. It was, as I'd gradually come to understand, a dazzling orchestral form for which the dancers' bodies themselves were its principal instruments, tuned to such near perfection that inflections of movement alone could extend their acts of bravura into something as poignant or sublime as whatever might be acted or sung.

Later, when I was high school, I'd try to explain that to a friend, Nicky Moore, who was built like an offensive lineman with hands that looked big and clumsy but could play the piano well, and, after hearing my effusion, he replied that, though it was pleasant enough seeing music visualized, as far as he was concerned the dancers were just an amusement like the hippos in tutus and toe shoes in Walt Disney's *Fantasia*. Whereupon I launched a grandiose protest, arguing that because inescapably— "like music itself," I said—we too are subject to time, there's a tragic bravado in dance that goes beyond the purely aesthetic "like matches lit in the dark." I'm certain I used those last six words because I remember him shaking his head before rumbling out a reply. "A lightning bug does that," he said.

But I remained enthralled and wasn't at all surprised when, a couple of decades later, I happened upon an essay by the painter, playwright, and critic Walter Sorrell in which he described having undergone anesthesia for surgery that he knew he mightn't survive and how, in a moment of panic, he'd grasped about in his mind for something to which he could cling—and what he'd seized upon was a sequence of steps from a pas de deux in *Swan Lake*, revealing when he was conscious again that he'd found what mattered most to him, which was somehow embodied in dance.

That had prompted in me a shock of recognition, though I'd probably have selected as my own flotation device the entrance of the Shades from Act III of *La Bayadère* with its hauntingly slow repetition of *arabesques penchées* in long zigzagging diagonals. Though the rest of the same ballet is less inspired, that passage is one of the most inexplicably and unfailingly ineffable that I know, and whenever I call it to mind something lights up in my brain—like a match, if you will, or a lightning bug. I can't account for the fact that there're some who find it insufferably dull, but I totally understand what Sorrell meant—to be launched into eternity with only that in mind would be like setting forth with a billowing sail.

My sister Mary took classes at the Foster School of Dance, and, despite a ghastly recital in which, with a polka-dot bow in her hair, she shuffled off to Buffalo in a tap routine called "Rag Mop," she was naturally talented. Her body was right for dance in every respect except for her feet, but when she went on pointe, her shoes were left so full of blood that, reluctantly, she quit.

Meanwhile, a goofy tall friend named Jimmy Maher took lessons from Ann Brodie, a Myrtle Court neighbor's niece who, after having studied in New York with Vitaly Fokine and Igor Schwezoff, had performed as a soloist and principal dancer with the Radio City Music Hall Ballet before returning with her husband to Columbia, where she initially taught ballet for Lanneau and Margaret Foster. Later she opened a studio of her own in partnership with a friend who specialized in tap, and during the 1960s, after they'd launched the Columbia City Ballet, she'd travel to Russia for further studies at the Bolshoi and the Kirov along with a lifelong friend and ABT principal, Michael Lland.

Vaguely aware that she idolized my mother, I remember the two of us—my mother and I, at some point during my early high school years—watching Ann dance the Black Swan pas de deux at the Township Auditorium either before or just after returning from New York. She was tiny and her legs were short, but she had an irrepressible musicality that, within a couple of years, my friend Jimmy and his partner for the occasion, a slightly older and enticingly gamine Kay Boswell, had clearly absorbed from Ann when I saw them perform the Bluebird pas de deux from *Sleeping Beauty*. I was astonished by how good they were and, talking to them afterwards in a hallway, I was no less surprised and intrigued by Kay's casual obscenities—the sort of locker-room talk that, in that genteel era, I'd never heard from a girl before.

"Oh, shit!" she asked in response to my praise. "Did you see me slip as I skipped offstage?"

I hadn't and mutely shook my head, but it occurred to me as a Friday night running back that, if language of that sort was the prerogative of those with athletic skills, she more than qualified. I was smitten on the spot, though with makeup that set her expression in a forbiddingly haughty glare, she seemed to be unapproachable for anyone not of her world in which grappling was done like jujitsu instead of in helmets and pads.

On the other hand, as I reminded myself, football wasn't my only sport and, once its season was over, I'd again be a sprinter in track for which my main event was balletic in a way and, if they'd awarded me style points, I'd have been the winner of every race. They didn't, of course, and I wasn't, but I kept on running and jumping in one way or another even as my increasing awareness of the alluring sensuality of dance made me envy

Jimmy Maher—especially after watching Moira Shearer in *The Red Shoes* as she wavered so entrancingly between what her emotions craved and what her art demanded. I sat through the movie twice in a single afternoon, emerging more hooked on ballet than ever for reasons not purely aesthetic and, caught up in that enthusiasm, I wrote to the great ballerinas of the day, getting autographed photos in return from Tallchief, Markova, Fonteyn and others, among them a glossy 8x10 from Tanaquil Le Clercq that I've had on my desk ever since. "To Bernie," it says, "with all best wishes," as if we'd really been close friends. When she was stricken onstage with polio less than two years later, I felt deeply aggrieved on her behalf—not only because she'd never dance again but because her generous spirit had nodded in my direction once.

I read Nijinsky's diary and Karsavina's *Theatre Street* along with biographies of Pavlova and anything else I could find in the public library or order from R.L. Bryan, a local bookseller uptown. Then, when the London Festival Ballet returned in 1954, featuring not only Tamara Toumanova performing "The Dying Swan" but the virtuosic Nora Kovach and Istvan Rabovsky in a recreation of the Ballet Russe's *Scheherazade*, I leapt at the chance to volunteer as a super.

I can't remember who put me on the list, but it must have been Ann Brodie because all the other male volunteers were dancers from her company. There was going to be a matinee with an entirely different program and an evening performance for which our work was the centerpiece, which was why we had to meet for a special rehearsal very early in the morning with the visiting company's ballet master, Nicholas Beriosoff—father of the beautiful young dancer, Svetlana Beriosova, soon to be prima ballerina of the Sadler's Wells Ballet. Muttering to himself, he quickly looked us over, then pointed to me and said in a heavily accented voice, "You!"

I stepped forward like a Marine recruit.

"You get the dancing part," he said. "The rest will recline and run about."

"He's not even a dancer!" one of the rival supers complained.

But I was apparently just the right size for the costume, which I'd later learn had been worn by one of Diaghilev's dancers in the ballet's sensational 1910 debut. Through a remarkable set of circumstances, both costumes and décor designed by Léon Bakst had, more than forty years later, come out of long-term storage and onto the stage again for Julian Braunsweg's company and, perhaps because of my being a football player, I looked the part of one of the Shahriar's vengeful guards who, on finding an orgy underway, would chase the miscreants down and slaughter them on the spot.

My emotions were somewhat mixed when I found that, if I'd appeared more effete, I'd have been among the Golden Slave's cronies—those who'd merely run about but would also "recline" on cushions while the scantily-clad harem women caressed and fondled them. But I'd been instructed instead to pursue a lascivious slave across the width of the stage, follow him up a number of steps to the top of a parapet, confront him when he turned, and do him in with my scimitar—after which I should descend the steps, taking murderous satisfaction in my deed. Though it wasn't exactly choreographed, I was also encouraged by Beriosoff to move "like a hungry panther."

I can recall the polyglot camaraderie of the men's dressing room with its peeling pale-yellow walls and ceiling high overhead, the bored indifference of the company member who'd been given the task of slapping my make-up on, and the envious resentment of my fellow supers. When my moment came in the ballet, I bounded out ferociously, pursued my prey across the stage and up the parapet, then mercilessly cut his throat. But as I was turning to descend, I found my knee in a vise-like grip and heard the *corpus delicti*'s voice hissing with Slavic urgency, "Don't drop me, you fool!"

I saw that I'd dumped him somewhat carelessly, and he was, in fact, about to fall some six or eight feet to the floor, so I hastily improvised. As if gloating over my handiwork, I raised his jerking body, gave it a disdainful shake, and tossed it back on the parapet prior to stalking back down the stairs with a maniacal grin. I'm told I was riveting, distracting everyone for a moment from what was happening center stage. Only Rabovsky was annoyed, but I got a distinct impression after the curtain had closed that, like my career as a singer, my ballet career was done—if not my fixation on dancers, which persisted throughout my early years of high school.

During that time, I dated the girl who'd caught my eye one day in junior high as, balanced on the ball of her foot like Artemis aiming an arrow, she sold a Nutty Buddy from a makeshift student canteen. That was before she'd begun to study dance, but she belonged to a social club called Les Petites Terpsichore and I found that waltzing with her in a ballroom was a lot like being in love—until in my senior year I met a German exchange student by the name of Ute Christensen who, despite a somewhat heavy-footed gait, was beautiful in a pure and simple way, enormously bright, and a performer as a cellist with an orchestra back in Berlin. But following our graduation, Ute returned to Germany, and after my sophomore year of college, my former girlfriend and I resumed our relationship.

She'd taken up modern dance by then and studied with Martha Graham but, much as I admired her grace and athleticism, I ranted in a letter to her that "Martha Graham is so artsy-fartsy" while betraying that very fault in my own bombastic prose, which I carefully copied out before putting it in the mail. "The connections between her static poses are so lacking in *enchaînement*," I pretentiously declared,

> and with all those overwrought contractions and releases, everything seems too much like silent-movie melodrama or Freudianism in motion as she ransacks ancient myths in search of flamboyant emotion—grief or greed or lust—expressing each one in turn as literally as a medieval allegory. I much prefer the creaky narrative frame of ballets like *Giselle* or the abstraction of Balanchine in which what's so moving to me lies not simply in acting out a plot (prince encounters a village girl or three dancers meet a fourth) but in the manner in which a gesture completely devoid of blatant mimetic meaning relates to the storyline. The poetry lies in the distance between the two.

I was trying to rephrase what I'd said to Nicky Moore, but, as the recipient of that diatribe couldn't have failed to notice, those were the pontifications of an insufferably self-important spectator addressed to an actual dancer. Unsurprisingly, despite our physical congruity, we eventually went our separate ways— I literally to England and she to North Carolina. I was totally unaware, of course, that at roughly the same time in a memorable *Peanuts* cartoon, Snoopy was saying to Lucy in words that might have reconciled us, "To live is to dance. . . to dance is to live," and in a comparably non-doctrinaire way, something similar would soon erupt at Judson Church in New York—though so far as I could tell, there was no modern dance in England while I was there.

Still, there was lots of ballet, and I attended every performance I could, sitting completely rapt at the pairings of Fonteyn and Somes, Sibley and Dowell, Seymour and Christopher Gable, and, in my final year, Fonteyn with Rudolf Nureyev for whom I heard cries from the balcony as I entered Covent Garden—"We want Rudy. . . preferably in the nudie!"— a crude reminder that, even beyond the dancer himself or the notion that all male dancers were gay, there's a sexual innuendo in nearly every pas de deux, one made cruelly explicit in Kenneth MacMillan's *The Invitation* which I saw Lynn Seymour enact with a harrowing intensity. It was after that very performance, in fact, that with an Oxford acquaintance whom I'd encountered in the lobby I tagged along to a Belgrave flat for a party attended by dancers from the corps who seemed as languidly exotic as the harem from *Scheherazade* nearly a decade before. Though most of them now seemed much closer to me in age, I felt as out of my depth as if I were at the Jockey Club during the Belle Époque, reflecting that neither my stipend nor my style would be up to keeping such company.

At Covent Garden itself, I generally sat in the topmost balcony "among the gods," but sometimes I'd spring for more expensive seats, and on one such special occasion—as if acting out Leopold Bloom's inner thoughts on the dive-bombing tactics of pigeons ("Who will we do it on? I pick the fellow in black.")— what must have been a ten-pound bird dropped a payload on my shoulder just as I was mounting the steps for a long-awaited *Swan Lake*. I tried to wipe the guano away, but it adhered like napalm, smearing and spreading across my suit. There was nothing to do but brazen it out to the obvious disgust of those seated near me in the balcony stalls—though I enjoyed the performance anyhow and even reflected as I did that, for lovers of that particular work, it went with the territory.

Sometimes, but only rarely, the debacle took place onstage—as was the case in Boston when my wife and I paid through the nose to see Fonteyn and Nureyev in Roland Petit's absurdly misbegotten *Paradise Lost*, rightly described by Clive Barnes as "paper thin and wispily trivial." After that disappointment, more than a decade would pass before, back in Columbia, I'd immerse myself in ballet again—and then only because, in 1978, I ran into Mimi Wortham at an ETV Christmas party just after completing *Cinematic Eye*.

I knew that Mimi herself had been a dancer, performing as Cinderella in Ann Brodie's adaptation of the evening-length Bolshoi production that my friend and collaborator Sidney Palmer had taped for a national feed nearly fifteen years before. That came up in the course of our conversation, and Mimi pointedly remarked that, since I seemed so interested, I really should take a look at some of the company's current performers.

I gathered from what she'd said that, in addition to working at SCETV, she'd also been standing in as an assistant ballet mistress, so I thought she probably meant at some sort of informal recital like the one I'd seen my sister in so many years before. But she told me they were presenting *Swan Lake* and, not having yet seen the tape of her previous *Cinderella*, I assumed that, however ardent the company's efforts were, the results would be amateurish.

"Scaled down?" I asked.

"Four acts," she said.

"Really?" I was surprised, but my immediate association was with a scene from *The Red Shoes* in which the impresario Boris Lermontov rebuffs Victoria Page in her eagerness to audition but goes to see her nevertheless on a tiny provincial stage performing in *Swan Lake*. I didn't expect another Moira Shearer.

"Look, Mimi," I told her, more or less as I'd written my girlfriend who'd studied with Martha Graham, "I don't want to sound like a snob, but . . ."

"Oh, perish the thought!" she cried, adroitly tweaking my vanity. "You just can't bear amateurs and, if you accept an invitation to a party, you don't expect to find yourself at an audition. I've seen that movie as many times as you have."

Since she had me so dead to rights, I politely heard her out. Ann Brodie's company was called the Columbia City Ballet— did I know that? I didn't, though I should have. Its ballet mistress was Adolfina Suarez-More who, when she was younger, had danced with Alicia Alonso. I didn't know that either, though the first ballet I'd ever seen was with Alonso and Youskevitch in *Giselle*. Also, Mimi continued, though it was true that most of Ann Brodie's dancers were still in high school, one or two would go on each year to the School of American Ballet or straight into the corps with Houston or ABT. As a matter of fact, in Ann's current production, Odette-Odile was being performed by one of Ann's former students who'd danced in Houston for Ben Stevenson but had just returned following some contretemps there. Her name was Lou Martin, I learned.

"She's really good," Mimi added.

I must have still looked skeptical.

"Just go and see," she urged.

So I went and had an experience that was much like Lermontov's when he finally sees his fetching soubrette perform. Lou Martin was a remarkably good Odette in a wistful ethereal way and good enough as Odile—with recorded music, of course, and uneven support from her partner, though some of the other dancers seemed quite accomplished too, especially given their age. Next day I confessed to Mimi how truly impressed I'd been.

"What did you think of the men?" she asked.

They'd been the weakest parts, I thought.

She said she generally agreed. The principal males were generally imported, but Walter Miller was good. . . and furthermore, she added, he was offering a men's class twice a week and might soon make it three if he got a good response. I could see she was sizing me up, but she was quicker than I was as, "So," she asked with a smile, "are you willing to give it a try?"

"What?" I said with exclamation points. I was forty years old, I objected, reminding myself of the fact that, though I'd taken up distance running and sporadically practiced yoga over the years, I was lamentably middle-aged and couldn't imagine getting into splits. "I'd look ridiculous," I added, "strutting about in tights."

"That's a coward's way out!" she scoffed. "I've heard you danced before or partnered some Martha Graham dancer and, whether that's true or not, I can see you're fit. . . and you've got a young body that'll match with most of our girls." She'd said that in a coolly appraising way and, despite my scoffing at her proposal, topped it off with an impish shrug. "Last chance, you know, if you don't do it now."

I would have been the right height for her—she was shorter than Gelsey Kirkland—but I knew she'd developed arthritis or something worse in both ankles and, like Tanaquil Le Clercq, been forced to give up dancing for good after her *Cinderella*. I was flattered by her efforts to enlist me.

"That's absurd," I said, "but I'll think about it."

I didn't, though. I was, after all, a semi-dignified professor with a wife and three children, the oldest of whom had just turned ten. That was my daughter Boykin who had the sort of body a commissar would have plucked from the steppe for the Kirov in Leningrad, but she had no interest at all in ballet. My other daughter was six and, though she was, as a matter of fact, taking beginner's classes at the Calvert-Brodie school, she was more compact than her sister and I was loath to impose my *grande folie* on her. My son was four and, despite an interest in climbing trees, had recently fallen and broken his arm—but soccer would be his game unless he did the same to a leg. And as my most important reason for refusing to take that on, I was teaching full-time at USC and working full-time at ETV with no room at all on my schedule for anything more.

And yet, I told myself, at almost exactly my same age, Nureyev was still as active as ever—and, as if to confirm what Mimi had said about my size, I happened to know that, although a decade younger, his fellow Russian Baryshnikov was allegedly my same height and maybe even shorter. Besides, it was a time when ballet was everywhere the rage. Balanchine and Suzanne

Farrell were at their peaks as choreographer and muse and, with the passing of Stravinsky and Picasso, Balanchine was by consensus the greatest living artist of any sort. Even closer to home for me, dance was hugely popular on PBS and, because ours was one of the four producing networks for the ongoing *Dance in America* series, Sidney Palmer had asked me to join him as his writer and co-producer for companies ranging as widely as Pilobolus, Lar Lubovitch, and Alwin Nikolais, taped at different festivals and locations. When Mimi got word of that, she found occasion to suggest that my credibility would be much greater if I were a dancer myself.

Not least among the causes of dance's prodigious vogue was a film called *The Turning Point*, a Hollywood romance about the world of ballet in which Baryshnikov and an ingenue Leslie Browne danced and smoldered across the screen. And a program would soon be aired on ABC in which Lynn Swann, a Pittsburgh Steelers superstar, would appear with Peter Martins, a principal for the New York City Ballet, duplicating a series of challenging steps before letting it be revealed that, prior to becoming the best wide receiver in football, he'd studied dance for fourteen years at his mother's studio. Together they'd make it clear that ballet wasn't for sissies—but the inescapable fact remained that, as a responsible husband-father-professor and writer-producer-presenter in an ultra-conservative southern town, my non-conformity, such as it was, had been mostly under the radar. . . and I was being importuned to blow what was left of my cover.

To my amazement, though, when I reported Mimi's preposterous proposition, my wife said Mimi was right and that I really should give it a try. I have no idea why except to note that she herself had once taught ballroom dancing throughout the state, and that, during her teenage years until her father had reined her in, she'd figured prominently in several children's theater productions—though, admittedly, at the pinnacle of her acting career in the title role of a non-balletic "Sleeping Beauty," she'd slept onstage through most of the play. But she loved the arts and, as I'd learned in our fifteen years of marriage while raising three children together, she loved more generously than seemed compatible with reason.

More than five years before, for example, when I'd taught a young cousin of hers named Susan Carrison—a bright and ebullient young woman who, like my mother when she was young, parted her hair in the middle—it happened that, late one spring, she was in my office at USC discussing a thesis project of hers when I got a call from the hospital. Our older daughter had had a fall at school and injured her head. They'd tried but couldn't reach my wife, who must have taken our only car to wherever she might have gone—the Piggly Wiggly, I supposed.

So my student, Susan, drove me in her V-W to the emergency room where I quickly learned that my daughter was not only fine but had been accompanied by a nurse's aide from her school. I wanted to stay nonetheless in order to take her home and, while we waited for the completion of paperwork, I thanked my student again for getting me there. She told me I was welcome of course but might have been better off in somebody else's hands because she was legally blind. I thought she must be joking until, as if to confirm the fact, she took her slightly tinted glasses off, looking at me with glazed unfocused eyes. With massive correction, she said, she'd gotten permission to drive.

I reported that to my wife, who was home by the time my student could drop us off, and she was equally surprised. I confessed that her cousin had told me once that I was one of the few older men in town who'd never made a pass at her. I suppose attractive women know at an early age when their beauty is being admired—our eyes dilate or something of the sort—so I must have come across as a paragon of virtue and restraint, and, in any case, her comment certainly wasn't an invitation for me to join the crowd. It was probably just a fact. . . though, as I said to my wife, it had been awkward enough in the ER explaining that Susan wasn't my wife, then strangely intimate when she told me about her eyesight.

"Don't be getting ideas," my wife advised.

"Don't worry," I assured her, though I felt irked in a way about the older men's presumption.

Several weeks later, we and our children were at Anne's parents' "briar-patch" house on the Wateree River while they were someplace else. When we woke on Monday morning, July

5th, my wife insisted on recounting the saddest dream she'd ever had.

"It was just before I woke up," she said.

I reminded her that she'd always objected to hearing somebody else's dreams and had never let me tell her any of mine.

"But this was different," she protested. "There was a sort of medieval cortege and a beautiful young woman on a sledge being drawn by a pair of horses. She was dead, and you were leading the procession."

I said it sounded like an Ingmar Bergman film. "And why was it so sad?"

"Because," she said, "I knew your heart was broken."

I was flabbergasted. How could anyone be so generous-spirited, even in her subconscious mind? By contrast I knew my soul was a hard black lump of self-centeredness.

"So, why are you telling me this? You don't believe in prophetic dreams."

"No," she said. "I don't know why."

It was hardly an hour before my brother called and said he'd been trying to track me down. My student Susan, whom he also knew, had been killed in an accident as she drove to meet her brother who resembled her so closely that I'd once thought they were twins. My brother reported that, at a construction site, she'd apparently failed to see some sort of obstruction that caused her to overturn in her Volkswagen Beetle. Her mother was arranging the funeral, he said, at a little country church in Rembert. . . and she wanted me to serve as the crucifer because, as she'd told my brother, her daughter had written in a journal left behind in her room that I'd helped her understand what she ought to do with her life. I was, her mother had concluded, the one to conduct her daughter to where she was going next. I had no choice but to agree.

Not a single detail of that account is even slightly embroidered. Furthermore, my wife had been right—though my heart wasn't truly broken, the death of that earnest, bright, and beautiful young woman was appallingly sad—and, like anyone confronted by such irrefutable evidence that he's living with his spiritual superior, I was stunned by what my wife had revealed about herself. I did my best to downplay it, of course, but it was very much in my mind when, some years after that, I repeated to her what Mimi Wortham had said and was somewhat less surprised that she was urging me to pursue something she knew I loved, no matter how crazy it seemed.

Still undecided, however, I went first to my running doctor who, when I presented him with a list of a dozen-odd physical feats I hoped that I could pull off in roughly six months or so, told me I'd had my last real shot at nearly all of them some twenty years before—which was just the incentive I needed. Then, newly resolved while doing my best to suppress my numerous inhibitions, I went, as my wife had advised, to Parklane Hosiery in the Dutch Square Mall where, finding myself the only male shopper in sight, I asked a clerk in a discreetly casual way if they happened to carry men's tights.

"Phyllis!" she shouted across the store. "He's looking for men's tights!"

I felt bombarded by curious stares as if I'd asked for something salacious, but Phyllis confirmed that what I wanted was, surprisingly, in stock. So I bought two pairs and left.

Still, that was easier to negotiate than my first class at Calvert-Brodie, which was the one for men on Tuesday and Thursday evenings that Mimi had described. After awkwardly donning my tights in the very small men's dressing room, overlaying them with running shorts and wearing a bulky sweatshirt with its sleeves pushed past my elbows, I had to wait in the lobby outside with a group of pre-teen girls whose parents were picking them up after their weekly class. I knew a lot of the parents and couldn't avoid their stares through the floor-to-ceiling windows or the thought that they must have deduced I'd either lost my mind or come gaudily out of the closet.

The class was tougher than I expected. My legs were strong enough—I'd been running six to eight miles each night as well as resuming my yoga and, with long Achilles tendons, I had enough *ballon*—at least, while going up—to feel as if I were soaring. But I kept landing with a thud and losing my balance attempting turns. The other half-dozen men, who'd clearly been dancing for years, seemed not to notice my awkwardness—though, of course, I knew they had, and the mirror along one wall made it woefully clear to me how ludicrous I appeared. Before the class was halfway through, I was sure it would be my last.

But the following day at ETV, Mimi asked me to write and produce a promo for the company's new production of *Cinderella*. She said there were public-service slots available on the schedule for segments of up to five minutes in length and, as a matter of fact, the lead part of Cinderella would be danced by Karen Gibbons whose father was a colleague of mine at USC— in Engineering, she added. Though I hadn't yet seen Karen dance, she was, according to Mimi, a bright and willowy twenty-two-year-old who, before returning home to teach, had performed with the Ballet Celeste in San Francisco.

It took no more to persuade me—and Ditsie Weynand, who'd been such an important part of *Cinematic Eye*, agreed to direct and help me edit the segment which we taped where we'd worked before, in the network's largest studio. I wrote a short script, and the following day Karen Gibbons with her partner Jeffrey Judson performed a portion of their *grand pas de deux* with such exuberant verve and finesse that I tossed in a bit of improvised voice-over saying she'd "notched her body to the music like an arrow to a bowstring"—after which, impelled by my own grandiloquence, I decided that I'd return to class.

At the end of four or five dogged months, I'd checked off everything on my dozen-item list except for "baby-doll" splits, though front splits I could manage with ease and my turns were getting steadier. There was always a shortage of men for partnering in recitals, so I took it as a sign of only modest progress when, shortly before the spring recital, one of the other instructors asked me to partner a student of hers who'd be heading off to college in the fall. Though not a lyrical dancer, the girl—whose name was Shelley Martin—was as statuesque as a girl of seventeen could be and the piece had been choreographed with that in mind, involving my striding about with a princely gait while holding her over my head, then putting her down, supporting a turn, and lifting her up again. With misgivings, I agreed.

I needn't have worried. We danced to the four-and-a-half-minute "Nimrod" section of Elgar's *Enigma Variations*, and, at its climactic moment, I dead-lifted her in arabesque and carried her downstage as the audience gasped and applauded. My part had consisted of little more than glorified weight-lifting set to music but, however ungainly I might have appeared, it was the first performance of my middle-aged dance career, and I was wholly committed to it—even though it was also true that, when Shelley asked for advice about where she should go to college, I felt in a way as if she was growing up while I was busy regressing. She chose to go to Duke, where I'm sure she must have soared even higher aloft on her own.

Meanwhile, in teaching my largest class at USC, which was held in an auditorium designed like a movie house, I'd taken to springing onto the stage in an effortless *jeté* instead of using the three or four carpeted stairs—and that was while wearing cowboy boots. One of my colleagues observed that I'd begun to look like a dancer who happened to be a professor as opposed to the other way around. That might have been an admonishment, though I took it as flattery.

I'd intensified my efforts in the twice-a-week classes for men and been invited to join the daily intermediate classes—at which point, out of the blue, Karen Gibbons approached me one day about another and bigger recital at the Township Auditorium, asking me to partner her in a much longer and more demanding pas de deux from Petipa's *Harlequinade*. When I asked if she thought I was up to it, she said it would be the Lopukhov revival that had aired on PBS—of Valery and Galina Panov, both formerly of the Kirov—but we could study her copy of the tape and adapt it as we saw fit. Then, noting my expression, she added that with a few adjustments, like subtracting Valery's *grandes pirouettes* while retaining all the jumps, it would mainly involve a lot of character dancing. Initially, I demurred, but she insisted that I was such a natural Harlequin that, suppressing the thought I'd merely be playing the fool, I finally agreed to do it.

My qualms had been partly based on the fact that, though *commedia dell'arte*—which is what we were talking about—may seem on its surface merely knockabout humor with an array of cartoonish stock characters, it can often take on as much R-rated freight as the opera *Pagliacci* amid its false naivete and whimsically amorous interludes. . . and in the version we'd be performing, Harlequin and Columbine weren't just animated dolls but frolicsome long-time lovers engaged in artful game-playing.

That might seem to have been a far-fetched concern on my part, but I'd taken it for granted from my very first class that, no matter what might have occurred in *The Turning Point*, I must never in any way even hint at an impropriety—and while Karen herself was a grown-up and properly businesslike, she was also strikingly good looking and, as I've just implied, that particular pas de deux in its sly and teasing way is all about seduction. So, no sooner had we started rehearsing than I began to have second thoughts about how things might appear.

But much younger though she was, Karen was way ahead of me and tactfully and expertly, as if detecting my reticence, set about coaxing me into the task we'd undertaken, insinuating herself so naturally and unselfconsciously that I came to understand that physical though our engagement was, we were solving a problem that wasn't all that dissimilar from the ones her father addressed in Chemical Engineering. That was a perception that helped allay my prudish if prudent anxiety and, in a journal of mine from the time, I've run across an entry that captures what followed from there:

> In the middle of our rehearsal yesterday, with much else going awry (her shoulder hurt, my leg and toe were killing me), I caught an elbow in my mouth during her quick supported turns and kicked her twice in the shins while reversing a ball-cross-change—after which Karen looked at me and said with her eyebrow raised and an exasperated shrug, "I feel like Adam and Eve." Though that struck me at first as disconcertingly enigmatic, what she meant, I think, in the nicest possible way, was that when dancing with a beginner, you too can make a beginner's mistakes—whereas my own interpretation is that, though I hope we make a plausible couple onstage, I'm as painfully inept as Adam banged-up in the Garden with a newly missing rib in the company of a far more knowing Eve. She

sometimes talks in riddles, but the English teacher
in me thinks what she's trying to get across is that
an ardent rogue is better suited to this ballet than
a hesitant ninny, or, in other words, that innocence
isn't what it's about—undoubtedly good advice,
though it's equally true that she ought to have kept
her elbows in. I might be slow on the uptake, but
the pain in my jaw doesn't lie.

In any case, with her persistence and my ability to take a
punch, we settled down to working things out together, and when
we performed onstage in the Township Auditorium in front of a
sizable audience, they resoundingly lapped it up. Ann Brodie
lavished me with praise and asked me to join the company which,
with my wife's encouragement, I did—though as I needlessly
noted, I was still a beginner.

Nonetheless, there was now no turning back. "After last
Monday's class," I noted in my journal, "my second with the
company, I felt I'd been so klutzy, so much a clumsy intruder,
that I drove home telling myself I was just a middle-aged fool.
But then, on the following day, Gary Oiler—who, I learned, is
actually twenty-nine, older than I'd supposed and taking some
graduate courses at USC—dropped by my office to talk, and
when I confessed my mortification about the night before, he
said, 'Oh, no, you have a *mission*!' That sounded a little
grandiose to me. He saw my expression and added, 'Think of it
this way, everybody knows what adolescent girls can do and,
anyhow, the truth of the matter is that only one or two out of a
hundred will be professional dancers. But who can tell what
somebody your age can do? Oh, they'll say you have to study
before a certain age, but what if you're in shape and know how
to discipline yourself? How far can you actually go? Nobody
really knows, and you. . . well, you can find out and show others
too.'"

"Thanks for the encouragement," I said, though I wondered
if that's what it was. On the other hand, it occurred to me that
Ann Brodie might have sent him to reassure me, and anyhow,
whether she had or hadn't, I'd decided by then to give it a try for
as long as I possibly could. A day or two later, I reflected in my

journal, "Well, there's not much risk of falling on my face—and
it'll hardly matter if I do because in classical ballet, it seems, all
the roles for dancers my age are basically as buffoons." I was
chafing at the discovery that, for my initial role in the company's
full-length *Coppélia*, I'd just learned that I'd be adorned with
mutton-chop whiskers and a wig, which came as something of a
let-down amidst my earnest attempts at dash and panache in my
bit-part as the burgomaster—but only to find it had been reduced
to no more than a comic walk-on involving a little mime. Though
I'd also briefly appear in a minor dancing role involving a few
basic steps, I felt I was regressing.

About that same disappointment, I'd afterwards take myself
to task in a marginal rebuke, "It's supposed to be funny—get over
it! It's not Antony Tudor, you know!" and not long after that,
probably in October, I was bursting with elation that, "I've now
begun taking five classes a week and am starting to get a bit of it
right, including a little real turn-out.

> My *développés* don't get very high, but my legs
> are feeling much stronger. Tonight, I took back-
> to-back classes, which was a mistake. I was tired
> in the company class (Mimi's class, with a lot of
> tough combinations), and I slipped near the end of
> one doing a *saut de basque* and twisted my ankle.
> I may find myself an ex-dancer in the morning,
> but at this moment I'm in the best shape of my
> life. I'm doing lifts—press lifts, fishes, running
> lifts, and have even managed a helicopter! It's
> hard to know what to make of this. In a way, I feel
> like an aging Hemingway back in Pamplona,
> following the bulls again for one last summer—so
> exhilarating and even, at times, so tantalizingly
> beautiful with, just below the surface, the faintest
> hint of comic pathos because I'm not merely
> watching from the stands but actually in the arena
> and, though I know in my heart I can't keep it up
> forever or even for very long, I'm loving every
> second, this sense of being so alive and so utterly
> in the moment! I took two classes on Saturday

morning and did pretty well, and, as I was leaving
the larger studio, another class was continuing in
the other. I could hear the piano playing that
wonderful pulsebeat music, so childishly simple
and buoyant, and, as I stepped into the cool
sunshine outside, I felt so happy. . . so *happy*! The
kind of happiness that makes you want to put it
into words for your children to read long after
you've caught the ferry that, "If all my life after
this should go awry and come to absolutely
nothing, to suffering and grief and spite,
remember that I was this happy once"—which is,
I think, as much as any creature can ask. May each
of them know the same.

Mid-life crises must come in many forms, and, though I can't
imagine Hemingway at the barre (as opposed to the one at the
Ritz), there's something going on in *Across the River and into
the Trees* that seems at least as giddily self-indulgent as my own
late-blooming career in tights, though mine came a decade sooner
in the form of a gift from my wife—for which I'd continue to
thank her over and over. I had good cause, as I explained again
in an entry a few months later:

I leave classes sometimes euphoric, at other times
despondent—but it's not how it was at first,
dawdling among the fourteen-year-olds waiting
for their parents to pick them up. All that's
irrelevant now. I study with former professionals
and partner those who'll be dancing with major
companies soon, one of whom—Stacey Calvert,
who'll shortly be off to SAB—told me after
Saturday's company class that she thinks it's
wonderful I'm not dancing for any reason other
than wanting so much to do it. "There're two
kinds of dancers," she said in the voice of a
teenaged sibyl, "those who want to be a dancer
and those who want to dance." She added that she
and I are in the second group. Then she shared

with me the secret of holding your stomach in. "You tuck in here!" she said, clutching the muscle under what, already in New York vein, she referred to as her tush. "Not here," she added helpfully, putting her hand on her abdomen. She's very determined and athletic, and what I share with her, with no delusions about how long it's going to last or where it'll someday get me, is feeling so vitally focused, so alert and aware of my body becoming so finely tuned that sometimes now in our center work for two or three combinations I truly know what it is to *dance* and my whole being seems to hum like a vibrating string as if I myself am the music.

In another undated entry from sometime late in my second year, I noted a new ability to individuate different muscles in a way I could never have done before—though like every diarist who harbors the thought that posterity might be listening in, I quickly added a wry rejoinder, "But so can any lizard on a rock," prompting a later reproof along with a rapturous claim, "No, that's the wrong comparison—*I burn like the seraphim!*"

I've got no idea in retrospect what I might have had in mind (and doubt if seraphim would be tucking their tushes in anyhow, having none to tuck), but I guess my comment must have derived from Walter Pater's dictum that "To burn always with this hard gem-like flame, to maintain this ecstasy, is success in life." And assuming that was the case, I'd now contend it wasn't so overblown after all—it was simply how it felt to be alive. I was undoubtedly on a continual endorphin and adrenalin high, and, if there was a wobble in my prose, I'd nonetheless become a more infectiously vibrant husband, father, and teacher—or so my family and students assured me.

My longtime friend from Oxford, Sam Holt, opined that I was adding decades to my life, and when, on a visit to Washington, I went with him to a party at the house of Peter Jay—a classmate of Sam's at Christ Church and, at exactly my same age, the British ambassador to the U.S.—I met another of Sam's friends named Bud McFarland, a former Marine and future National Security Advisor who was also my same age and was playing a major role in the Salt II Treaty negotiations. In such company as theirs, I was wholly unprepared for my conversation with Bud who was, again like me, godfather to one of Sam's daughters and roughly my same height with his face habitually set in a look of grim resolve.

"Sam tells me that you're studying ballet," he said in what I took to be a growl.

"That's right," I said by way of reply to what had sounded like a challenge.

"Well, that's really interesting," he said without a change of expression, "because I'm studying tap with my daughter. . . and it's one of the best and hardest and things I've ever done."

We agreed it was better than playing golf.

Meanwhile, back at the barre, Ann Brodie's assistant, Fina Suarez-More, who had a heavy Cuban accent and always called me "Barney," was the toughest of my teachers, and, even now, I can hear her in my mind singling me out for reprimands when I'd just begun her classes. "No! No, Barney!" she'd erupt. "Don't be trying to do three! One pirouette's enough for you!"

I'd go for a double anyhow, tilting like a spinning top.

"Think with your body!" Fina would bark to everyone in the class. "If you're waiting for messages from your brain, your arms and legs will be getting there too late."

I wondered what she was talking about—the autonomous nervous system? Muscle memory was something I'd heard about, mainly involving tennis. . . but thinking like an octopus? It struck me as implausible at first, though I'd noticed while running track how the minds of gifted runners appeared to be floating above whatever their bodies were doing as if they were merely looking on while I was so frantically thrashing about. There might be something to it, I thought, but I'd have to be good before I was great.

So day after day I'd struggle in Fina's class with combinations ending in *tours jetés* and, if I managed to nail one, she'd shake her head and say, "No, Barney, no! You're behind the music again!" She was always right, partly because I was tossing my leg so high I was almost upside down in the air. But athleticism alone clearly meant little to her.

As far as I knew, she was a spinster and, judging from something she once said, I think she harbored a notion that I must have studied dance before and, having forgotten whatever I'd learned in the wake of a wartime injury (hence the long scimitar of a scar across my torso), had given it up for a decade or so before deciding on a whim with nothing really at stake, to take it up again—which, in view of my turn in *Scheherazade*, was just barely less than totally wrong, though as a former dancer herself with nothing so harebrained in her past, I think she'd also dismissed me at first as a dabbler who'd soon regret my mistake and take up some easier hobby. To allay that sort of suspicion, I told her that my motivation was simple: I was co-producing dance programs for Public Television and needed a better sense of what I was doing. She nodded at that rationale and became even harder on me.

But as I improved, I sometimes won looks of approval and even a winsome smile or two. She wasn't that much older— maybe fifteen years, I guessed—and I gradually came to think she regarded what I was up to in terms that Gary Oiler had predicted, as a chance to see what older dancers could do. . . notwithstanding the fact that Fonteyn was dancing still at sixty, and I'd seen films of Ruth St. Denis performing well into her eighties and, in 1981, during our coverage of the American Dance Festival for PBS, I'd finally meet Martha Graham who, though at eighty-seven wasn't exactly dancing, was nevertheless performing in a sense with a sort of stately hauteur—from which I concluded we already knew what dancers much older than I could do, which was less about pyrotechnical feats than what I called in my journal "the wisdom of the body."

It dawned on me then that, like any Zen master from whom one seeks *satori*, what Fina was trying to convey—to me in particular—by those endless *ronds de jambe* inflicted on us at the barre was what I suspect she knew so well in herself. . . an awareness that only comes from never ceasing to love what we can't any longer possess. "Like Tithonus," I wryly mused, "still embraced by the ever-renewing dawn while helplessly growing older." But I wasn't quite there yet. . . and, in fact, what was truly extraordinary for me about that portion of my life was not a false feeling of youth but the realization that, at just the point in middle-age when I might have begun to stand on my dignity, I'd suddenly find myself again not only in the company of those not old enough to vote but getting scolded myself like a errant schoolboy—regarding which, as I'd gradually come to understand, nothing could have been more salutary, especially for my creative work.

That was increasingly the case in performing arts television for, no matter how amateurish the level at which I'd performed, dance companies trusted me as essentially one of their tribe and welcomed the chance to work together—as Mimi had said they would, and as Erick Hawkins did near the end of his long career when, on the verge of 80, he and I would collaborate.

But other benefits were accruing across the board, as not since my college years had my schedule been so full. I was not only taking two classes a day with rehearsals and performances interspersed but maintaining two full-time jobs, winning accolades in both and—most importantly to me as it was, of course, to my wife—helping to raise three children, one of whom was by then already in a tutu.

As my technique got much better, I took on bigger roles in more of the classic ballets. I was listed as a soloist and even for a brief while a principal of sorts, dancing on national television as well as at high schools and shopping malls. For a special event at the Township Auditorium, Leslie Saunders, who'd returned from SAB, taught Dorita Strasburger and me a pas de deux from Balanchine's *Who Cares?* which we once performed at a local TV station following a lengthy commercial for a product called Hairaway used to remove unwanted hair from somebody's upper lip. It didn't matter when or where, I simply wanted to dance, and my partners did as well.

Dorita, with her arsenal of witty and elegant moves, would afterwards change her name to Kyra Strasburg and become the prima ballerina of the Boston Ballet. Stacey Calvert became a soloist for the New York City Ballet where, while on a mission for PBS, I'd visit her in 1982, meeting Merrill Ashley and Jacques D'Amboise—who was three years older than I and wouldn't retire until nearly 50 and only then because, as he stressed, there were too few roles for dancers his age—though I wouldn't meet Balanchine because, with seismic consequences, he'd already begun a decline from which he wouldn't recover.

But despite the loss of such dancers as Stacey, Dorita, and Karen, our company grew and flourished with successors like Ashley Tuttle who, even as a devil-doll at twelve, was so spectacular that none of us was surprised when she subsequently moved to ABT and became a principal dancer, and Elizabeth Walker too who, though tiny at the time, was so entrancing as Clara in *The Nutcracker* that no one could look at anyone else as long as she was onstage, an aura that would accompany her to the New York City Ballet.

As for those who remained in Columbia, we continued to take our *Nutcracker* on the road in December, traveling to smaller towns throughout the state, and over the course of time, I'd dance nearly all the second-act divertissements. But, in Act I, I always appeared as an Actors-Studio Rat King, dying with such a melodramatic flair that, following my galvanic demise, adults would cheer as loudly as the kids. Elizabeth once wrote to me at the height of her career, declaring me to have been her favorite Rat King, a bit of praise I treasure, but I can't recall if she was performing as Clara on a night that became for me an absurd reprise of my very first role with a sword more than twenty-five years before.

I'm semi-ambidextrous, and, during my epic fight with the unbeatable Nutcracker Prince, I used to toss my rapier back and forth, slashing with either hand. During my next-to-last season, when our visiting Prince was William Starrett—who, though he'd danced with Joffrey and ABT as well as the Royal Winnipeg and been a medalist at the International Ballet Competition, was unprepared for my legerdemain—I switched my weapon from right to left and brought it down hard as he was lunging towards me, catching him accidentally on the wrist. He instantly dropped his sword and, with an agonized howl, went down like a shot to both knees, wincing and wringing his hand. Once more I had to improvise as I had in *Scheherazade*—so, as the music moved on, I leapt downstage in exultant *tours* and *grands jetés* while William lurched unsteadily to his feet and children began to wail with alarm.

For some reason known only to him, he attacked me with his fists and pummeled me to death. For obvious reasons of time, I died more quickly than usual, though I'd come very close to rewriting the whole scenario so that a triumphant Rat King might have shared on that one night a pas de deux with Clara. Ah, Elizabeth, if only!

Four years had passed by then with so many of my partners moving on while I remained where I was, extending my skills and repertoire and reappearing as Harlequin—this time in Fokine's *Carnaval* with Schumann's lyrically manic score sending me over the stage in a series of spring-loaded *grands pas de chat* that drove Gary Oiler's Pierrot into the wing ahead of me and, in each of our performances, to his intense irritation, prompting a burst of applause.

I felt I could bound like that to the very ends of the earth as long as the music played, reminding myself in a valedictory way that, as T.S. Eliot had said in his *Four Quartets*, "You are the music while the music lasts." But sooner or later, of course, the music always stops—and, at one point during that spring I had a dream in which I was weeping inconsolably and woke up in the middle of the night, remembering that what I'd dreamed was that something or other had happened and I could no longer dance.

With that still troubling my thoughts, I contended in my journal that, even if I should later become a very successful author, my longtime aspiration, I'd feel whenever encountering dance "like someone long in exile who suddenly hears his native tongue, a sort of 'knowing already' as opposed to a 'figuring out.'" Then, as if to shrug off my emotion, I wrote in a self-critical way, "Ha! Remember in the fairy tale when the ugly duckling sees those strange and beautiful creatures flying high overhead and, while turning his head to follow them with his eyes, is alarmed by the heartfelt cry he hears his own throat utter?"

It occurs to me now that, mawkish as that is, I must have been thinking as I wrote it about the magical rush of strings when, at the end of *Swan Lake*'s first act, Tchaikovsky conveys the wonderment Albrecht feels as he traces a flight of swans across the sky, presaging all sorts of things—love and death among them as well as transfiguration—too weighty a burden for my dream to bear. But I knew I was nearing an end.

When we undertook a newly choreographed version of Stravinsky's *Rite of Spring*, largely reconstructed by Leslie Saunders, I was cast in the leading male role, partnering Sarah Funderburk who'd danced with the Washington Ballet. She was good but much too tall for me and, out of sheer trepidation, failed to hold her back on our more acrobatic lifts, making them dangerous as well as difficult. After a bad rehearsal one night with a couple of near falls, I worked off my frustration with a series of *double tours*, coming down on the last of them with one of my feet bent under itself. I heard a sound like a pistol crack and discovered my foot was broken.

My doctor wanted to put it in a cast, but I refused, explaining that learning Stravinsky's counts had been like trying to memorize the Manhattan phonebook, which I couldn't let go for naught—and, in any case, I was going to dance at the premiere which was less than three weeks away. He told me that, unfortunately, that would require a miracle, but thinking of Alonso in her blindness, I sat for long sessions every night, propping my foot on a hassock while staring at it fixedly, visualizing the broken bones as they knitted back together. I could literally feel the metatarsals healing.

I dressed out for the dress rehearsal. No one could believe I was actually there, and my understudy appeared to be disappointed. At my expansive opening solo, which began with a jump from *plié* to *à la seconde*, I leapt with total confidence— only to hear a sickening splat as I came to earth again. There were some things the mind alone couldn't do.

That needn't have ended my career, but, not long afterwards, I was awarded a major grant by the National Endowment for the Humanities to write and produce a series of dramatic adaptations. It was an opportunity I'd long been seeking, and—consoling myself with the half-facetious thought that, having already received the "Most Improved Dancer" award from Ann Brodie, I had little more to achieve—I concluded that I should stop while I was at my best. . . or as good as I would get.

It was like walking out on someone I loved. It sounds affected to say I missed it in an excruciating way, but I did, feeling full of a guilty apostasy from what I'd described to my wife as the Church of the Holy Sweat. At the beginning of every barre, as soon as the *tendus* had begun, I'd been thrown into an instant alpha state, and, towards the end of class, when big jumps were unleashed in exuberant combinations, I'd felt as if I were literally taking flight. Perhaps, in a strictly musical sense, I may have consorted too much with the likes of Minkus and Drigo, but at least I'd begun to understand what Fina must have meant by repeatedly urging all of us to learn to think with our bodies. As I wrote near the end of my journal, "It's hard to put into words but, when thoughts and acts so perfectly coincide as they do for me now when I dance, I'm full of a sense of pure being and wholeness of the self that, if I could only sustain it, would be an ecstatic way of life."

What proved most difficult for me when I finally gave it up was going cold turkey, I think—so difficult in fact that in that journal entry I could have described what I'd lost as an addictive way of life—though it had been both, of course, and it occurs to me now in a more reflective vein that I was circling back, in effect, to what I'd felt when sipping my cosmic ginger ale or even to what I'd glimpsed in the eye of a fox at Uffington. What in time would matter most was feeling more gratitude than regret that, against all odds and common sense, I knew and remembered in my bones what dancing had really been like—and I was delighted to learn that when George Washington, who'd taken great pride in dancing a mean minuet, was nearing the end of his life, he responded to an invitation to a ball with the plaintive declaration, "Alas, our dancing days are no more."

Mine were over as well, of course—except for one flawless triple pirouette unleashed two decades later as an aging college president dressed in a Snoopy suit for my part in a Christmas revel, provoking general astonishment, and, during the years after that, some musical creds I earned delivering pre-concert lectures in places like Severance Hall. Such heady adventures as those— from the ludicrous to the sublime—would culminate in between with one that ran the full gamut beginning, unexpectedly, with an invitation from Ed Betsill, the former tenor soloist at Trinity Cathedral (the church's status having been raised by then). He was hosting an intimate dinner for his very good friend Joan

Sutherland—among operatic divas, the foremost of her time—
and he wanted my wife and me to join him and his brother George
in welcoming her to Columbia.

As part of my line of work by then, I'd grown accustomed to
holding forth in Aspen, Cleveland, and elsewhere on subjects for
which my fervor exceeded my knowledge—a skill I'd observed
at Oxford and tried to master myself. Because it so often had
served me well, I presumed it would work again when dining
with La Stupenda. Besides, I owned many of her recordings and
listened to them again.

Anne and I were the first to arrive at the small private dining
room reserved at the Palmetto Club, followed by Ed and George
who appeared in the narrow passageway as if hauling Dame
Joan's chariot while, looming like a titaness in tow, she recounted
a raucous anecdote with an accent like those of my Aussie friends
in a long-ago rugby scrum. It involved an accident that she'd had
an hour or so before when she sat on a toilet seat and, as she said
with a guffaw, "smashed it to *smithereens!*"

I was totally taken aback. I'd prepared myself for all sorts of
high-cultural palaver but not for such boisterous gusto or, for that
matter, the sheer dimensions of her presence. Desperately casting
about for something witty to say, I said I hoped the seat had been
padded.

"Wot?" she shrilled. "The kind that *farts*?"

I surmised I was being told that the last thing she wanted to
hear that night was the sort of arty chitchat she'd so often had to
endure before her recent retirement, but I was nonetheless
undone. As I sought to regain my composure, the five of us had
barely taken our seats at a round well-appointed table when one
of the waiters tripped with a gravy boat in hand, dumping its
sludge-like contents down the front of George's shirt. He dealt
with the mishap admirably, but a moment or two later, when I
launched into what must have been an equally blundering
expression of admiration for Maria Ewing's widely telecast
Salome, Dame Joan shrieked again, declaring the shortcomings
of Ewing's voice to have been "appallingly exposed. . . along
with everything else"—a reference to Ewing's final split-second
appearance devoid of any veils.

"And those lips!" she added with a howl. "Those *lips!*" smearing her hand across her mouth in a gesture that showed in equal measure dislike for Maria Ewing and disdain for my opinion.

Ed Betsill looked distressed, so, in an apologetic effort to be ingratiating, I mentioned a spellbinding video I'd seen of Dame Joan herself singing with Tito Gobbi.

"Tee-tow Go-bee," she corrected.

"Yes, Tito Gobbi," I said. "In *Tosca.*"

"No," she insisted, biting off the consonants. "*Tee*-tow *Go*-bee!" and I understood that we were inescapably at loggerheads.

I fell mostly silent after that, hoping to wreak no further damage to the shambles of Ed's dinner party, but things didn't improve at all when I confessed as we were leaving that, though it might not qualify as grand opera, I still loved Offenbach's *Tales of Hoffmann* as much as I had as a boy. Dame Joan responded by telling me in no uncertain terms that it was a very difficult work to sing, and I concluded correctly that, no matter how important music might be to me, I was, in the eyes of one who ought to know, an irredeemable ignoramus.

But that was okay, I tried to tell myself. My love of music was authentic enough, and I'd truly been a dancer of sorts—even a professional one, if only in a brief and technical sense—and nothing could alter that. I've often reflected on that thought and come to several conclusions. Mimi Wortham-Brown, the friend who'd instigated that whole quixotic pursuit, once told me that former dancers, when watching a ballet, experience it from the inside—as if some long-term muscle memory was reflexively kicking in. I can hardly compare myself to those who danced for decades, but I find it's true that something inside me traces the dancers as they move. . . not just my eyes and mind but, even so many years later, what Fina must have meant by thinking with my body. I don't know if I'm fantasizing.

But with her photograph still on my desk, I think as well of Tanaquil Le Clercq after her legs were paralyzed at the age of twenty-six—"at the peak of her powers," as *The New York Times* would observe—and through all those years that followed, remembering herself onstage and, maybe as Mimi had said, still dancing in her mind unless that had proved too painful for her. I know she wrote a *Ballet Cookbook* during that afterlife, and, twenty-one years ago, as I was beginning another new career and donning the Snoopy suit, I read that she had died. Other than name and dates, her epitaph says "Ballerina," which occurred to me when, in Moscow four or five years ago, I visited the Novodevichy Cemetery where Russia has interred its most illustrious countrymen—leaders like Khrushchev and Yeltsin; composers like Rimsky-Korsakov, Shostakovich, and Prokofiev; filmmakers like Dovzhenko, Pudovkin, and Eisenstein; writers like Gogol and Bulgakov, and, above all, Anton Chekhov.

I stood there in the cold October rain, musing on the fact that whatever else might be said of that complicated land, it's a country where politicians seek to bolster their prestige among the dead by their proximity to artists. I turned from Chekhov's grave and saw, a short distance away, the bas relief of a dancer in a tutu. It was Galina Ulanova not far from her former pupil, Ekaterina Maximova, and I lowered my umbrella to let the rain conceal the tears on my still living cheek.

The week before in St. Petersburg, I'd attended a performance of *Paquita* at the Mariinsky—the theater of Karsavina, Pavlova, and Nijinsky where Ulanova too had studied and danced. My wife and I had been given the best seats in the orchestra, but, during an intermission, a Russian friend, who'd been a dancer herself, asked if we'd like to look down at the stage from the imperial box. I said I hardly thought that would be permitted, and, sure enough, we found a scowling matron at the door whose function was clearly that of repelling interlopers.

"Nyet!" she said with finality, shaking her head and blocking our way.

But my Russian friend spoke to her rapidly and confidentially, and the matron moved aside. We ourselves stood where the tsar and his party had sat gazing down at the same sumptuously ornate Aleksandr Golovin curtain, and I asked our friend what she'd told that Carabosse at the door. She looked at me and smiled.

"That you're Ben Dunlap," she said, "the great American dancer."

CODA

Energy Is Eternal Delight

Looking back from my present perspective at the first half of my life, I can see how many persistent traits were evident from the start, a prime example being the fact that, though I was born with one foot on the accelerator, it took me quite a while to find the brakes. If I'd grown up a half-century later, I'd almost certainly have been sedated into near catatonia—and, as if to prove that point when, well into my sixties, I became the president of Wofford College, my wealthiest trustee insisted that on his tab I should undergo an exorbitantly expensive check-up at the Duke Executive Health Program, a suggestion I resisted because, since having my gall bladder extracted by mistake, I'd kept myself in good shape and stayed away from physicians. In the end, however, I complied, and, after innumerable tests which I passed with flying colors, I encountered a doctor with an Irish name and suspiciously rubicund face who told me that, though my numbers were fine, he'd recommend some heavy medication.

"Why on earth?" I asked, being vain about my fitness.

He craned his neck to the side and said, "You're very excitable."

"Energetic, yes," I acknowledged.

"I can help you smooth out the peaks and valleys,"

Those were his very words. I was aghast. "Why in heaven's name would I want to do that?"

"To adjust your metabolism."

"I like it the way it is," I said. "'Energy is eternal delight.'"

He looked at me blankly.

"William Blake," I explained.

He still looked blank.

"The Marriage of Heaven and Hell," I added, knowing that wouldn't clarify anything.

He wanted to perform a heart catheterization, but I declined. As things turned out, from a medical point of view, I should have listened, although from a philosophical perspective—or, at least, a psychological one—his proposal was unthinkable.

You might as well tell a fox not to trot—"Slow down, okay? Just take it easy!"—which is, in fact, an admonition that's been leveled at me at every stage of my life. . . though it's one I've learned to dismiss as the protest of lotus-eaters or, now and then, of cardiologists. But I am what I am, and it's too late now to alter that.

My friend George Garrett, who lived with an unfailing intensity matched only by his generosity, wrote a wonderful historical novel about Sir Walter Raleigh which he entitled *The Death of the Fox*. I thought of that turn of phrase when I got word of George's death, summoning to mind a favorite poem of another close friend of mine, Keith Berwick, who'd introduced me to the rousingly seditious lines of Wendell Berry's "Manifesto: The Mad Farmer Liberation Front," the last few words of which might serve as my valedictory here.

"Go with your love to the fields," Berry urges—precisely what my wife and I belatedly chose to do in Western North Carolina, though with a mailing address in my native state as one-foot-in and one-foot-out had always been an essential part of how we'd lived our lives.

The next lines resonate too:

> Lie easy in the shade. Rest your head
> in her lap. Swear allegiance
> to what is nighest your thoughts.

This memoir holds a lot that's nighest to my thoughts along with the hope that some of the things I've done have made a difference—not so much the funny stories as the day-to-day sharing of things that have mattered so much to me. But having said all that, it's what follows in the poem that, as I meant to imply in my epigraph at the start, defines the ruling impulse of my life and returns me to my totem once again:

As soon as the generals and the politicos
can predict the motions of your mind,
lose it. Leave it as a sign
to mark the false trail, the way
you didn't go. Be like the fox
who makes more tracks than necessary,
some in the wrong direction.

Though Berry himself—a southerner by birth like me, just slightly older than I—has stuck even closer to home as foxes are prone to do, I find that, in a larger sense, he's been a longtime fellow traveler, the essence of whose advice resounds in a final line:

Practice resurrection.

—which, so long as I keep slipping the snare, I hope to go on doing.

TO BE CONTINUED

Camden, South Carolina, 1938. Shortly before my encounter with a percolator, I'm amused by the photographer in what will remain, despite occasional mishaps, my default mood for the rest of my life. "My life has not only included a great deal of fun but lots of people who were funny."

Camden, South Carolina, 1941. Apparently dressed for the Italian front in World War I, I'm standing in front of a very large dog pen with only one of our 16 Dalmatians in view as it tussles with another that's just out of camera range. "Fussed over still as an only child, content with all my arrangements at home and lacking even a vague idea of what might lie beyond, I decided to set forth nonetheless to see a bit more of the world. . . knowing as I did that it was full of relatives who, if I needed help along the way, would gladly provide it."

Camden, S.C., 1941. With my older Savage cousins: from left to right, Bill, Carroll, and me at 3½—all in hodgepodge military attire—plus Hope in a costume inspired by *The Belgian Twins*, one of our mothers' favorite childhood books from World War I. "Back then my cousins were like a small army with me, as an only child, a mere camp follower in the rear. In addition to an older half-brother known by his childhood nickname of Bill Will, Hopey's other older brother was, like our Columbia cousin, named for our mothers' father, Carroll Jones."

Camden, S.C., 1941-42. The "beautiful, elusive Hopey" Savage, head up and heels down, on the mare named Belle which she shared with her older brother Carroll, who would later recall in a memoir of his own that, frustrated though he was by the horse's stubborn defiance, it passively submitted "to her strong will." "That was Hopey's intransigent way. She couldn't be coerced, not then or ever."

Atlanta, Georgia, 1943. My mother and I are captured by a street photographer on a downtown sidewalk on our way to a special occasion, probably for my birthday. For whatever reason, my top half looks a good deal spiffier than the rest of me, but, typically, we both appear to be wholly absorbed in talking at the same time. "My mother took me to the lavishly ornate Fox Theater to see my very first movie, a rerun of *The Invisible Man* which, though it seemed a curious choice, was ironically apt in a way because I myself, having begun attending school at Williams Street Elementary two or three months before, would become a ghostly presence there."

Columbia Backs

Columbia, S.C., 1953. The Columbia High School starting backfield from a game program at the beginning of the season during my junior year. From left to right, me, Jesse Smarr, Bobby Thomas, and W.C. West. Note the condition of both our uniforms and our practice field. "Those weren't boom years for the old Red & Gold. During my sophomore year we'd lost eight games in a row before finally scratching out a win against a leaderless Eau Claire team whose quarterback, on the night before, got sick from some ribs at a barbecue shack that, according to rumors never confirmed, was managed by Benny Utterback's aunt."

Washington, D.C., 1954. Delegates to Boys Nation with President Eisenhower in the Rose Garden of the White House. At that point, as the pseudo-Governor of South Carolina, I myself was a candidate for the Presidency before settling for an appointment to the Supreme Court. I'm in a gap at the center of the picture over the shoulder of the actual president "whom I'd seen from a distance four years before at the Boy Scout Jamboree—just as nine years after my White House photo op, a Boys State Governor from Arkansas would share a similar moment with JFK, though the impact on our future careers would differ considerably."

Sewanee, Tennessee, 1957. Norman McSwain is fourth from the left and Jim McKeon on the extreme right. In the center, posed like a bridal couple, Wemple Lyle is on the left and I on the right. "Sewanee in those days was still an all-male institution stuck in the middle of nowhere, so we had lots of practice time in the humid old gymnasium with sabers glinting and puttees shining in the dim shellac of the basketball floor. By mid-spring we were looking good. Even Norman could wheel about the gym with the menacing grace of a medium-range tank. And somehow. . . word got around that something of martial note was taking place in East Tennessee."

New York City, 1957. Only seconds before the fateful performance is to begin. "We stood rigidly at attention as a resentful hush fell over the barricades where thwarted fans were restlessly maneuvering and aggressively waving their signs. Then the camera lights came on, and Cadet Commander Wemple Lyle barked out the single savage command that set us irretrievably in motion."

New York City, 1959. I've been posed by a newspaper photographer to look like Paul Henreid in *Now Voyager*. "We'd departed on the same day that Eisenhower launched extended talks with his Soviet counterpart, Nikita Khrushchev, with what he'd described for the press as an 'open heart and good intentions'— which was on the whole our frame of mind as well for what we were undertaking. I knew I wouldn't see home again for a minimum of two years."

Oxford, England, 1960. Daryl Canfill and I are at the far end of Magdalen Bridge, he in a scholar's gown and I in a barely detectable commoner's gown. Note my recently altered coiffure. "Actually setting foot on English soil would strike me as so momentous that, to commemorate the event on the morning we reached Southampton, I impulsively brushed my hair from right to left instead of left to right and parted it on the other side. I was going to be a new person."

Columbia, S.C., 1954. Anne Boyd as a stage-struck thespian. "She herself had once taught ballroom dance throughout the state, and during her teenage years until her father had reined her in, she'd figured prominently in several children's theater productions—though, admittedly, at the pinnacle of her acting career in the title role of a non-balletic 'Sleeping Beauty,' she'd slept onstage through most of the play."

Camden, S.C., 1963. Doing my best to look jaunty at the annual Carolina Cup steeplechase event, I and Anne have just told my uncle, Henry Savage, that we're planning to marry. Our engagement would be announced the following day. "We kissed and meant it at last, and I was thinking I'd like to pursue things further when she looked me in the eyes and asked if I was really serious—'because,' she said in a no-nonsense way, 'I've got a rent-controlled apartment in New York, and I'm not risking it on a whim.' I realized that I'd caught my heart's desire and didn't know what to do with it. 'Is this a proposal?' I jokingly asked, but Anne's expression didn't change. 'Okay,' I said, 'give me twenty-four hours to work things out.'"

Nantucket, Mass., 1963. Posing nonchalantly as one of the "native drivers" at the taxi and touring service's downtown lot just off the town's cobblestoned Main Street, I'm leaning against the pride of our fleet in the mid-morning sun. "Accompanied by my endlessly patient wife, I went to the Hospital Thrift Shop—again in my Green Line uniform—hoping to find some interesting cast-off books. But shortly after entering, my eyes fell on a glass-topped case in which, amid some floridly engraved flat silver, I spotted a pair of serving spoons. Then, squinting to read them, I indignantly howled, 'These were stolen from my family!'")

Columbia, S.C., 1978. In a publicity shot for the PBS series *Cinematic Eye* at the very beginning of its production. I'm not yet wearing my official wardrobe. "Among those who'd seen my screen test, there were a few misgivings—though not about my vocabulary or even my odd southern accent. It was my artless haircut and the style-averse cut of my jib that made the front office nervous. So they brought a very mod hairdresser in from an Atlanta salon as well as a local haberdasher who specialized in revamps for rural legislators."

Monhegan Island, Maine, 1978. On location with Larry
Lancit for *Cinematic Eye*. I'm pointing to a cliff ledge where
I'm about to risk my life for my art. "With a national slot
locked in, our network was suddenly thinking big, offering to
underwrite such remote location sites as Monhegan Island off
the coast of Maine for a program on Robert Flaherty's *Man of
Aran*. My scripts were nearly intelligible, my delivery less
spasmodic, and I was almost cocky by the time we took our
crew on the road for that particular shoot—though I should
have known better, of course."

Columbia, S.C. 1979. Taking bows with Karen Gibbons after our performance at the Township Auditorium. "Karen Gibbons approached me one day about another and bigger recital, asking me to partner her in a much longer and more demanding pas de deux from Petipa's *Harlequinade*. When I asked if she thought I was up to it, she said it would be the Lopukhov revival that had aired on PBS— of Valery and Galina Panov, both formerly of the Kirov—but we could study her copy of the tape and adapt it as we saw fit. Initially, I demurred, but she insisted that I was such a natural Harlequin that, suppressing the thought I'd merely be playing the fool, I finally agreed to do it."

Columbia, S.C. 1981. With Ann Richardson in the Arabian Dance from *The Nutcracker*. "As my technique got much better, I took on bigger roles in more of the classic ballets. I was listed as a soloist and even for a brief while as a principal of sorts, dancing on national television as well as at high schools and shopping malls. It didn't matter when or where, I simply wanted to dance, and my partners did as well."

Columbia, S.C. 1981. With my daughter Susannah, who'll be one of the children in Act I of the *The Nutcracker.* "Four years had passed by then while I remained where I was, extending my skills and repertoire and reappearing as Harlequin—this time in Fokine's *Carnaval* with Schumann's lyrically manic score sending me over the stage in a series of spring-loaded *grands pas de chat.* I felt I could bound like that to the very ends of the earth as long as the music played, reminding myself in a valedictory way that, as T.S. Eliot had said in his *Four Quartets*, 'You are the music while the music lasts.' But sooner or later, of course, the music always stops."

Author's Note

Some real events in this memoir have been mined for episodes in my fiction, but nothing in this book is fictional. Dogged efforts have been made to maintain factual accuracy throughout, especially in humorous passages and those involving apparent improbability or coincidence. In one minor instance, a name has been changed in the interest of privacy, and though I've found that the name of my high school teammate Sonny Serio was omitted in printed programs at the end of the season in question, it had appeared in earlier ones—suggesting that, at some point during that season, he seems to have permanently disappeared over an embankment as we all must do in time. Otherwise, every detail of this memoir is as close to what actually happened as memory and exhaustive research can make it.

Many thanks to my friend, the poet and painter Tamsin Smith, for acting once again as my editor, and, for her invaluable help in proofreading, to my daughter Boykin Bell—who's outstripped me in so many things, including her long success as a backyard poulterer.

Ben Dunlap has been a novelist, librettist, writer-producer for Public Television, dancer, teacher, college president, and Senior Moderator for the Aspen Institute. A former Rhodes Scholar, he has also been the recipient of numerous awards and honorary degrees. His celebrated TED Talk has been watched by millions, and he's among those profiled in Waqās Ahmed's *The Polymath: Unlocking the Power of Human Versatility.* His recent publications include two works of fiction, *Famous Dogs of the Civil War* and *Sunshine Bell: The Autobiography of a Genius.* More volumes of his memoirs are forthcoming.

THE DIVERS COLLECTION

Number 1
Hôtel des Étrangers, poems by **Joachim Sartorius**
translated from German to English by **Scott J.
Thompson**

Number 2
Making Art, a memoir by **Mary Julia Klimenko**

Number 3
XISLE, a novel by **Tamsin Spencer Smith**

Number 4
Famous Dogs of the Civil War, a novel by **Ben Dunlap**

Number 5
Now Let's See What You're Gonna Do by **Katarina Gogou**
translated from Greek to English by **A.S.**
with an introduction by **Jack Hirschman**

Number 6
Sunshine Bell / The Autobiography of a Genius,
an annotated edition by **Ben Dunlap**

Number 7
The Glint in a Fox's Eye & Other Revelations,
a memoir by **Ben Dunlap**

Made in the USA
Las Vegas, NV
17 May 2022

49023971R00198